**READINGS FROM THE
ASSOCIATION FOR
PSYCHOLOGICAL SCIENCE**

Current
Directions
in
SOCIAL
PSYCHOLOGY

SECOND EDITION

EDITED BY

Janet B. Ruscher

Tulane University

Elizabeth Yost Hammer

Xavier University of Louisiana

Upper Saddle River, NJ
Columbus, OH

Library of Congress Cataloging-in-Publication Data
Current directions in social psychology / edited by Janet B. Ruscher,
Elizabeth Yost Hammer.—2nd ed.
    p. cm.
"Readings from the Association for Psychological Science."
ISBN-13: 978-0-13-606280-6
ISBN-10:   0-13-606280-6
1. Social psychology.   I. Ruscher, Janet B.   II. Hammer, Elizabeth Yost.
  HM1033.C87 2009
  302—dc22   2008006678

Editorial Director: Leah Jewell
Executive Editor: Jeff Marshall
Project Manager: LeeAnn Doherty
Associate Managing Editor: Maureen Richardson
Full Service Production Liaison: Joanne Hakim
Senior Marketing Manager: Jeanette Koskinas
Marketing Assistant: Laura Kennedy
Senior Operations Supervisor: Sherry Lewis
Cover Art Director: Nancy Wells
Cover photo/illustration: "Faces '98" by Diana Ong/SuperStock, Inc.
Manager, Cover Visual Research & Permissions: Karen Sanatar
Full-Service Project Management: Doug Korb/TexTech International
Composition: TexTech International
Printer/Binder: RR Donnelley & Sons Company

Credits and acknowledgments borrowed from other sources and reproduced, with
permission, in this textbook appear on appropriate page within text.

Pearson Education LTD., London   Pearson Education North Asia Ltd., Hong Kong
Pearson Education Singapore, Pte. Ltd.   Pearson Educación de Mexico, S.A. de C.V.
Pearson Education Canada, Inc.   Pearson Education Malaysia, Pte. Ltd.
Pearson Education–Japan   Pearson Education Upper Saddle River,
Pearson Education Australia PTY, Limited   New Jersey

10   9   8   7   6   5   4   3   2   1
ISBN 13:   978-0-13-606280-6
ISBN 10:   0-13-606280-6

Contents

Section 4: The Interpersonal Extremes: Prosocial Behavior and Aggression   *97*

Section 5: Stereotyping and Prejudice   *131*

Section 1: The Social Self: Evaluation, Perception, and Regulation

Social psychology examines how situational factors influence the individual, as well as how the individual influences the situation. A critical question, then, is who is the person in the situation? Traditionally, social psychologists have addressed this question by considering the Self. The Self comprises beliefs about one's own characteristics, such as abilities, preferences, and possessions, as well as an evaluation of those characteristics (i.e., self-esteem). Beyond these characteristics, the Self also provides an executive function: it is self-aware, renders decisions, exercises self-control, and executes intentions. Roughly speaking, the content and control aspects of the Self respectively correspond to what William James referenced as the "me" and the "I."

Although each individual possesses a unique set of characteristics, abilities, and possessions, the majority of people view their own set in a favorable manner. In fact, most of us believe that we are above average with respect to socially-desirable characteristics. We are better, smarter, funnier, kinder, and apt to have a happier future than the average person (or, at least, that is what we think!!). Interestingly, people also extend this positive evaluation to possessions, including trivial items that they possess only momentarily (i.e., the mere ownership effect). People also extend this positive evaluation to self-relevant characteristics such as the first letter of their names or to numbers resembling their birthdays. Thus, Francine likes the letter "F" more than Sophie does and, perhaps, Francine describes herself as "friendly" rather than "sociable" simply because she likes words that begin with "fr." These positive associations to self-relevant characteristics are relatively implicit, meaning that such associations generally operate outside conscious awareness.

An intriguing extension of the work on positive associations to self-relevant characteristics is reported by Pelham and his colleagues (Pelham, Carvallo, & Jones, 2005). They find, for example, that the likelihood that married couples share names beginning with the same first letter is higher than chance would predict (e.g., Francine James' likelihood of being married to a man named Fred or Johnson is higher than chance.) Francine's likelihood of moving to cities such as Franklin, Frederick, or Frankfort also exceeds mere chance. Recognizing that many extraneous uncontrollable factors could underlie such choices in natural settings, Pelham and his colleagues also demonstrated similar relations under carefully controlled laboratory conditions. For example, they paired a two-digit number subliminally with participants' own names, so that participants formed a nonconscious positive association to that number. Later, they found that participants' perceptions of someone wearing an athletic jersey with that

1

number were more positive than if the jersey contained another number. Pelham and colleagues refer to such effects as "implicit egotism:" a relatively unconscious preference for self-relevant qualities.

Thus, most people hold relatively positive views of the Self and of self-relevant qualities, characteristics, and possessions. Moreover, most people prefer to maintain these positive self-views over time, defending or bolstering as circumstances allow. Sometimes, people simply take serendipitous advantage of life-events to bolster their own self regard: they bask in the success of their beloved sports team or in their child's recent accolades. At other times, people work actively to keep the Self view shining: They intentionally may select challenging but attainable tasks or may drop thinly-veiled hints of recent accomplishments to supervisors, neighbors, and friends. The active approach also predominates when circumstances diminish or threaten positive self views. Hurting another person's feelings, receiving criticism, or scoring poorly on an examination, for instance, temporarily reduces positive self-regard. Efforts to restore positive regard take myriad forms. People may compare themselves to a person less successful than themselves (i.e., downward social comparison). Alternatively, people may reaffirm their deeply-held personal values by engaging in behaviors that reflect those values or simply by thinking about those values (as predicted by self-affirmation theory). Consequently, after receiving a poor but passing grade on an exam, one student might compare herself to fellow students who received failing grades. Alternatively, another student might reaffirm her personal value of social justice by organizing a food-drive or by donning the t-shirt from a recent outreach operation in which she participated.

Clearly, maintaining positive views of the Self—having high self-esteem—is important to most people. But some researchers argue that the relation of self-esteem to various outcomes is not simply a matter of how high or low it is. Instead, other dimensions and aspects of self-esteem also are critical to consider. For example, is self-esteem relevant to specific domains (e.g., academic achievement; physical attractiveness) or is self-esteem a more global assessment of self-worth? Is the positive view of the Self excessively inflated or relatively accurate when compared to objective indices or sociometric measures (i.e., perceptions of acquainted peers)? Is the evaluation of the self relatively stable or does it vary dramatically from day-to-day in response to life experiences? Tackling a question especially relevant to the latter, Crocker and Knight (2005) argue that self-esteem can be unstable when it is contingent upon successes and failures in particular domains. Students who base their self-esteem on academic success, for example, are particularly vulnerable to academic failures: they may experience depression or select unchallenging tasks to avoid failure and guarantee success. Similarly, first-year students who base their self-esteem on physical attractiveness may engage in healthy behaviors such as exercise, but also can be vulnerable to alcohol use and disordered eating patterns. In their article, Crocker and Knight not only discuss the pitfalls of contingent self-esteem, but also offer ideas for fostering high self-esteem that is relatively resilient to day-to-day threats.

Research on implicit egotism and on self-esteem maintenance clearly illustrate the importance that people attach to the Self. Although people occasionally report the experience of "losing" the Self (e.g., in a huge, emotional crowd; when intoxicated; when overwhelmed by the enormity of the universe), people—at least when they are awake—usually have some level of awareness of themselves. The Self is regularly salient to people, so they are cognizant of their own appearance, their own past actions, and their own true intentions. Egocentrically, we believe that other people are similarly attentive to our own Selves: we believe that there is a spotlight upon us. (And, meanwhile, everyone else proceeds as though they are in the spotlight!!) As Gilovich and Savitsky (1999) suggest, we believe that peers notice changes in our appearance from day to day, and that strangers notice embarrassing qualities such as an unusual t-shirt choice or facial blemish. But they don't, at least not to the extent that we expect!! In this vein of research, one sees the interface between the "I" and the "me": The person is self-aware of his or her personal characteristics and true intentions, and infers that these characteristics (components of the "me") are transparent to on-lookers.

That belief in transparency underlies, in part, people's occasional efforts to conceal their true attitudes or feelings. Many people believe that they are "an open book," and that others easily can see their dislike of a suite-mate, anger at their professor, desperate attraction to a neighbor, and the like. Because these feelings may be socially inappropriate in some settings, people exert considerable energy to conceal them. Efforts to hide one's feelings involve the Self's executive function, along with exercising self-control, making difficult decisions, or focusing on a complex or tiring task. These tasks of self-regulation can deplete cognitive resources, diminishing success on subsequent tasks that also require self-regulation. For example, after foregoing chocolates and cookies, people show reduced persistence on a cognitive task. Examining self-regulation of emotion in particular, Richards (2004) discusses memory deficits, negative impacts on social interactions, and decrements in task performance. Conceivably, people suppress emotional expression to avoid negative social consequences, but they may be unaware of the costs of doing so.

Thus, the person in the situation is an active one: striving to maintain self-esteem, gathering information about the Self, interpreting how others see the Self, and endeavoring to change undesirable characteristics. Active, yes. Perfectly accurate, no. The person in the situation often is egocentric and can be ego-protective to boot. As you progress through other topics of social psychology—most of which focus strongly upon situational forces—try to keep the person in situation in mind.

Implicit Egotism

Brett W. Pelham,[1] and Mauricio Carvallo
University at Buffalo, State University of New York
John T. Jones
U.S. Military Academy, West Point

Abstract

People gravitate toward people, places, and things that resemble the self. We refer to this tendency as *implicit egotism*, and we suggest that it reflects an unconscious process that is grounded in people's favorable self-associations. We review recent archival and experimental research that supports this position, highlighting evidence that rules out alternate explanations and distinguishes implicit egotism from closely related ideas such as mere exposure. Taken together, the evidence suggests that implicit egotism is an implicit judgmental consequence of people's positive self-associations. We conclude by identifying promising areas for future research.

Keywords

implicit; egotism; self-esteem

Researchers have long known that how people view themselves plays an important role in virtually every aspect of their daily lives, including phenomena as diverse as personal achievement, interpersonal attraction, and even physical well-being. In recent years, however, researchers have argued that people's conscious self-evaluations provide an incomplete view of the self-concept. Specifically, researchers have argued that people's implicit (i.e., unconscious) self-evaluations also influence their judgment and behavior (Greenwald & Banaji, 1995; Hetts & Pelham, 2001). Implicit self-evaluations are not beliefs that a Freudian homunculus has banished to the unconscious. Instead, such beliefs are probably best conceptualized as part of the cognitive or adaptive unconscious (Kihlstrom, 1987). Presumably, some implicit self-evaluations consist of beliefs that were once conscious but have become highly automatized. Other implicit self-evaluations might be unconscious because they were formed prior to the individual's acquisition of language. Although few researchers have acknowledged the possibility, it may also be that implicit self-evaluations are a product of defensive processes to which people have little or no conscious access. Finally, implicit self-evaluations may be a product of classical conditioning or implicit learning, that is, associative learning that occurs in the absence of conscious awareness. Thus, just as puppies do not know why they salivate, people may not always know why they trust a stranger who sounds vaguely like Garrison Keillor.

It is now well documented that people possess implicit self-evaluations—that is, unconscious associations about the self. It is also well-documented that most implicit self-associations are highly favorable. Two decades ago, Nuttin (1985) showed that people like the letters that appear in their own names much more than other people like these same letters—a phenomenon Nuttin called the *name-letter effect*. Nuttin also showed that people who preferred the letters in their own names were typically unaware of the basis of this preference. Similarly, Beggan (1992) showed that once people are given an object people evaluate the object more favorably than they would otherwise—a phenomenon called the *mere-ownership effect*. Give Ivan a puppy, and he will overestimate the puppy's worth, presumably because the puppy has become an extension of the self.

It is now well established that people possess positive implicit associations about themselves. Until very recently, however, it was unclear whether people's implicit self-associations ever predict meaningful social behaviors (but see Dijksterhuis, 2004; Shimizu & Pelham, 2004; Spalding & Hardin, 1999). To address this question, we investigated the role of implicit self-associations in major life decisions. Our primary hypothesis was simple. If Dennis adores the letter *D*, then it might not be too far-fetched to expect Dennis to gravitate toward cities such as Denver, careers such as dentistry, and romantic partners such as Denise. Pelham, Mirenberg, and Jones (2002) referred to this unconscious tendency to prefer things that resemble the self as *implicit egotism*. In a series of articles (Jones, Pelham, Carvallo, & Mirenberg, 2004; Pelham, Mirenberg, & Jones, 2002; Pelham, Carvallo, DeHart, & Jones, 2003), we reported the results of numerous archival studies (i.e., studies relying on public records such as birth, marriage, or death records) and experiments suggesting that implicit egotism influences major life decisions. As suggested by the list in Table 1, which summarizes many of our recent studies, implicit egotism appears to influence a wide variety of important decisions. In the remainder of this report, we address some of the strengths and limitations of our research on implicit egotism and then offer some suggestions for future research.

STUDYING IMPLICIT EGOTISM

In our initial article (Pelham et al., 2002), we argued that implicit egotism influences both where people choose to live and what people choose to do for a living. For instance, in Study 1 of this article, we identified four common female first names that strongly resembled the name of a Southeastern state. The names were Florence, Georgia, Louise, and Virginia, corresponding with the states Florida, Georgia, Louisiana, and Virginia. We then consulted Social Security Death Index (SSDI) records (kept since the advent of the Social Security system) to identify women who had died while living in each of the four relevant Southeastern states. This design yielded a 4 × 4 matrix of name–state combinations, and a total sample size of more than 75,000 women. Women named Florence, Georgia, Louise, and Virginia were all disproportionately likely (on average, 44% above chance values) to have resided in the state that closely resembled their first name.

Ruling Out Confounds

This study raised many concerns about possible confounds. One concern was the possibility that these women disproportionately resided in states whose names resembled their own first names simply because they had been named

Table 1. *A Selective Summary of the Most Comprehensive Studies Providing Support for Implicit Egotism*

Pelham, B.W., Mirenberg, M.C., & Jones, J.K. (2002):
1. Four most common female first names that resemble Southeastern state names
2. Four most common male first names that resemble Southeastern state names
3. Eight largest U.S. states and surnames resembling these state names
4. Eight largest Canadian cities and surnames resembling these city names
5. Four most common male and female names that resemble the occupations "dentist" and "lawyer"
6. All U.S. cities that prominently feature number words in the names (matched with numbers corresponding to people's day and month of birth)

Pelham, B.W., Carvallo, M., DeHart, T., & Jones, J.T. (2003):
1. The 30 most common European American surnames and all U.S. cities that include the surname anywhere in the city name (e.g., Johnson City, Johnsonville, Fort Johnson, etc.)
2. The three most common U.S. surname pairs (e.g., Smith–Johnson) and street names that include these surnames (each pair was replicated individually in each U.S. state)
3. Three sets of surnames chosen to avoid spurious name–street matches (e.g., Hill–Park) and street names that included these names or words (each pair also replicated individually in each U.S. state)

Jones, J.T., Pelham, B.W., Carvallo, M., & Mirenberg, M.C. (2004):
1. Matches for first letter of surname in two large counties, covering approximately 150 years
2. Single initial surname matches for parents of every birth occurring in Texas in 1926
3. Systematic surname match studies of four large Southeastern states over about 150 years
4. Nationwide joint telephone listing study of 12 systematically chosen male and female first names
5. Laboratory experiments involving (a) birthday numbers, and (b) first three letters of surname
6. Subliminal conditioning study using participants' full names as conditioning stimuli

after the states in which they had been born (and had never moved). Although SSDI records do not indicate where the deceased were born, these records do indicate the state in which they resided when they applied for social security cards (typically as adults). Using these records, we were able to focus on people who got their social security cards in one state and died while residing in another—that is, people who had moved into the states in which they died. An analysis of these interstate immigrants yielded clear and consistent evidence for implicit egotism.

Another concern about this study is that the results might reflect explicit rather than implicit egotism. It would be extremely surprising if Virginia failed to notice the resemblance between her first name and the state name that appeared on her driver's license. Archival research methods do not always lend themselves well to documenting implicit effects. Nonetheless, we have tried. In other studies summarized in the same article (Pelham et al., 2002), we focused on names that, unlike Georgia and Virginia, shared only their first few letters with the states or cities to which people with those names gravitated. When Samuel Winters moves to Winnipeg, for example, it seems unlikely that he will conclude that the first few letters of his surname are the reason for his move.

Watering down a manipulation in this fashion tends to water down the size of the effect obtained. But to our surprise, implicit egotism proved to be sufficiently robust that it survived systematic tests involving relatively subtle manipulations. We were able to show, for example (Pelham et al., 2002; Study 6), that people disproportionately inhabit cities whose names feature their birthday numbers. Just as people born on February 2 (02-02) disproportionately inhabit cities with names such as Two Harbors, people born on May 5 (05-05) disproportionately inhabit cities with names such as Five Points. This birthday-number study also illustrated that implicit egotism is not limited to name-letter preferences. Presumably, any meaningful self-attribute can serve as a source of implicit egotism. Another finding that seems likely to reflect implicit preferences comes from studies of street addresses. Whereas people whose surname is Street tend to have addresses that include the word Street (e.g., Lincoln Street), people whose surname is Lane tend to have addresses that include the word Lane (e.g., Lincoln Lane; Pelham et al., 2003).

Moderators of Implicit Egotism

Can archival studies such as these shed any light on the psychological mechanisms behind implicit egotism? We believe so. To the degree that archival studies yield support for meaningful moderators of implicit egotism, such studies can suggest, albeit indirectly, that implicit egotism is based on self-evaluation. For example, laboratory research has shown that women show stronger first-name preferences than men do (perhaps because many women realize that their first name is the only name they will keep forever). In keeping with this established finding in the laboratory research, behavioral first-name preferences have also proven to be stronger for women than for men (Pelham et al., 2002).

The distinctiveness of a person's name also appears to moderate the strength of implicit egotism. Implicit egotism is more pronounced for rare (i.e., more self-defining) than for common names. The fact that rare names do a better job of distinguishing their owners from other people than common names do suggests that implicit egotism is grounded in identity. By definition, people with rare names are also exposed to their own names slightly less often than are people with common names (e.g., Zeke meets other people named Zeke less often than John meets other people named John). The fact that implicit egotism is stronger among those with statistically rare names also suggests that implicit egotism is not grounded exclusively in the mere exposure effect, that is, the tendency for people to prefer stimuli to which they have been exposed more often (see also Jones et al., 2002, where this issue is addressed in other ways).

The Problem of Sampling

One of the limitations of archival research on implicit egotism is that it is often impossible to sample people randomly in such studies. The researcher is usually forced to sample names systematically. In some studies, we tackled this problem by sampling surnames and city or street names from all 50 U.S. states (Pelham et al., 2003). For example, by systematically sampling the same common surname pairs (e.g., Smith–Johnson, Williams–Jones) in all 50 U.S. states, we were able to document robust name–street matching in six different nationwide samples. Thus, we were able to show, for instance, that the surname pair Smith–Johnson yielded supportive data for 45 out of 50 individual U.S. states.

Another way in which we have tackled the sampling problem is by sampling names exhaustively within large geographical units. In studies of interpersonal attraction, we were sometimes able to sample entire states or counties. For example, using exhaustive statewide birth records, Jones et al. (2004) were able to show that people are disproportionately likely to marry others who happen to share their first or last initial. (Moreover, in samples in which it has been possible to determine people's ethnicity, we have also been able to control for ethnic matching (the tendency for people to marry others of their own ethnic group) by testing our hypothesis within specific ethnic groups (e.g., among Latinos only). Although archival studies of interpersonal attraction raise their own methodological problems, we have gone to great lengths to rule out alternative explanations, including not only ethnic matching but also age-group matching and proximity. For instance, we ruled out the possibility that people married those who were seated near them in high school (based on surname) by showing that our findings remained robust among couples whose ages differed by 5 years or more. Our studies have consistently yielded evidence for implicit egotism.

Assessing Implicit Egotism in the Laboratory

Thomas Edison once said that genius is 1% inspiration and 99% perspiration. With a little inspiration and a great deal of perspiration, researchers who rely on archival research methods can go a long way toward ruling out alternate explanations for a particular effect. But as Edison's contemporary, the methodologist R.A. Fisher, might have put it, neither inspiration nor perspiration is a match for randomization. The researcher who wishes to rule out numerous alternate explanations for a phenomenon, while gaining insights into its underlying mechanisms, must occasionally conduct experiments. In our research on implicit egotism and interpersonal attraction (Jones et al., 2004), we have done exactly that.

In one experiment, we introduced participants to a bogus interaction partner whose arbitrarily assigned experimental code number (e.g., 02-28) either did or did not happen to resemble their own birthday number. Participants were more attracted to the stranger when his or her code number resembled their own birthday number. This study suggests that implicit egotism is not merely a corollary of the principle that people are attracted to others who are similar to them. After all, participants did not think that their interaction partner actually shared their birthday. In a second experiment, we found that implicit egotism is most likely to emerge under conditions of self-concept threat (i.e., when people have been forced to think about their personal weaknesses). Men who had just experienced a mild self-concept threat (by writing about their personal flaws as a potential dating partner) were especially attracted to a woman in a "Yahoo personals" ad when her screen name happened to contain the first few letters of their surname (e.g., Eric Pelham would prefer STACEY_PEL to STACEY_SMI). Together with past research suggesting that self-concept threats temporarily

Fig. 1. Stimulus person from subliminal conditioning study (Jones, J.T., Pelham, B.W., Carvallo, M., & Mirenberg, M.C., 2004). Participants evaluated this woman after the number on her jersey (16 or 24) had or had not been subliminally paired with their own names.

increase people's positive associations to the self, this study suggests that implicit egotism is grounded in self-evaluation (Beggan, 1992; Jones et al., 2002).

In a third experiment on interpersonal attraction (Jones et al., 2004, Study 7), we found the most direct evidence yet for the underpinnings of implicit egotism. Male and female participants evaluated an attractive young woman on the basis of her photograph. The woman was depicted wearing a jersey that prominently featured either the number 16 or the number 24 (see Fig. 1). Prior to evaluating the woman, participants took part in 30 trials of a computerized decision-making task in which they made simple judgments about strings of random letters. At the beginning of each judgment trial, a row of Xs appeared briefly in the center of the computer monitor, to focus participants' attention. This task was actually a subliminal conditioning task: The row of Xs was always followed (for 14 ms) by either the number 16 or the number 24. One of these two numbers (16 or 24) was always followed by the individual participant's own full name (for 14 ms), and the other number was always followed by one of several gender-matched control names. Participants liked the woman more, and evaluated her more favorably when her jersey number had been subliminally paired with their own names. Implicit egotism appears to be implicit.

FROM IMPLICIT EGOTISM TO IMPLICIT SELF-EVALUATION

We believe that we have established beyond a reasonable doubt that implicit egotism influences important decisions. Thus, we believe that future research should attempt to identify meaningful boundary conditions (i.e., predictable limitations) of implicit egotism. Along these lines, some questions that seem ripe for investigation involve close relationships, culture, and implicit self-esteem.

Do name-letter preferences apply exclusively to the self, or do the names of people to whom one is close also affect one's preferences? Do such preferences grow stronger as relation-ships grow closer? If Bill truly loves Virginia, will he be highly interested in moving to Virginia, just as she might be? Given recent developments in the psychology of culture, it might also be profitable to assess cultural influences on implicit egotism. One might expect that in collectivistic cultures (i.e., ones that celebrate collective as opposed to individual identities), name-letter preferences would be exaggerated for collective aspects of the self (e.g., surnames might have a greater effect than forenames). We are currently planning studies to test this idea. We have also begun to address the implications of implicit egotism for more mundane decisions. Specifically, we (Brendl, Chattopadhyay, Pelham, & Carvallo, in press) recently found that people prefer products (e.g., teas, crackers, chocolate candies) whose names share one or more letters with their own names.

If unconscious self-evaluations influence both mundane and important daily decisions, it is important to understand the origins and nature of these implicit self-evaluations—that is, to understand implicit self-esteem. Do negative social interactions early in life cause some people to develop low implicit self-esteem? Apparently they do. In three separate studies, DeHart, Pelham, and Tennen (in press) asked parents, their adult children, or both to report on parent–child interactions in the family when the children were growing up. Both the children's and their parents' reports of how nurturing the parents had been were associated with the adult children's levels of implicit self-esteem. This association still held true after controlling for participants' levels of explicit self-esteem. Studies such as these raise the question of whether we have observed consistent evidence for implicit egotism merely because most people are fortunate enough to possess positive implicit associations to the self. It is possible that our typical findings would be reversed among people who possess truly negative self-associations (i.e., for those with very low levels of implicit self-esteem). Such findings might have implications not only for theories of self-regulation but also for clinical theories of the etiology of depression and self-destructive behaviors. Of course, broad speculations such as these await empirical scrutiny. However, we hope that our research on implicit egotism will inspire re-searchers to take a closer look at the nature of implicit self-esteem. A complete understanding of the self-concept may hinge, in part, on a better understanding why Jack loves both Jackie and Jacksonville.

Recommended Reading

Fazio, R.H., & Olson, M.A. (2003). Implicit measures in social cognition research: Their meaning and uses. *Annual Review of Psychology, 54*, 297–327.

Koole, S.L., & Pelham, B.W. (2003). On the nature of implicit self-esteem: The case of the name letter effect. In S. Spencer, S. Fein, & M. Zanna (Eds.), *Motivated social perception: The Ontario Symposium on Personality and Social Psychology* (Vol. 9, pp. 93–116). Mahwah, NJ: Erlbaum.

Wilson, T.D., & Dunn, E.W. (2004). Self-knowledge: Its limits, value and potential for improvement. *Annual Review of Psychology, 55*, 493–518.

Acknowledgments—We thank the many friends and colleagues who have encouraged us to pursue this research.

Note

1. Address correspondence to Brett Pelham, Department of Psychology, SUNY, Buffalo, Buffalo, NY 14260; e-mail: brettpel@buffalo.edu.

References

Beggan, J.K. (1992). On the social nature of nonsocial perception: The mere ownership effect. *Journal of Personality and Social Psychology, 62*, 229–237.

Brendl, C.M., Chattopadhyay, A., Pelham, B.W., & Carvallo, M. (in press). Name letter branding: Valence transfers when product specific needs are active. *Journal of Consumer Research.*

DeHart, T., Pelham, B.W., & Tennen, H. (in press). What lies beneath: Early experiences with parents and implicit self-esteem. *Journal of Experimental Social Psychology.*

Dijksterhuis, A. (2004). I like myself but I don't know why: Enhancing implicit self-esteem by subliminal evaluative conditioning. *Journal of Personality and Social Psychology, 86*, 345–355.

Greenwald, A.G., & Banaji, M.R. (1995). Implicit social cognition: Attitudes, self-esteem, and stereotypes. *Psychological Review, 102*, 4–27.

Hetts, J.J., & Pelham, B.W. (2001). A case for the non-conscious self-concept. In G. Moskowitz (Ed.), *Cognitive social psychology: The Princeton Symposium on the Legacy and Future of Social Cognition* (pp. 105–123). Mahwah, NJ: Erlbaum.

Jones, J.T., Pelham, B.W., Carvallo, M., & Mirenberg, M.C. (2004). How do I love thee? Let me count the Js: Implicit egotism and interpersonal attraction. *Journal of Personality and Social Psychology, 87*, 665–683.

Jones, J.T., Pelham, B.W., Mirenberg, M.C., & Hetts, J.J. (2002). Name letter preferences are not merely mere exposure: Implicit egotism as self-regulation. *Journal of Experimental Social Psychology, 38*, 170–177.

Kihlstrom, J.F. (1987). The cognitive unconscious. *Science, 237*, 1445–1452.

Nuttin, J.M. (1985). Narcissism beyond Gestalt and awareness: The name letter effect. *European Journal of Social Psychology, 15*, 353–361.

Pelham, B.W., Carvallo, M., DeHart, T., & Jones, J.T. (2003). Assessing the validity of implicit egotism: A reply to Gallucci. *Journal of Personality and Social Psychology, 85*, 800–807.

Pelham, B.W., Mirenberg, M.C., & Jones, J.K. (2002). Why Susie sells seashells by the seashore: Implicit egotism and major life decisions. *Journal of Personality and Social Psychology, 82*, 469–487.

Shimizu, M., & Pelham, B.W. (2004). The unconscious cost of good fortune: Implicit and explicit self-esteem, positive life events, and health. *Health Psychology, 23*, 101–105.

Spalding, L.R., & Hardin, C.D. (1999). Unconscious unease and self-handicapping: Behavioral consequences of individual differences in implicit and explicit self-esteem. *Psychological Science, 10*, 535–539.

Critical Thinking Questions

1. Distinguish between archival and experimental research methods. How do the authors use both to support their theory of implicit egoism?

2. Compare and contrast implicit egoism and mere exposure. Explain how the authors rule out other alternative explanations of implicit egoism.

3. Why do the authors call their concept *implicit* egoism, as opposed to explicit egoism or simply egoism? Draw on specific research from the article to defend your response.

This article has been reprinted as it originally appeared in *Current Directions in Psychological Science*. Citation information for this article as originally published appears above.

Contingencies of Self-Worth

Jennifer Crocker[1] and Katherine M. Knight
University of Michigan

Abstract

We argue that the importance of self-esteem lies in what people believe they need to be or do to have worth as a person. These contingencies of self-worth are both sources of motivation and areas of psychological vulnerability. In domains of contingent self-worth, people pursue self-esteem by attempting to validate their abilities and qualities. This pursuit of self-esteem, we argue, has costs to learning, relationships, autonomy, self-regulation, and mental and physical health. We suggest alternatives to this costly pursuit of self-esteem.

Keywords

self-esteem; motivation; vulnerability; self-regulation; mental health

High self-esteem is often regarded as the holy grail of psychological health—the key to happiness, success, and popularity. Low self-esteem, on the other hand, is blamed for societal problems ranging from poor school achievement to drug and alcohol abuse. However, this rosy view of high self-esteem has detractors who argue that the objective benefits of high self-esteem are small and limited. Although high self-esteem produces pleasant feelings and enhanced initiative, it does not cause high academic achievement, good job performance, or leadership, nor does low self-esteem cause violence, smoking, drinking, taking drugs, or becoming sexually active at an early age (Baumeister, Campbell, Krueger, & Vohs, 2003). Many parents, educators, and policymakers are confused, with some holding steadfastly to the idea that low self-esteem is the root of much, if not all, evil, and others concluding that self-esteem is, at best, irrelevant.

Although high self-esteem does little to cause positive outcomes in life, and low self-esteem is not to blame for most social and personal problems, we disagree that self-esteem is irrelevant. People want to believe that they are worthy and valuable human beings, and this desire drives their behavior (Pyszczynski, Greenberg, Solomon, Arndt, & Schimel, 2004). We suggest that the importance of self-esteem lies less in whether it is high or low, and more in what people believe they need to be or do to have value and worth as a person—what we call contingencies of self-worth.

SELF-ESTEEM AND CONTINGENT SELF-WORTH

Over a century ago, William James (James, 1890) suggested that self-esteem is both a stable trait and an unstable state; momentary feelings of self-esteem fluctuate around a person's typical or trait level in response to good and bad events. James also noted that people are selective about what events affect their self-esteem: They invest their self-esteem in—that is, are ego-involved in succeeding at—some things, whereas their success at other endeavors has no impact on their self-esteem. Instability of self-esteem is the result of being ego-involved in events, or having contingent self-worth (Deci & Ryan, 1995; Kernis, 2003).

Crocker and Wolfe (2001) proposed that good and bad events in domains of contingent self-worth raise or lower momentary feelings of self-esteem around a person's typical or trait level of self-esteem, and these fluctuations in state self-esteem have motivational consequences. Increases in self-esteem feel good, and decreases in self-esteem feel bad. Therefore, regardless of whether people typically have high or low self-esteem, they seek the emotional high associated with success in domains of contingent self-worth and strive to avoid the emotional lows that accompany failure in these domains. Consequently, contingencies of self-worth regulate behavior.

Contingencies of self-worth also shape long-term and short-term goals. People want to prove that they are a success, not a failure, in domains of contingent self-worth, because that would mean they are worthy and valuable; in other words, they have self-validation goals in these domains (Crocker & Park, 2004). When they are not sure that success is possible or failure can be avoided, they will disengage from the task, deciding it doesn't matter, rather than suffer the loss of self-esteem that accompanies failure in these domains.

Students who base their self-esteem on their academic accomplishments typically have self-validation goals in this domain, viewing their schoolwork as an opportunity to demonstrate their intelligence. Because failure in domains of contingency threatens self-esteem, people try to avoid failure by increasing effort; if they are still uncertain of success, they may abandon their self-validation goal and become unmotivated, or prepare excuses that will soften the blow to self-esteem in case they fail. Making excuses or blaming others are defensive maneuvers by which people deflect the threat to self-esteem when they do fail. When failure in domains of contingency cannot be dismissed with defensive responses, self-esteem decreases. Consequently, contingencies of self-worth are both a source of motivation and a psychological vulnerability (Crocker, 2002).

We have investigated the domains in which college students commonly invest their self-esteem, including appearance, others' approval, outperforming others, academics, family support, virtue, and religious faith or God's love (Crocker, Luhtanen, Cooper, & Bouvrette, 2003). Our research indicates that contingencies of self-worth shape students' emotions, thoughts, and behavior. In a sample of college seniors applying to graduate school, the more students based their self-esteem on their academic success, the higher their self-esteem was on days they were admitted to graduate school and the lower their self-esteem was on days they were rejected (see Fig. 1; Crocker, Sommers, & Luhtanen, 2002). The more students' self-esteem is contingent on their academic success, the more it decreases on days they receive worse-than-expected grades; this is particularly true for women majoring in engineering, who face negative stereotypes about their ability (Crocker, Karpinski, Quinn, & Chase, 2003). Contingencies of self-worth are strongly related to the goal of validating one's abilities in the domain of contingency (Crocker & Park, 2004), and students report spending more time on activities that are related to their contingencies of self-worth (Crocker, Luhtanen, et al., 2003).

This approach extends or challenges existing models of self-esteem in several ways. First, our argument that the importance of self-esteem lies in what it is

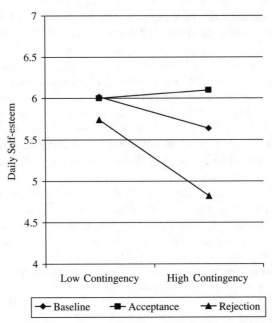

Fig. 1. Students' self-esteem on days they were accepted or rejected by a graduate school (compared to a baseline) as a function of how contingent their self-esteem was on academic success.

contingent upon stands in contrast to decades of research focused on whether trait self-esteem is high or low. Furthermore, we are not simply shifting the focus to whether people have high or low self-esteem in specific domains such as academics or athletics, but rather suggesting that regardless of people's level of domain-specific self-esteem, contingent self-worth in these domains has predictable consequences. Although our research is complementary to research that focuses on the stability of self-esteem over time (Kernis, 2003), we extend that work by showing that instability of self-esteem results from experiencing positive and negative events in those domains in which self-esteem is contingent. Other scholars have argued that people vary as to whether their self-esteem is contingent or not (Deci & Ryan, 2005; Kernis, 2003). We argue that nearly everyone has contingencies of self-worth but that people differ as to what their self-esteem is contingent on. Basing self-esteem on external factors such as appearance, others' approval, or academic achievement has more negative consequences than basing it on internal factors such as virtue or God's love. And in contrast to most researchers who argue that self-esteem is a fundamental human need that people need to pursue (Pyszczynski et al., 2004; Sheldon, 2004), we argue that pursuing self-esteem by attempting to prove that one is a success in domains of contingency is costly (Crocker & Park, 2004).

THE COSTS OF PURSUING SELF-ESTEEM

Successful pursuit of self-esteem has short-term emotional benefits, such as increased happiness and decreased anxiety (Pyszczynski et al., 2004). The emotional boosts associated with success in domains of contingency are pleasant but do not satisfy fundamental human needs for learning, relatedness, and autonomy. Rather, we think of boosts to self-esteem as analogous to sugar: tasty but not nutritious. Indeed, the boosts to self-esteem that accompany success in contingent domains can, we think, become addictive, and pursuing self-esteem by attempting to validate one's abilities has costs for learning, relatedness, autonomy, self-regulation, and, over time, physical and mental health (Crocker & Park, 2004).

Costs to Learning

When people have self-validation goals, mistakes, failures, criticism, and negative feedback are self-threats rather than opportunities to learn and improve. Consequently, when self-esteem is contingent on a domain, people either adopt performance goals to succeed and avoid failure, or they disengage entirely from the endeavor. Focusing on performance increases stress and anxiety, which can undermine learning, whereas disengagement from a domain also leads to a withdrawal of effort, which is essential to learning.

Costs to Autonomy

Autonomy refers to the sense of choice, or being the causal origin of one's behavior. When autonomy is low, people feel pressured by internal or external demands, expectations, and standards—they feel that they are "at the mercy" of people and events. When self-esteem is contingent, autonomy tends to be low. As Deci and his colleagues suggest, "The type of ego involvement in which one's 'worth' is on the line—in which one's self-esteem is contingent upon an outcome—is an example of internally controlling regulation that results from introjection. One is behaving because one feels one has to and not because one wants to, and this regulation is accompanied by the experience of pressure and tension" (Deci, Eghrari, Patrick, & Leone, 1994, p. 121).

Costs to Relationships

Pursuing self-esteem interferes with establishing and maintaining mutually supportive relationships, because people become focused on themselves at the expense of others' needs and feelings (Crocker & Park, 2004). Relationships become a means of validating the self, rather than an opportunity to give to and support others.

Costs to Self-Regulation

The pursuit of self-esteem interferes with achieving important goals both because efforts to protect self-esteem can undermine success and because the intense emotions associated with failure in contingent domains can disrupt efforts to achieve goals. The more contingent their self-worth is on academics, the more time students spend working on an easy verbal task, but the less time they spend working on a difficult verbal task; apparently, more contingent students want to work on tasks that make them feel accomplished and, hence, worthy.

Costs to Mental Health

The stress and anxiety associated with contingent self-esteem may also affect mental health. When people experience positive and negative events in domains of contingency, their self-esteem fluctuates over time; these fluctuations in self-esteem predict increases in symptoms of depression (Crocker, Karpinski, et al., 2003). We hypothesize that these fluctuations in self-esteem are accompanied by elevated cortisol levels triggered by the stress response, which is strongly linked to the development of depression.

Costs to Physical Health

Contingencies of self-worth can affect physical health directly, through stress, and indirectly, through self-destructive behavior. For example, college freshmen who base their self-esteem on their physical appearance report greater levels of alcohol consumption, drug use, unsafe sexual practices, and binge drinking (Crocker, 2002), all of which can affect physical health over time.

Do Some Contingencies Have More Costs?

The costs of pursuing self-esteem depend on what people think they need to be or do to have worth and value. Basing self-esteem on external contingencies of self-worth, such as appearance or others' approval, requires continual validation from others. Consequently, people who base their self-esteem on external sources may more chronically adopt self-validation goals and consequently experience greater costs (Crocker & Park, 2004). In a longitudinal study of college freshmen, external contingencies of self-worth at the start of college were associated with more problems such as binge drinking and symptoms of disordered eating during the freshman year, whereas internal contingencies, such as virtue or religious faith, were associated with lower levels of these problems. Thus, it matters how one pursues self-esteem. More research is needed to identify why this is the case and to find out whether people with external contingencies have chronic self-validation goals that account for these findings.

ALTERNATIVES

If the pursuit of self-esteem is costly, what is the alternative? One solution might be to replace self-validation goals with learning goals. Priming incremental theories of ability (i.e., exposing people to the idea that intelligence can be improved) eliminated the drops in self-esteem that usually accompany failure in a contingent domain (Niiya, Crocker, & Bartmess, 2004). However, incremental theories of ability do not eliminate concerns with self-esteem; rather, they shift the conditions under which failure threatens self-esteem. Specifically, Niiya and Crocker (2004) found that, relative to less contingent students or students who do not believe that improvement is possible, highly contingent incremental theorists practice less when an upcoming task is difficult, presumably because practice followed by failure suggests lack of ability, and for highly contingent students, this implies they are worthless.

We think that adopting goals that are good for others as well as for the self may lessen the costs of contingent self-esteem. For example, instead of focusing on achieving success to boost self-esteem, focusing on how success at one's goals can contribute to others may reduce the costs of contingent self-esteem for learning, relationships, autonomy, self-regulation, and mental and physical health.

CONCLUSION

Recently, in a backlash against the self-esteem movement, researchers have suggested that rather than trying to raise self-esteem by giving indiscriminate praise or ensuring that every child receives an award or trophy, parents, educators, and athletic coaches should encourage "warranted" self-esteem, based on actual accomplishments. We think their approach validates the idea that some children deserve high self-esteem whereas others do not, and encourages the development of contingent self-esteem. Contingent self-worth is an ineffective source of motivation; although boosts to self-esteem feel good, they can become addictive, requiring ever greater success to avoid feelings of worthlessness. The resulting relentless quest for self-esteem may be narrowing and limiting, and choices may be guided by their implications for self-esteem rather than by more essential goals. Rather than trying to raise self-esteem by helping children find domains of contingency in which they can succeed, parents and educators may help children more by focusing on what they want to contribute, create, or accomplish and what they need to learn or improve in themselves to do so.

This research has implications for the treatment of depression and perhaps other disorders. Ultimately, people might benefit from shifting their motivational "driver" from self-esteem to contribution goals that are larger than the self. Helping people identify where they have invested their self-esteem and how such investment creates costs to their relationships, learning, feelings of autonomy, and ability to accomplish their goals is a crucial step in making this motivational shift, in our view.

Research on contingencies of self-worth is still in its infancy; much research examining the costs of contingencies of self-worth relative to other sources of motivation needs to be done. Developmental psychologists could explore how these contingencies develop and change across the lifespan. To what extent are contingencies of self-worth related to early attachment experience, traumatic childhood events, parenting styles, and peer influences? Cultural psychologists could examine whether there are cultural differences in contingencies of self-worth, and whether the consequences of contingent self-worth differ across cultures. The concern with validating self-worth might be a very Western, or even North American, phenomenon. Finally, research could explore how to intervene to reduce the costs of contingencies of self-worth. Are there learning orientations that reduce vulnerability of contingent self-esteem and enable people to exert effort on difficult tasks in contingent domains without protecting the self from the possibility of failure? Do goals that are larger than the self, such as contribution goals, reduce the costs of contingent self-esteem? Shifting from a focus on level of self-esteem to the contingencies on which self-esteem depends may yield new insights into the importance of self-esteem in people's lives.

Recommended Reading

Baumeister, R.F., Campbell, J.D., Krueger, J.I., & Vohs, K.D. (2003). (See References)
Crocker, J., & Park, L.E. (2004). (See References)
Crocker, J., & Wolfe, C.T. (2001). (See References)
Pyszczynski, T., Greenberg, J., Solomon, S., Arndt, J., & Schimel, J. (2004). (See References)

Note

1. Address correspondence to Jennifer Crocker, Department of Psychology, University of Michigan, Ann Arbor, MI 48109-1109; e-mail: jcrocker@umich.edu.

References

Baumeister, R.F., Campbell, J.D., Krueger, J.I., & Vohs, K.D. (2003). Does high self-esteem cause better performance, interpersonal success, happiness, or healthier lifestyles? *Psychological Science in the Public Interest, 4*, 1–44.

Crocker, J. (2002). Contingencies of self-worth: Implications for self-regulation and psychological vulnerability. *Self and Identity, 1*, 143–149.

Crocker, J., Karpinski, A., Quinn, D.M., & Chase, S. (2003). When grades determine self-worth: Consequences of contingent self-worth for male and female engineering and psychology majors. *Journal of Personality and Social Psychology, 85*, 507–516.

Crocker, J., Luhtanen, R., Cooper, M.L., & Bouvrette, S.A. (2003). Contingencies of self-worth in college students: Measurement and theory. *Journal of Personality and Social Psychology, 85*, 894–908.

Crocker, J., & Park, L.E. (2004). The costly pursuit of self-esteem. *Psychological Bulletin, 130*, 392–414.

Crocker, J., Sommers, S.R., & Luhtanen, R.K. (2002). Hopes dashed and dreams fulfilled: Contingencies of self-worth and admissions to graduate school. *Personality and Social Psychology Bulletin, 28*, 1275–1286.

Crocker, J., & Wolfe, C.T. (2001). Contingencies of self-worth. *Psychological Review, 108*, 593–623.

Deci, E.L., Eghrari, H., Patrick, B.C., & Leone, D.R. (1994). Facilitating internalization: The self-determination theory perspective. *Journal of Personality, 62*, 119–141.

Deci, E.L., & Ryan, R.M. (1995). Human autonomy: The basis for true self-esteem. In M.H. Kernis (Ed.), *Efficacy, agency, and self-esteem* (pp. 31–49). New York: Plenum.

James, W. (1890). *The principles of psychology* (Vol. 1). Cambridge, MA: Harvard University Press.

Kernis, M.H. (2003). Toward a conceptualization of optimal self-esteem. *Psychological Inquiry, 14*, 1–26.

Niiya, Y., Crocker, J., & Bartmess, E. (2004). From vulnerability to resilience: Learning orientations buffer contingent self-esteem from failure. *Psychological Science, 15*, 801–805.

Pyszczynski, T., Greenberg, J., Solomon, S., Arndt, J., & Schimel, J. (2004). Why do people need self-esteem? A theoretical and empirical review. *Psychological Bulletin, 130*, 435–468.

Sheldon, K.M. (2004). The benefits of a "sidelong" approach to self-esteem need satisfaction: A comment on Crocker and Park. *Psychological Bulletin, 130*, 421–424.

Critical Thinking Questions

1. Explain what is meant by "contingencies of self worth." How does this concept differ from general self-esteem? Does the distinction matter? Explain.

2. Drawing on research using college students, explain how contingencies of self worth regulate behavior.

3. Describe the costs of pursuing self-esteem in terms of learning, autonomy, relationships, self-regulation, mental health, and physical health.

4. Discuss some of the educational and mental health implications of the research on contingent self-worth.

This article has been reprinted as it originally appeared in *Current Directions in Psychological Science*. Citation information for this article as originally published appears above.

The Spotlight Effect and the Illusion of Transparency: Egocentric Assessments of How We Are Seen by Others

Thomas Gilovich[1]

Department of Psychology, Cornell University, Ithaca, New York (T.G.)

Kenneth Savitsky

Department of Psychology, Williams College, Williamstown, Massachusetts (K.S.)

Abstract

We review a program of research that examines people's judgments about how they are seen by others. The research indicates that people tend to anchor on their own experience when making such judgments, with the result that their assessments are often egocentrically biased. Our review focuses on two biases in particular, the spotlight effect, or people's tendency to overestimate the extent to which their behavior and appearance are noticed and evaluated by others, and the illusion of transparency, or people's tendency to overestimate the extent to which their internal states leak out and are detectable by others.

Keywords

egocentrism; spotlight effect; transparency

Everyday social interaction often requires that people try to anticipate how they are seen by others. Does my boss know how hard I've worked? Did I come across as badly as I fear? The accuracy of such judgments and the processes by which they are made have recently sparked strong interest among social psychologists (Kenny & DePaulo, 1993). In this article, we describe our own work on the topic. The overriding theme of our research is that people's appraisals of how they appear to others tend to be egocentrically biased. Because people are so focused on their own behavior, appearance, and internal states, they overestimate how salient they are to others. Thus, others are less likely than one suspects to notice an embarrassing faux pas or a meritorious personal triumph, and one's internal states, such as nervousness, disgust, or alarm, seldom leak out as much as one thinks.

THE SPOTLIGHT EFFECT

In a memorable scene from the not-so-memorable film *The Lonely Guy*, the comedian Steve Martin arrives at a restaurant and is asked by the maitre'd, How many in your party, sir? When Martin replies that he is dining alone, the maitre'd raises his voice and asks with astonishment, Alone? The restaurant falls silent as everyone stares at Martin in disbelief. To make matters worse, a spotlight suddenly appears from nowhere and follows Martin as he is escorted to his seat.

Although farcical, the scene captures the fear many people have of how their awkward moments look to others. Whether dining out alone, fumbling with change at the front of the bus, or momentarily having no one to talk to at a cocktail party, people are typically afraid that they will stick out like a sore thumb. How realistic are these fears? We maintain that they tend to be overblown that people often overestimate the extent to which others notice them. They do so, furthermore, not just for their mishaps and awkward moments, but for their triumphs as well. The efforts that an individual views as extraordinary whether a brilliant comment after a scholarly presentation or a no-look bounce pass on the basketball court often go unnoticed or underappreciated by others. We have dubbed this phenomenon the spotlight effect (Gilovich, Medvec, & Savitsky, in press). People tend to believe that the social spotlight shines more brightly on them than it actually does. We have documented the spotlight effect in a number of contexts. In one study, individual participants were asked to don a T-shirt featuring a picture of pop singer Barry Manilow (a figure of dubious renown among college students). In each session, one such participant was escorted to another room in the laboratory and instructed to knock on the door. A second experimenter answered and ushered the participant into the room, where 4 to 6 other (normally dressed) participants were seated filling out questionnaires. After a brief interchange, the second experimenter escorted the participant back out of the room and into the hallway. There, the participant was asked to estimate how many of those seated in the room would recall who was pictured on his or her shirt. As expected, participants overestimated the actual accuracy of the observers (by a factor of 2). The T-shirt wearers were noticed far less than they suspected (Gilovich et al., in press).

We have also demonstrated this effect in a number of other experiments. We have shown, for example, that participants tend to overestimate the salience of their own contributions both positive and negative to a group discussion. And we have shown that participants who were absent for a portion of an experiment expected their absence to be more apparent to the other participants than it actually was. Once again, people expected others to notice them (even their absence) more than was actually the case (Gilovich et al., in press; Savitsky & Gilovich, 1999).

Finally, we have explored a corollary of the spotlight effect: We propose that beyond overestimating the extent to which others are attentive to their momentary actions and appearance, people also overestimate the extent to which others are likely to notice the variability of their behavior and appearance over time. For the individual performer, it is often the differences in performance across time that are salient, with the constancies relegated to the back-ground. For observers, the pattern is often reversed. To examine this issue, we have asked participants to estimate how they would be judged on successive occasions and then compared the variations in those predictions with variations in how they were actually rated by their peers. Thus, we asked college students to predict, on a number of occasions, how their personal appearance would be judged, relative to their usual appearance (were they having a good or bad day on that occasion?). We also asked collegiate volleyball players to rate how their performance would be judged by their teammates after numerous scrimmages. In both studies, participants expected their peers ratings of them to be more variable than they actually were. What one takes to be an outstanding performance or a bad hair day, for instance, and expects others to notice, may be largely indistinguishable from what others perceive to be one's typical performance or appearance (Gilovich, Kruger, Medvec, & Savitsky, 1999).

Having established the existence of the spotlight effect, we examined the obvious next question: Why do people overestimate the salience of their own appearance and behavior? Our answer emphasizes the difficulty of getting beyond one's own phenomenological experience. To be sure, people are often aware that others are less focused on them than they are on themselves, and that some adjustment from their own experience is necessary to capture how they appear in the eyes of others. Even so, it can be difficult to get beyond one's own perspective. The adjustment that one makes from the anchor of one's own phenomenology (Jacowitz & Kahneman, 1995), or, in Gilbert's (1989) terms, the correction from an initial characterization, tends to be insufficient. The net result is that estimates of how one appears to others are overly influenced by how one appears to oneself (Kenny & DePaulo, 1993).

We have obtained support for this interpretation in a number of ways. In one experiment, some participants were given an opportunity to acclimate to wearing an embarrassing shirt prior to confronting their audience. Others were not. Because the habituation period tended to decrease the extent to which participants were themselves focused on the shirt, the estimates of participants who became accustomed to wearing the shirt began from a less powerful internal state or a lower anchor than the estimates of participants who had no habituation period, and their predictions of the number of observers who had noticed their shirt were diminished. Note that the objective nature of the stimulus was unchanged across conditions it was, after all, the same shirt. But because participants phenomenological experience of wearing the shirt had changed, so did their sense of being in the spotlight (Gilovich et al., in press).

ANTICIPATING HOW ONE WILL BE JUDGED BY OTHERS

Recall the predicament of individuals who must dine alone in a restaurant. They are made anxious not simply by the prospect that they will be noticed, but by the anticipation that, once spotted, they will be judged harshly as outcasts who lack social appeal. Our current research suggests that these concerns, too, are overblown. We have demonstrated that after a failure (whether a social faux pas or an intellectual downfall), individuals expect others to judge them more harshly than they actually do. Participants who fail to perform well at solving anagrams, for instance, expect their faulty performance to garner more condemnation than it actually does, and expect observers to rate them more harshly on attributes such as intelligence and creativity than they actually do (Savitsky, Epley, & Gilovich, 1999).

Anchoring and adjustment may be at work here, too. There is evidence that individuals often condemn themselves more harshly for a failure than they expect others to, and such harsh self-recriminations can then serve as their starting point in attempting to discern how harshly they will be judged by others. Even if individuals realize that their self-recriminations are more acute than what they will receive from others, their adjustments from their own feelings are typically insufficient. Consequently, there may be some residual effect of how individuals judge themselves when they anticipate how they will be judged by others.

We suspect, however, that people's excessive concern about the severity of others judgments is also due to a failure to anticipate a particular type of judgmental charity on the part of observers the charity that comes with having experienced similar failures themselves. People often commiserate with those they witness dining alone, losing their train of thought during a presentation, or forgetting the name of an acquaintance in part because they have suffered similar embarrassments themselves.

We have collected evidence indicating that, on average, people think they are more prone to such embarrassing episodes than their peers, and that they fail to appreciate the extent to which those who have been there, done that are likely to empathize with their misfortune and withhold judgment. In one study, participants attempted challenging word problems and failed in view of two observers. One of the observers possessed (and was known by the participants to possess) the answers to the word problems; the other did not. Not surprisingly, the observers who were given the answers considered the questions to be easier than did those who were not, and thus judged the participants more negatively. But this difference was lost on the participants, who expected the two observers to judge them equally harshly. The participants apparently failed to anticipate the extent to which the uninformed observers would simply conclude that the problems were difficult. We suspect that this failure to anticipate the extent to which others will empathize with one's plight is at work in many situations in which individuals expect to be judged more harshly than they actually are (Eply, Savitsky, & Gilovich, 1999).

THE ILLUSION OF TRANSPARENCY

In addition to being acutely aware of their own appearance and behavior, individuals are often quite focused on their internal states and emotional sensations. Sometimes these states are apparent to others, but other times they are well hidden and it is often important to know whether such states are apparent to others or not.

Can he tell I'm not interested?

Was my nervousness apparent? We propose that in making these determinations, people are likewise egocentrically biased. Once again, people realize that others are less aware of their sensations than they are themselves they know that others cannot read their minds. But the adjustments that individuals make to try to capture other people's perspectives tend to be insufficient. As a result, people tend to overestimate the extent to which their internal sensations leak out and are apparent to others. We refer to this as the illusion of transparency (Gilovich, Savitsky, & Medvec, 1998).

We have shown in a number of investigations that individuals are typically less transparent than they suspect. In one study, participants were asked to conceal their disgust over a foul-tasting drink, and then to estimate how successfully they had done so. Specifically, we asked participants to taste five specially prepared drinks while we videotaped their reactions. Four of the drinks were pleasant tasting and one randomly placed amidst the other four was decidedly unpleasant.

After tasting all five, participants estimated how many of 10 observers would be able to guess which drink had been the foul-tasting one after watching a videotape of their facial expressions. As expected, tasters overestimated the extent to which their disgust was transparent: The observers were far less accurate than the tasters predicted (Gilovich et al., 1998).

We have demonstrated the illusion of transparency in a host of other paradigms as well. We have shown, for example, that people tend to think that their nervousness over telling lies leaks out more than it actually does, and so they overestimate the extent to which their lies are detectable. We have also shown that witnesses to a staged emergency believe their concern about the situation is more apparent than it actually is, and that negotiators overestimate the extent to which their negotiation partners can discern their preferences (Gilovich et al., 1998; Van Boven, Medvec, & Gilovich, 1999). In these studies, we have employed a number of control conditions to rule out various alternative interpretations, such as the curse of knowledge (i.e., the belief that what one knows is known to others as well) or the fact that people may have inaccurate abstract theories about how easily internal states not just one's own, but anyone's can be detected. The results have consistently supported the critical role of the illusion of transparency.

CONCLUSION

Across three lines of inquiry, we have demonstrated that individuals have difficulty anticipating how they appear in the eyes of others. When it comes to predicting whether one will be noticed, how one will be judged, or whether one's internal sensations are detectable, there is often a considerable gap an egocentric gap between one's intuitions and the actual judgments of others. Much work, of course, remains to be done. Although our research has shown that the spotlight effect and illusion of transparency exist for both positive and negative experiences, there surely are differences in how the two phenomena are played out for positive versus negative experiences, and an understanding of these differences should increase understanding of both phenomena. It is also important to determine whether the spotlight effect and illusion of transparency vary with development, as has been shown for egocentrism more generally. Finally, there are a host of applied implications that await exploration. Does the illusion of transparency contribute to marital miscommunication? Can the spotlight effect shed light on social phobia and anxiety? Does the spotlight effect contribute to the perception that one has lost face, and to the humiliation and violence that such a perception engenders? We hope that it is not too egocentric to suggest that these are important questions waiting to be addressed.

Recommended Reading

Gilovich, T., Savitsky, K., & Medvec, V.H. (1998). (See References)
Kenny, D.A., & DePaulo, B.M. (1993). (See References)
Keysar, B., Barr, D.J., & Horton, W.S. (1998). The egocentric basis of language use: Insights from a processing approach. *Current Directions in Psychological Science, 7,* 46–50.
Vorauer, J.D. (in press). Transparency estimation in social interaction. In G.B. Moskowitz (Ed.), *Future directions in social cognition.* Mahwah, NJ: Erlbaum.

Acknowledgments—This research was supported by Research Grants SBR9319558 and SBR9809262 from the National Science Foundation.

Note

1. Address correspondence to Thomas Gilovich, Department of Psychology, Cornell University, Ithaca, NY 14853, e-mail: tdg1@cornell.edu, or to Kenneth Savitsky, Department of Psychology, Bronfman Science Center, Williams College, Williamstown, MA 01267, e-mail: kenneth.k.savitsky@ williams.edu.

References

Eply, N., Savitsky, K., & Gilovich, T. (1999). *Anticipating overly harsh judgments of the self: On the failure to anticipate the empathic discounting of others.* Unpublished manuscript, Cornell University, Ithaca, NY.

Gilbert, D.T. (1989). Thinking lightly about others: Automatic components of the social inference process. In J. Uleman & J.A. Bargh (Eds.), *Unintended thought* (pp. 189–211). New York: Guilford Press.

Gilovich, T., Kruger, J., Medvec, V.H., & Savitsky, K. (1999). *Biased estimates of how variable we look to others.* Unpublished manuscript, Cornell University, Ithaca, NY.

Gilovich, T., Medvec, V.H., & Savitsky, K. (in press). The spotlight effect in social judgment: An egocentric bias in estimates of the salience of one's own actions and appearance. *Journal of Personality and Social Psychology.*

Gilovich, T., Savitsky, K., & Medvec, V.H. (1998). The illusion of transparency: Biased assessments of others ability to read our emotional states. *Journal of Personality and Social Psychology, 75,* 332–346.

Jacowitz, K.E., & Kahneman, D. (1995). Measures of anchoring in estimation tasks. *Personality and Social Psychology Bulletin, 21,* 1161–1166.

Kenny, D.A., & DePaulo, B.M. (1993). Do people know how others view them? An empirical and theoretical account. *Psychological Bulletin, 114,* 145–161.

Savitsky, K., Epley, N., & Gilovich, T. (1999). *The spotlight effect revisited: Overestimating the extremity of how we are judged by others.* Unpublished manuscript, Cornell University, Ithaca, NY.

Savitsky, K., & Gilovich, T. (1999). *Is our absence as conspicuous as we think?* Unpublished manuscript, Cornell University, Ithaca, NY.

Van Boven, L., Medvec, V.H., & Gilovich, T. (1999). *The illusion of transparency in negotiations.* Unpublished manuscript, Cornell University, Ithaca, NY.

Critical Thinking Questions

1. This line of research focuses on our egocentric bias in judging how others see us. Explain how both the spotlight effect and the illusion of transparency illustrate the egocentric bias.

2. The authors claim that the spotlight effect holds for both positive and negative ocurrences. Explain this claim and describe some research evidence that supports it.

3. Explain how the anchoring and adjustment heuristic relates to the spotlight effect. Reflect on at least one other heuristic that might be at work in either the spotlight effect or the illusion of transparency.

This article has been reprinted as it originally appeared in *Current Directions in Psychological Science*. Citation information for this article as originally published appears above.

The Cognitive Consequences of Concealing Feelings

Jane M. Richards[1]
University of Texas at Austin

Abstract

When emotions arise, we are not powerless to overcome them: Adults actively regulate the extent to which their emotions are experienced and expressed in everyday life. Often, these efforts are aimed at looking and feeling better. However, theories of self-regulation and emotion suggest that some forms of emotion regulation may have unintended consequences for cognitive functioning. This article reviews studies that link expressive suppression, which involves concealing outward signs of emotion, with degraded memory, communication, and problem solving. Explanations for these consequences are considered, along with the possibility that not all forms of emotion regulation are cognitively costly. Recent research suggests that reappraisal, which entails changing how we think about an event to neutralize its emotional impact, leaves cognitive functioning intact. Thus, the cognitive consequences of keeping one's cool may vary according to how this is done.

Keywords

cognition; emotion; memory; regulation; suppression

Are you an open book—always showing what you feel? Or do you take great pains to keep your inner emotional states from showing to the people around you? For example, you might try to look calm and composed during a job interview despite feeling so anxious you want to throw up. Or you might strive to appear unfazed by a friend's awful culinary experiment that you would much rather feed to a dog. And not your own dog, either.

If you occasionally (or frequently) try to decrease the extent to which your emotions show, you likely are hoping to produce beneficial affective consequences, such as looking or feeling good despite emotionally trying times. There is mounting evidence, however, that these emotion-regulatory efforts may have unintended cognitive consequences. My goal in this article is to consider whether keeping emotions one feels on the inside from showing on the outside has cognitive consequences, and if so, why this might be.

EXPRESSIVE SUPPRESSION: A COMMON EMOTION-REGULATORY STRATEGY

Emotions can be regulated in many ways, but expressive suppression, or the conscious inhibition of emotion-expressive behavior, is a particularly common staple in our emotion-regulatory repertoire. For example, undergraduates who kept diaries of their emotion-regulatory experiences over 14 days reported inhibiting outward signs of emotion one quarter of the time (Gross, Richards, & John, in

27

press). Similarly, researchers have shown that more than one third of individuals' efforts to deceive others involve inhibiting feelings (DePaulo, Kashy, Kirkendol, Wyer, & Epstein, 1996).

Typically, people conceal feelings to foster the illusion that they are calm, cool, and collected. But impression management is not all that matters in emotional situations. Peak cognitive performance is also important. In view of increasing evidence that emotional and cognitive processes are tightly intertwined in everyday life (Damasio, 1994), researchers have begun to examine whether concealing feelings influences our ability to perform common cognitive tasks, such as forming memories and communicating with other people.

COGNITIVE CONSEQUENCES OF EXPRESSIVE SUPPRESSION

How might expressive suppression influence cognitive functioning? One possibility, of course, is that suppression has no cognitive consequences whatsoever. After all, the motivation and skills necessary to control emotions emerge early in life and become commonplace by adulthood (Gross, 1998). These considerations might lead one to expect that expressive suppression is so overlearned and effortless that it has no discernible effect on cognitive performance in adults.

Other considerations, however, lead to a rather different conclusion. Cybernetic control models of self-regulation (e.g., Carver & Scheier, 1981; Larsen, 2000) suggest that efforts to maintain or change behavior evoke a negative-feedback loop whereby the existing condition of a system (e.g., the expression on one's face) is compared to a behavioral standard or goal (e.g., wanting to appear emotionally neutral). If a discrepancy between the two is detected (e.g., grimacing when one wishes to appear neutral), an operating process is evoked to lessen this discrepancy and achieve the desired state or behavior (e.g., appearing emotionally neutral). Although these self-monitoring and self-corrective processes may permit us to conceal feelings successfully, they could end up diverting finite attentional resources away from other things we may be doing at the same time, thereby disrupting how well we can do those other tasks. Does this mean that concealing feelings actually might have cognitive costs?

Consequences for Memory

To test whether expressive suppression affects cognitive functioning, several interlocking studies have focused on memory—a cognitive process that is particularly crucial in everyday life. In two initial studies (Richards & Gross, 1999), participants viewed several slides of injured men that produced transient increases in negative emotions. As slides were presented, information concerning each man (i.e., name, occupation, injury he sustained) was presented orally with his slide. Expressive suppression was manipulated by randomly assigning participants to one of two instructional conditions: Suppressors were asked to refrain from showing emotion while watching the slides; control participants were not given any regulatory instructions. Results showed that suppressors were successful at appearing unfazed by the upsetting slides. As predicted by the cybernetic model of self-regulation, suppressors also showed significantly worse performance on a memory test for the orally presented information.

The generality of these initial findings has been demonstrated in several related studies. For example, Bonanno, Papa, O'Neill, Westphal, and Coifman (2004) showed that people who concealed emotional facial expressions in response to unpleasant and pleasant slides remembered the slides less well than control participants. Thus, the effects of expressive suppression on memory appear to generalize to emotionally positive experiences and visual details. The effects of suppression on memory have also been studied in socially relevant contexts. For example, people who have been asked to conceal facial expressions while watching others argue have been found to remember the argument less well than control participants (Richards & Gross, 2000, Study 1). Similarly, a study of conversations revealed that romantic partners who were instructed to conceal both facial and vocal cues of emotion while talking about important relationship conflicts with each other remembered less of what was said than did partners who received no suppression instructions (Richards, Butler, & Gross, 2003).

These laboratory-based investigations manipulated suppression, thereby permitting a causal interpretation of results. However, one might wonder whether spontaneously occurring suppression in everyday life has cognitive costs as well. After all, suppression may be quite automatic and unlikely to consume attentional resources among people who do it habitually. One study addressed this possibility by examining links between memory ability and individual differences in expressive-suppression tendencies (Richards & Gross, 2000, Study 3). Results showed that individuals who reported habitual efforts to inhibit outward signs of their emotions reported more memory problems than individuals who rarely suppressed their emotions. Suppressors also performed more poorly on an objective memory test of emotional experiences they had recorded in a daily diary 1 week earlier. Thus, even when suppression is presumably well practiced, it is still associated with cognitive costs.

Why does expressive suppression impair memory? Expressive suppression does not influence self-reported negative emotion, so subjective emotional experience cannot be the culprit. By contrast, successful expressive suppression does lead to increases in some markers of physiological stress (e.g., constriction of blood vessels and electrical conductivity of the skin). However, research shows that the physiological work of suppression is uncorrelated with memory and, therefore, unlikely to explain why suppression impairs memory (Richards & Gross, 1999, Study 2).

A more promising explanation may be the one suggested by the cybernetic control model of self-regulation discussed earlier. A recent study (Richards et al., 2003) demonstrated that self-reported self-monitoring efforts were heightened among suppressors relative to control participants. That is, suppressors were more likely to report thinking about their behavior and the need to control it during a conversation. Further, increases in self-monitoring predicted decreases in memory for what was said. That is, people who reported thinking a lot about controlling their behavior had particularly impoverished memories. However, additional research is needed to confirm whether self-monitoring actually exerts a causal effect on memory.

Consequences for Social Interaction

If expressive suppression consumes attentional resources—by way of either self-monitoring or some other process—its effects should extend beyond the realm of memory. Recent research has focused specifically on whether inhibiting emotions disrupts the flow of communication during face-to-face interactions. In one study (Butler et al., 2003), unacquainted pairs of women were asked to view an upsetting film and then talk about their reactions with each other. In one type of pairing, neither partner was given instructions about how to express herself during the conversation. In another type of pairing, one partner was instructed to suppress outward signs of emotion (unbeknownst to her partner); the other partner was given no instructions. Results showed that suppressors were less responsive than nonsuppressing participants, as evidenced by being less likely to acknowledge what their partner was saying during the conversation. Moreover, when suppressors did respond, they were slower to do so. Unfortunately, these speech disturbances appear to have adverse social consequences. Partners of suppressors reported reduced feelings of rapport during the conversation. Analyses confirmed that this effect was explained by suppressors' deficits in responsiveness.

These findings are broadly consistent with studies on interpersonal deception, which have linked efforts to suppress truthful thoughts and feelings with reduced responsiveness, reduced complexity of utterances, increased rates of grammatical errors, and decreased verbal fluency (DePaulo, Stone, & Lassiter, 1985). A recent statistical analysis combining the results of numerous studies showed that one particular type of speech disturbance, namely, repetitions of words and phrases, appears to be the most reliable verbal marker of deception (DePaulo et al., 2003). Although the cognitive disturbances associated with deception typically are attributed to people's efforts to control what they say during the lie, the research on expressive suppression suggests that "simply" controlling what we show on our faces is sufficient to degrade at least some aspects of communication.

EXPRESSIVE SUPPRESSION AND ENERGY DEPLETION

The research reviewed so far is generally consistent with the theoretical proposition that suppressing emotional responses consumes attentional resources. This would explain why concealing feelings disrupts simultaneous performance of cognitive tasks. Taking this line of reasoning one step further, we might ask whether concealing feelings also compromises performance on subsequent cognitive tasks.

According to the ego-depletion view (Baumeister, Bratslavsky, Muraven, & Tice, 1998), self-regulatory efforts of many types consume some limited resource akin to "strength" or "energy." As a result, one act of self-regulation should reduce the self's capacity or willingness to engage in a subsequent act of self-regulation. To test this prediction, Baumeister et al. (1998) asked some participants to "conceal or suppress any emotional reaction" while viewing an upsetting film. Results revealed that suppressors showed poorer performance on a subsequent anagram problem-solving task (i.e., unscrambling letters to form words) than control participants did. In fact, an ego-depletion effect has been found for multiple forms of self-regulation, ranging from suppressing particular kinds of thoughts to resisting temptation.

COGNITIVE COSTS FOR EXPRESSIVE SUPPRESSION BUT NOT COGNITIVE REAPPRAISAL?

Research on both the immediate and the delayed cognitive consequences of expressive suppression paints a consistently grim picture of its effects on memory and social interactions. Are such consequences common to all forms of self-regulation, as predicted by the ego-depletion view of Baumeister and his colleagues? Or is there something especially costly about suppression, as compared with other forms of emotion regulation? It would be poor design indeed if all emotion-regulatory strategies we use in everyday life degraded ongoing and vital cognitive processes.

On the basis of an analysis of when different emotion-regulation strategies intervene in the generation of emotion, my colleagues and I have predicted that some forms of emotion regulation should not be cognitively costly. This prediction follows from a theoretical model of emotion that distinguishes between cognitively focused reappraisal and behaviorally focused expressive suppression (Richards & Gross, 2000). According to this model, reappraisal is evoked at the front end, or very early on during a potentially emotional event. Specifically, reappraisal involves reinterpreting a potentially emotional situation up front in a way that neutralizes its emotional impact. Suppression, by contrast, occurs at the back end, or after emotions have been triggered. Thus, suppression can be thought of as mopping up one's emotions; reappraisal keeps them from spilling in the first place. For example, suppression during a job interview would entail chronic efforts to conceal feelings that press constantly for expression. By contrast, successfully reappraising the interview beforehand as nothing to worry about should keep full-blown emotions from arising in the first place, thereby obviating the need for chronic regulatory effort during the interview. Thus, suppression should consume attentional resources as an event unfolds, but reappraisal should not. If this reasoning is correct, we might expect that suppression—but not reappraisal— has cognitive costs.

Results of several experiments that manipulated reappraisal support this hypothesis. For example, participants who adopted the neutral perspective of a medical doctor while watching slides of injured people (i.e., reappraisers) felt less emotional than control participants who received no regulation instructions but remembered the slides just as well (Richards & Gross, 2000, Study 2). Similarly, romantic partners who reappraised potentially upsetting conversations about relationship problems by thinking about the positive aspects of their relationship beforehand showed better memory for the conversations than partners who were asked to suppress their emotions while the conversations took place (Richards et al., 2003). Moreover, another study showed that reappraisal in the context of an upsetting conversation did not compromise verbal engagement or responsiveness (Butler et al., 2003). Finally, research taking an individual differences approach has shown that people who habitually regulate their emotions by altering how they think about life events (e.g., looking on the bright side) have no better or worse memory than people who do not habitually reappraise (Richards & Gross, 2000, Study 3).

DIRECTIONS FOR FUTURE RESEARCH

Research on the cognitive consequences of emotion regulation is of relatively recent vintage. On balance, the available evidence suggests that expressive suppression can interfere with memory, aspects of discourse, and problem solving. However, not all forms of emotion regulation are cognitively costly. Reappraisal appears to be a strategy that allows people to look and feel better emotionally without impairing the areas of cognitive functioning studied thus far.

Despite recent empirical progress in understanding how emotion regulation influences cognitive functioning, a number of important questions remain unanswered. The first group of questions pertains to the scope of the cognitive consequences of expressive suppression. For example, is the cognitive load of concealing feelings sufficient to undermine a job applicant's performance during a stressful interview? Might jurors' efforts to appear stoic during a trial compromise their ability to make evidence-based decisions? Do students' efforts to appear calm and collected during an exam degrade their performance? Additional research is necessary to uncover the generality and limits of the cognitive consequences of suppression.

A second group of questions concerns the relative effects of different forms of emotion regulation. After all, reappraisal and suppression are not the only strategies people use to decrease unwanted emotions. Future research should examine the cognitive consequences of other emotion-regulatory strategies, such as thought suppression, rumination, and masking (i.e., showing an emotion other than the one that is actually felt). Only by studying multiple strategies can we begin to learn which strategies may be most preferable to use when peak cognitive performance is important to us.

A third group of questions concerns methodology. How should the cognitive consequences of emotion regulation be studied? The research reviewed here relied almost exclusively on explicit instructions to manipulate the regulatory processes of interest. This approach permits a high degree of control. However, future research should also use less explicit manipulations. For example, one might introduce or remove critical situational factors (e.g., the presence of other people, social norms, goals) to prompt spontaneous efforts to alter emotional responding. This approach is crucial not only for documenting the cognitive consequences of emotion regulation, but also for clarifying the types of situations that inspire people to regulate their emotions in the first place.

Several other important questions await attention. It is still not known precisely how people go about regulating their emotions in everyday life or when these strategies are particularly likely to degrade cognitive functioning. Moreover, it is not known whether people can overcome any deleterious consequences of emotion regulation. If people are aware that suppression can impair cognition, can they preserve cognitive functioning by trying harder to remember something or to be an articulate conversationalist?

Answers to these and other questions about the intersection of emotion regulation and cognition subserve not only the practical goal of knowing when and how emotion regulation may promote or degrade optimal functioning in everyday life, but also the broader theoretical goal of clarifying what it means to be "emotionally intelligent."

Recommended Reading

Gross, J.J. (1998). (See References)
Richards, J.M., & Gross, J.J. (1999). (See References)
Richards, J.M., & Gross, J.J. (2000). (See References)

Acknowledgments—I would like to thank Dawn DeGere, James Gross, and Donna Whitsett for their helpful comments.

Note

1. Address correspondence to Jane M. Richards, Department of Psychology, University of Texas, Austin, TX 78712-0187; e-mail: richards@psy.utexas.edu.

References

Baumeister, R.F., Bratslavsky, E., Muraven, M., & Tice, D.M. (1998). Ego depletion: Is the self a limited resource? *Journal of Personality and Social Psychology, 74*, 1252–1265.

Bonanno, G.A., Papa, A., O'Neill, K., Westphal, M., & Coifman, K. (2004). The importance of being flexible: The ability to enhance and suppress emotional expressions predicts long-term adjustment. *Psychological Science, 15*, 482–487.

Butler, E.A., Egloff, B., Wilhelm, F.H., Smith, N.C., Erickson, E.A., & Gross, J.J. (2003). The social consequences of expressive suppression. *Emotion, 3*, 48–67.

Carver, C.S., & Scheier, M.F. (1981). *Attention and self-regulation: A control-theory approach to human behavior.* New York: Springer-Verlag.

Damasio, A.R. (1994). *Descartes' error: Emotion, reason, and the human brain.* New York: Grossett/Putnam.

DePaulo, B.M., Kashy, D.A., Kirkendol, S.E., Wyer, M.M., & Epstein, J.A. (1996). Lying in everyday life. *Journal of Personality and Social Psychology, 70*, 979–995.

DePaulo, B.M., Lindsay, J.J., Malone, B.E., Muhlenbruck, L., Charlton, K., & Cooper, H. (2003). Cues to deception. *Psychological Bulletin, 129*, 74–118.

DePaulo, B.M., Stone, J.I., & Lassiter, G.D. (1985). Deceiving and detecting deceit. In B.R. Schlenker (Ed.), *The self and social life* (pp. 323–370). New York: McGraw-Hill.

Gross, J.J. (1998). The emerging field of emotion regulation: An integrative review. *Review of General Psychology, 2*, 271–299.

Gross, J.J., Richards, J.M., & John, O.P. (in press). Emotion regulation in everyday life. In D.K. Snyder, J.A. Simpson, & J.N. Hughes (Eds.), *Emotion regulation in families.* Washington, DC: American Psychological Association.

Larsen, R.J. (2000). Toward a science of mood regulation. *Psychological Inquiry, 11*, 129–141.

Richards, J.M., Butler, E.A., & Gross, J.J. (2003). Emotion regulation in romantic relationships: The cognitive consequences of concealing feelings. *Journal of Social and Personal Relationships, 20*, 599–620.

Richards, J.M., & Gross, J.J. (1999). Composure at any cost? The cognitive consequences of emotion suppression. *Personality and Social Psychology Bulletin, 25*, 1033–1044.

Richards, J.M., & Gross, J.J. (2000). Emotion regulation and memory: The cognitive costs of keeping one's cool. *Journal of Personality and Social Psychology, 79*, 410–424.

Critical Thinking Questions

1. Define expressive suppression and give an example from your own experience. Drawing on research presented in the article, describe the cognitive consequences of emotional suppression for memory and social interaction.

2. Describe the theory of ego-depletion. How does this theory contribute to an understanding of expressive suppression?

3. Compare and contrast expressive suppression and cognitive reappraisal. Why is one more costly than the other?

This article has been reprinted as it originally appeared in *Current Directions in Psychological Science*. Citation information for this article as originally published appears above.

Section 2: Influences on Social Knowledge: Biases, Unconscious Processes, and Culture

Considering an ancient volcano like the one that formed the island of Santorini, an earth scientist may examine the landscape, life, and weather impacted by its eruption, as well as the factors that precipitate eruption in present-day volcanoes. A contemporary earth scientist does not, however, consider the volcano's intentions, unconscious biases, or awareness of its emotions. Aspects of the physical world can be active, but they obviously are distinct from the social world. Human beings draw inferences about their own behavior as well as the behavior of others, and can reflect upon their own mental processes. They behave in the service of social goals, but sometimes do not recognize the true sources of those goals. Indeed, many influences on social knowledge and behavior occur outside conscious awareness, and operate through cultural and inferential biases.

Some social inferences fall under the general umbrella of metacognitive experiences. Metacognition involves thinking about one's own thought processes, such as mentally monitoring whether one is grasping a difficult concept, wondering why one just mentally compared a new acquaintance to one's sibling, and recognizing that one is having difficulty remembering a past event. The hindsight bias is a well-known metacognitive experience that involves bias in social inference; if an outcome seems unsurprising and inevitable, people have the experience that they "knew it all along." People also have metacognitive experiences about social events that may or will occur in the future: their graduation from college, marriage, death of a parent, or winning the lottery. An undergraduate senior may observe that she is worried about performing well in law school, a teacher who imagines winning the lottery may be surprised that his "plans" do not include quitting his job, a soon-to-be-homeowner performs a mental checklist of plans that need to be made. In a related vein, when people are thinking about the future, they often infer their likely emotional experiences and even base their decisions upon those inferences. A familiar example is experienced during multiple choice exams: students may not change an answer because they expect to feel worse if the new response is incorrect than if they retain the original answer.

The process of projecting future emotional reactions is called "affective forecasting" (Wilson & Gilbert, 2005). Generally speaking, people are relatively accurate in forecasting whether future emotional reactions will be positive or negative. Most people know, for example, that death of a loved one will be unpleasant and that dinner at a favorite restaurant likely will be pleasant. People are considerably less skilled at forecasting the duration and intensity of their emotions. Professors know, for example, that earning tenure is a happy event, but fail to recognize how quickly that experience recedes to mundane contentment. Similarly, people overestimate how long they will feel miserable after a romantic relationship ends, and discover that they are less miserable than they anticipated. Wilson and Gilbert argue that most people make sense of unusual events relatively quickly, and adapt to them as the "new normal." Many of the mental processes that help this adjustment operate nonconsciously once the event has occurred, so people do not anticipate the role of such processes. For example, after a romantic break-up, people may be less likely to remember the positive aspects of the relationship and may become especially attentive to the advantages of life as a single person. These mental defenses actually help them adjust more quickly than they expected to adjust. The anticipated emotion of "I can't live without him" dissipates as life indeed continues without the partner.

In addition to forecasting about the future (and believing that we could have forecast the past), people also think about the reasons why events and behaviors occur. The process by which people ascertain the causes of social events is called attribution. Perceivers wonder whether others caused an event intentionally and possess personality characteristics that could have caused that event. Alternatively, they may observe that external circumstances played a significant role in the event, and assign less responsibility to the actor. For instance, if one witnesses a mother scolding her child, one may think that the mother is impatient or unkind, rather than observing that the child had been pulling the tail of an angry sharp-clawed feline. For decades, social psychologists theorized that people drawing attributions were likely to make the fundamental attribution error (also known as the correspondence bias), which involves an over-reliance upon dispositional factors and under-reliance upon situational factors. This tendency to focus first on dispositional explanations, though, varies across cultures. Social scientists have come to recognize that cultural experience influences how people think about the very heart of social knowledge: intent and underlying dispositional causes. Norenzayan and Nisbett (2000) detail a number of studies that show how East Asians are much more sensitive to situational explanations (i.e., less likely to make the fundamental attribution error) than are Westerners. [East Asians can and do recognize intent and personality, of course, just as Westerners can recognize situational factors. Each group simply has a different default that has priority in attribution.]

When people consider their own behavior or events that befall them, they tend to make self-serving attributions: internal characteristics are credited for positive behaviors and outcomes (e.g., "I earned an "A" because I am smart and worked hard") and external characteristics are invoked to explain negative behaviors and outcomes (e.g., "I got a "D" because the test was unfair"). The fact that people draw attributions about their own behavior does not necessarily mean that their inferences are accurate. Behavior can be caused by subtle environmental cues which people may not consciously notice. For example, priming test-takers with the stereotype of a professor increases scores, but one scarcely imagines students saying "I earned an A because I was primed to think about professors!!"

Priming goals and behavioral concepts also can influence behavior, without actors realizing that these primes are affecting them. Bargh and Williams (2006) show, for example, that priming people with goals such as politeness or cooperation can encourage behaviors relevant to those concepts. The effects of primes are not equal or identical across people, either. For college-aged individuals who want to make their mothers proud of them, subliminally priming the concept of their mother will increase task persistence. Similarly, for communally-oriented people, exposure to primes about power encourage concern about the outcomes of their subordinates. Of course, in natural settings people are exposed to myriad stimuli, some of which might be additive and others which might exert opposite influences. The point is not that human beings are at the mercy of whatever strong prime crosses their paths, but rather that human behavior can be influenced by factors outside awareness.

Research that seeks to understand nonconscious influences on behavior and inference, inferential biases, and the perceptual filters provided by culture helps provide insight into how the human mind works. Why did an event occur, was it inevitable, how will people feel about the event in three months? Why did that person behave in a particular way, and is that identified reason the actual cause or simply the preferred attribution made by perceivers? The answers to these questions are unlikely to be found by taking behavior and inference at face value. Instead, like the volcanologist, the social psychologist must probe beneath the surface to understand the phenomenon in question.

Affective Forecasting: Knowing What to Want

Timothy D. Wilson[1]
University of Virginia

Daniel T. Gilbert
Harvard University

Abstract

People base many decisions on affective forecasts, predictions about their emotional reactions to future events. They often display an impact bias, overestimating the intensity and duration of their emotional reactions to such events. One cause of the impact bias is focalism, the tendency to underestimate the extent to which other events will influence our thoughts and feelings. Another is people's failure to anticipate how quickly they will make sense of things that happen to them in a way that speeds emotional recovery. This is especially true when predicting reactions to negative events: People fail to anticipate how quickly they will cope psychologically with such events in ways that speed their recovery from them. Several implications are discussed, such as the tendency for people to attribute their unexpected resilience to external agents.

Keywords

affective forecasting; prediction; emotion; sense making

Many cultures have myths in which people can make their wishes come true. The story of Aladdin and his lamp is best known to readers of the *Arabian Nights* (and to Disney fans); in Irish legends, it is leprechauns who make wishes come true; whereas in a Chinese fable it is an obliging dragon that has the head of a camel, the eyes of a hare, the neck of a snake, the claws of an eagle, and the ears of a buffalo (McNeil, 2003).

Common to these myths is the notion that if people (perhaps with the help of a genie) could make their wishes come true, they would achieve everlasting happiness. Sometimes, however, people are disappointed by the very things they think they want. Research on *affective forecasting* has shown that people routinely mispredict how much pleasure or displeasure future events will bring and, as a result, sometimes work to bring about events that do not maximize their happiness.

These mispredictions can take a number of forms. People can be wrong about how positive or negative their reactions to future events will be, particularly if what unfolds is different from what they had imagined. Prospective dog owners might predict that Rover will bring nothing but joy because they picture a faithful companion who obediently fetches the newspaper each morning instead of an obstinate beast who chews shoes and demands 6:00-a.m. walks in the freezing rain. Generally, however, humans are adept at predicting whether events are likely to be pleasant or unpleasant. Even a rat can readily learn that pressing one bar will produce a food pellet and another an electric shock and will vote with its paws for the more pleasant option. People know that a root beer will be more pleasant than a root canal.

People are less adept at predicting the intensity and duration of their future emotional reactions. Occasionally they underestimate intensity and duration; this may happen, for example, when a person is in a "cold" emotional state at the time of prediction and is trying to imagine being in a "hot" emotional state in the future. Satiated shoppers underestimate how much they will want ice cream later in the week, and addicts who have just injected heroin underestimate how much they will crave the drug when they are deprived of it later (Gilbert, Gill, & Wilson, 2002; Loewenstein, O'Donoghue, & Rabin, 2003).

THE IMPACT BIAS

More common than underestimating future emotional reactions, however, is the *impact bias,* whereby people overestimate the intensity and duration of their emotional reactions to future events—even when they know what the future event is likely to entail and they are not in a particularly "hot" or "cold" emotional state at the time of making their forecast. This error has been found repeatedly in a variety of populations and contexts. College students overestimated how happy or unhappy they would be after being assigned to a desirable or undesirable dormitory (see Fig. 1), people overestimated how unhappy they would be 2 months after the dissolution of a romantic relationship, untenured college professors overestimated how unhappy they would be 5 years after being denied

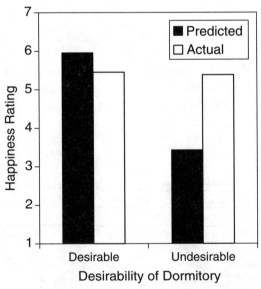

Fig. 1. College students' predicted and actual levels of happiness after dormitory assignments. Participants predicted what their overall level of happiness would be a year later if they were randomly assigned to a desirable or undesirable dormitory (on a 7-point scale, with 1 = *unhappy* and 7 = *happy*). Students predicted that their dormitory assignment would have a large positive or negative impact on their overall happiness (solid bars); but a year later, those living in undesirable and desirable dormitories were at nearly identical levels of happiness (open bars). Adapted from Dunn, Wilson, & Gilbert (2003).

tenure, women overestimated how unhappy they would be upon receiving unwanted results from a pregnancy test, and so on (see Loewenstein et al., 2003; Mellers & McGraw, 2001; Wilson & Gilbert, 2003). The impact bias is important because, when deciding what to work for, people need to predict not only the valencé (positivity or negativity) of their emotional reactions ("Will I feel good or bad?"), but also the intensity and duration of these reactions (e.g., "Will I feel good for a few seconds or a few months?"). If consumers overestimate the intensity and duration of the pleasure they will get from purchasing a new car, for example, they may be better off spending their money in some other way.

One cause of the impact bias is focalism, the tendency to overestimate how much we will think about the event in the future and to underestimate the extent to which other events will influence our thoughts and feelings (Schkade & Kahneman, 1998; Wilson, Wheatley, Meyers, Gilbert, & Axsom, 2000). When football fans think about how they will feel after their favorite team wins an important game, for example, they are likely to focus exclusively on the game and neglect to think about the many other things—such as upcoming deadlines at work, the need to get the car fixed, or a visit from old family friends—that will influence their thoughts and feelings. Focalism is a straight forward and, we suspect, quite common source of the impact bias. It can be corrected, to some degree, by asking people to think carefully about the many other events that will demand their attention in the future; studies have found that this exercise tempers people's predictions about the impact of a victory or loss by their favorite football team on their happiness (Wilson et al., 2000).

SENSE MAKING AND PEOPLE'S IGNORANCE OF IT

Another cause of the impact bias is that forecasters fail to recognize how readily they will make sense of novel or unexpected events once they happen. Research across a variety of fields suggests that such events trigger four processes in sequence: attention, reaction, explanation, and adaptation.

- First, people are especially likely to attend to events that are self-relevant but poorly understood. For example, a student who unexpectedly receives an A on an important exam will initially think about little else.
- Second, people react emotionally to self-relevant, poorly understood events. The student who receives an unexpected A will initially feel overjoyed.
- Third, people attempt to explain or make sense of self-relevant, poorly understood events. For example, the overjoyed student will begin to search for reasons why she received a better-than-expected grade.
- Fourth, by making sense of events, people adapt emotionally to them. Once the student has explained the reasons for her grade, she will think about her achievement less and experience less happiness when she does think about it. The event will come to be seen as more normal and inevitable then it actually was, and hence it will lose some of the emotional power that it had when it still seemed extraordinary.

These four processes may seem relatively uncontroversial to psychologists, but research suggests that people neglect to take them into account when forecasting

41

their future emotions. In particular, because the processes by which people explain or make sense of unexpected events are often quick and nonconscious, people do not recognize beforehand that such processes will occur; thus they do not consider how quickly their tendency to explain events will reduce the impact of those events. When a student tries to predict how she will feel if she receives an unexpected *A,* she has little trouble imagining herself feeling overjoyed but a lot of trouble imagining herself explaining the event in a way that makes it seem ordinary and predictable.

The Pleasure of Uncertainty About Positive Events

If making sense of positive events reduces the duration of the pleasure they cause, then inhibiting the sense-making process should prolong people's pleasure. In one study, for example, students who were studying in a library were unexpectedly given an index card with a dollar coin attached, and results showed that they were in a better mood 5 minutes later if the text on the card made it difficult rather than easy for them to explain why they had received the money. Yet people did not anticipate this effect; in fact, "forecaster" participants predicted that they would be happier if the card made explanation easy rather than difficult (Wilson, Centerbar, Kermer, & Gilbert, 2005). People do not realize how quickly they will make sense of unexpected positive events and how doing so will make their positive emotions dissipate.

A Pleasure Paradox

Most organisms avoid that which has previously caused them pain and approach that which has previously given them pleasure. Humans are better at this than most other animals because they do more than merely associate stimuli with their affective consequences. People are naive scientists who explain events to themselves, and the sophisticated causal theories people generate allow them to pursue pleasures and avoid pains with an unusual degree of success. But an ironic consequence of this inveterate sense making is that events tend to lose some of their hedonic impact as they become more sensible. People work to understand events so that they can repeat the good ones and avoid repeating the bad ones, but in understanding these events people may reduce their ability to be moved by them. True, some explanations of events make people feel better than other explanations do; taking credit for a major success is more pleasurable, for example, than attributing it to luck. Independent of the favorability of the explanation, however, sense making hastens emotional "recovery" from events. Things are rarely as good or bad as people expect them to be because people do not realize that by explaining the things that happen to them, they drain these things of the hedonic qualities that caused them to focus on the events in the first place.

NEGATIVE EVENTS: MOTIVATED SENSE MAKING

People are motivated to recover from negative emotional events, and the kind of sense making they engage in often involves coping, psychological defenses, and rationalization. Like the physiological immune system that fights threats to physical health, people have a psychological immune system that fights threats to emotional well-being. These defenses have been well documented by social and personality psychologists and include dissonance reduction, motivated reasoning, self-serving attributions, self-affirmation, and positive illusions.

A feature that all these defenses have in common is that they are largely unconscious, and in fact are more effective by operating behind the mental scenes. When trying to cope with a romantic breakup, for example, people usually will not be able deliberately and consciously to adopt a more negative view of their partner in order to make themselves feel better. Instead, the expartner will come to seem less suitable, with no awareness that one's own psychological immune system was responsible for this shift in view. Because people are generally unaware of the operation of these defenses, they tend not to take them into account when predicting their future emotional reactions—an oversight we have termed *immune neglect*.

In one study, for example, participants who failed to get a desirable job were less upset 10 minutes later when the failure was attributable to a single capricious interviewer (easy to rationalize: "The guy's a jerk") rather than to a team of interviewers (difficult to rationalize: "How could they all dislike me?"). In another study, participants were less upset when they received negative personality feedback from a computer (easy to rationalize: "Computers make mistakes") than from a clinician (difficult to rationalize: "How could I have scored so badly on the personality test?"). In both cases, people had stronger reactions when unexpected negative events were difficult to rationalize and explain, but in both cases they failed to anticipate that this would happen (Gilbert, Pinel, Wilson, Blumberg, & Wheatley, 1998).

Implications of Immune Neglect

People's failure to anticipate their natural tendency to make the best of bad outcomes has a number of consequences:

- Because people do not recognize that they have reduced the impact of negative events by explaining and rationalizing them, they sometimes attribute their unexpected resilience to the work of powerful, insightful, and benevolent external agents (Gilbert, Brown, Pinel, & Wilson, 2000). For example, employees who are transferred to undesirable locations might be surprised by how happy they are; by failing to recognize that they produced their own happiness with nonconscious coping and defensive processes, they might attribute their good fortune to the guiding hand of an external agent, such as God.
- When people make a decision that is difficult to reverse, such as buying a sweater from a store with a "no returns" policy, they are strongly motivated to rationalize the decision and make the best of it. When people can more easily undo a decision, such as buying a sweater they can return, they are less motivated to rationalize their choice, because they can always change their minds. Consequently people are often happier with irrevocable choices because they do the psychological work necessary to rationalize

what they can't undo. Because people do not realize in advance that they will work harder to rationalize irreversible decisions, however, they often avoid the binding commitments that would actually increase their satisfaction (Gilbert & Ebert, 2002). For example, many people pay more to purchase clothing from stores with a liberal return policy, when they would more satisfied with clothes they bought that they could not return.

- Not surprisingly, people believe that major traumas will have a more enduring emotional impact than minor ones will. Because people are more strongly motivated to make sense of major traumas than minor ones, however, the pain of minor traumas can sometimes last longer than more serious ones. It seems like it would be worse, for example, to be insulted by a close friend than a stranger. Because people are more motivated to cope with (and perhaps rationalize) the insult from the friend, however, they may recover from it more quickly (Gilbert, Lieberman, Morewedge, & Wilson, 2004).

- It is well-known that people weigh potential losses more heavily than corresponding gains, which often leads to economically illogical decisions. Kermer, Driver-Linn, Wilson, and Gilbert (2005), for example, found that most people refused a gamble in which they had a 50% of winning $5 and a 50% chance of losing only $3, demonstrating classic loss aversion. Loss aversion seems to involve a faulty affective forecast: Although participants predicted that losing a gamble would have a larger emotional impact than winning, they were wrong; the magnitude of unhappiness caused by losing was no greater than the magnitude of happiness caused by winning (Kermer et al., 2005).

SUMMARY AND FUTURE DIRECTIONS

Affective forecasts are important because people base many decisions on them. Decisions about who to marry, what career to pursue, and whether to donate money to the local homeless shelter are based, at least in part, on predictions about how these decisions will make one feel. To the extent that people's predictions about what will make them happy are flawed, people fail at maximizing their happiness.

One unanswered question is whether the impact bias is advantageous in some way. It could be argued that exaggerating the impact of emotional events serves as a motivator, making people work hard to obtain things that they predict will have large positive consequences and avoid things that they predict will have large negative consequences. It may be, however, that overestimating the impact of negative events creates unnecessary dread and anxiety about the future. And there are other costs to affective-forecasting errors. People suffering from debilitating digestive disorders who underestimate how quickly they will adapt to an ostomy bag might make less-than-optimal treatment decisions. People who overestimate the positive emotional impact of undergoing cosmetic surgery might be too willing to get an extreme makeover. Finding ways to increase the accuracy of affective forecasts is a worthy enterprise—though not, we suspect, a particularly easy one (Ubel et al., 2001). It is difficult to place oneself in the future and imagine what it will be like to have made sense of an event that, in the present, seems extraordinary. Such mental time traveling, however, might ultimately lead to better decisions.

Recommended Reading

Gilbert, D.T., Driver-Linn, E., & Wilson, T.D. (2002). The trouble with Vronsky: Impact bias in the forecasting of future affective states. In L.F. Barrett & P. Salovey (Eds.), *The wisdom in feeling: Psychological processes in emotional intelligence* (pp. 114–143). New York: Guilford.
Loewenstein, G., O'Donoghue, T. and Rabin, M. (2003). (See References)
Mellers, B.A., & McGraw, A.P. (2001). (See References)
Wilson, T.D. (2002). *Strangers to ourselves: Discovering the adaptive unconscious.* Cambridge, MA: Harvard University Press.
Wilson, T.D., & Gilbert, D.T. (2003). (See References)

Acknowledgments—Much of the research discussed in this article was supported by research grant #RO1-MH56075 from the National Institute of Mental Health to the authors.

Note

1. Address correspondence to Timothy D. Wilson, P.O. Box 400400, 102 Gilmer Hall, University of Virginia, Charlottesville, VA 22904-4400, e-mail: twilson@virginia.edu, or to Daniel Gilbert, Department of Psychology, William James Hall, 33 Kirkland Street, Harvard University, Cambridge, MA, 02138, e-mail: gilbert@wjh.harvard.edu.

References

Dunn, E.W., Wilson, T.D., & Gilbert, D.T. (2003). Location, location, location: The misprediction of satisfaction in housing lotteries. *Personality and Social Psychology Bulletin, 29,* 1421–1432.
Gilbert, D.T., Brown, R.A., Pinel, E.C., & Wilson, T.D. (2000). The illusion of external agency. *Journal of Personality and Social Psychology, 79,* 690–700.
Gilbert, D.T., & Ebert, J.E. (2002). Decisions and revisions: The affective forecasting of changeable outcomes. *Journal of Personality and Social Psychology, 82,* 503–514.
Gilbert, D.T., Gill, M., & Wilson, T.D. (2002). The future is now: Temporal correction in affective forecasting. *Organizational Behavior and Human Decision Processes, 88,* 430–444.
Gilbert, D.T., Lieberman, M.D., Morewedge, C., & Wilson, T.D. (2004). The peculiar longevity of things not so bad. *Psychological Science, 15,* 14–19.
Gilbert, D.T., Pinel, E.C., Wilson, T.D., Blumberg, S.J., & Wheatley, T.P. (1998). Immune neglect: A source of durability bias in affective forecasting. *Journal of Personality and Social Psychology, 75,* 617–638.
Kermer, D.A., Driver-Linn, E., Wilson, T.D., & Gilbert, D.T. (2005). *Loss aversion applies to predictions more than experience.* Unpublished raw data, University of Virginia.
Loewenstein, G., O'Donoghue, T., & Rabin, M. (2003). Projection bias in predicting future utility. *Quarterly Journal of Economics, 118,* 1209–1248.
Mellers, B.A., & McGraw, A.P. (2001). Anticipated emotions as guides to choice. *Current Directions in Psychological Science, 10,* 210–214.
McNeil, D.G. Jr. (2003, April 29). Dragons, a brief history in long miles. *New York Times* (p. F2).
Schkade, D.A., & Kahneman, D. (1998). Does living in California make people happy? A focusing illusion in judgments of life satisfaction. *Psychological Science, 9,* 340–346.
Ubel, P.A., Loewenstein, G., Hershey, J., Baron, J., Mohr, T., Asch, D., & Jepson, C. (2001). Do non-patients underestimate the quality of life associated with chronic health conditions because of a focusing illusion? *Medical Decision Making, 21,* 190–199.

Wilson, T.D., Centerbar, D.B., Kermer, D.A., & Gilbert, D.T. (2005). The pleasures of uncertainty: Prolonging positive moods in ways people do not anticipate. *Journal of Personality and Social Psychology, 88,* 5–21.

Wilson, T.D., & Gilbert, D.T. (2003). Affective forecasting. In M.P. Zanna (Ed.), *Advances in experimental social psychology* (Vol. 35, pp. 345–411). San Diego, CA: Academic Press.

Wilson, T.D., Wheatley, T.P., Meyers, J.M., Gilbert, D.T., & Axsom, D. (2000). Focalism: A Source of durability bias in affective forecasting. *Journal of Personality and Social Psychology, 78,* 821–836.

Critical Thinking Questions

1. What is affective forecasting and are we good at it? Explain how affective forecasting relates to the impact bias.

2. Describe two causes of the impact bias. Clearly explain how each leads to the bias.

3. Define immune neglect and discuss some implications of demonstrating immune neglect.

4. The authors state that "one unanswered question is whether the impact bias is advantageous in some way." Explain how a *bias* could be advantageous and describe some ways this particular bias might serve forecasters.

This article has been reprinted as it originally appeared in *Current Directions in Psychological Science*. Citation information for this article as originally published appears above.

Culture and Causal Cognition

Ara Norenzayan and Richard E. Nisbett[1]
Centre de Récherche en Epistemologie Appliquée, Ecole Polytechnique, Paris, France (A.N.), and Department of Psychology, University of Michigan, Ann Arbor, Michigan (R.E.N.)

Abstract

East Asian and American causal reasoning differs significantly. East Asians understand behavior in terms of complex interactions between dispositions of the person or other object and contextual factors, whereas Americans often view social behavior primarily as the direct unfolding of dispositions. These culturally differing causal theories seem to be rooted in more pervasive, culture-specific mentalities in East Asia and the West. The Western mentality is analytic, focusing attention on the object, categorizing it by reference to its attributes, and ascribing causality based on rules about it. The East Asian mentality is holistic, focusing attention on the field in which the object is located and ascribing causality by reference to the relationship between the object and the field.

Keywords

causal attribution; culture; attention; reasoning

Psychologists within the cognitive science tradition have long believed that fundamental reasoning processes such as causal attribution are the same in all cultures (Gardner, 1985). Although recognizing that the content of causal beliefs can differ widely across cultures, psychologists have assumed that the ways in which people come to make their causal judgments are essentially the same, and therefore that they tend to make the same sorts of inferential errors. A case in point is the fundamental attribution error, or FAE (Ross, 1977), a phenomenon that is of central importance to social psychology and until recently was held to be invariable across cultures.

The FAE refers to people's inclination to see behavior as the result of dispositions corresponding to the apparent nature of the behavior. This tendency often results in error when there are obvious situational constraints that leave little or no role for dispositions in producing the behavior. The classic example of the FAE was demonstrated in a study by Jones and Harris (1967) in which participants read a speech or essay that a target person had allegedly been required to produce by a debate coach or psychology experimenter. The speech or essay favored a particular position on an issue, for example, the legalization of marijuana. Participants' estimates of the target's actual views on the issue reflected to a substantial extent the views expressed in the speech or essay, even when they knew that the target had been explicitly instructed to defend a particular position. Thus, participants inferred an attitude that corresponded to the target person's apparent behavior, without taking into account the situational constraints operating on the behavior. Since that classic study, the FAE has been found in myriad studies in innumerable experimental and naturalistic contexts, and it has

47

been a major focus of theorizing and a continuing source of instructive pedagogy for psychology students.

CULTURE AND THE FAE

It turns out, however, that the FAE is much harder to demonstrate with Asian populations than with European-American populations (Choi, Nisbett, & Norenzayan, 1999). Miller (1984) showed that Hindu Indians preferred to explain ordinary life events in terms of the situational context in which they occurred, whereas Americans were much more inclined to explain similar events in terms of presumed dispositions. Morris and Peng (1994) found that Chinese newspapers and Chinese students living in the United States tended to explain murders (by both Chinese and American perpetrators) in terms of the situation and even the societal context confronting the murderers, whereas American newspapers and American students were more likely to explain the murders in terms of presumed dispositions of the perpetrators.

Recently Jones and Harris's (1967) experiment was repeated with Korean and American participants (Choi et al., 1999). Like Americans, the Koreans tended to assume that the target person held the position he was advocating. But the two groups responded quite differently if they were placed in the same situation themselves before they made judgments about the target. When observers were required to write an essay, using four arguments specified by the experimenter, the Americans were unaffected, but the Koreans were greatly affected. That is, the Americans' judgments about the target's attitudes were just as much influenced by the target's essay as if they themselves had never experienced the constraints inherent in the situation, whereas the Koreans almost never inferred that the target person had the attitude expressed in the essay.

This is not to say that Asians do not use dispositions in causal analysis or are not occasionally susceptible to the FAE. Growing evidence indicates that when situational cues are not salient, Asians rely on dispositions or manifest the FAE to the same extent as Westerners (Choi et al., 1999; Norenzayan, Choi, & Nisbett, 1999). The cultural difference seems to originate primarily from a stronger East Asian tendency to recognize the causal power of situations.

The cultural differences in the FAE seem to be supported by different folk theories about the causes of human behavior. In one study (Norenzayan et al., 1999), we asked participants how much they agreed with paragraph descriptions of three different philosophies about why people behave as they do: (a) a strongly dispositionist philosophy holding that "how people behave is mostly determined by their personality," (b) a strongly situationist view holding that behavior "is mostly determined by the situation" in which people find themselves, and (c) an interactionist view holding that behavior "is always jointly determined by personality and the situation." Korean and American participants endorsed the first position to the same degree, but Koreans endorsed the situationist and interactionist views more strongly than did Americans.

These causal theories are consistent with cultural conceptions of personality as well. In the same study (Norenzayan et al., 1999), we administered a scale designed to measure agreement with two different theories of personality: entity theory, or the belief that behavior is due to relatively fixed dispositions such as traits, intelligence, and moral character, and incremental theory, or the belief that behavior is conditioned on the situation and that any relevant dispositions are subject to change (Dweck, Hong, & Chiu, 1993). Koreans for the most part rejected entity theory, whereas Americans were equally likely to endorse entity theory and incremental theory.

ANALYTIC VERSUS HOLISTIC COGNITION

The cultural differences in causal cognition go beyond interpretations of human behavior. Morris and Peng (1994) showed cartoons of an individual fish moving in a variety of configurations in relation to a group of fish and asked participants why they thought the actions had occurred. Chinese participants were inclined to attribute the behavior of the individual fish to factors external to the fish (i.e., the group), whereas American participants were more inclined to attribute the behavior of the fish to internal factors. In studies by Peng and Nisbett (reported in Nisbett, Peng, Choi, & Norenzayan, in press), Chinese participants were shown to interpret even the behavior of schematically drawn, ambiguous physical events—such as a round object dropping through a surface and returning to the surface—as being due to the relation between the object and the presumed medium (e.g., water), whereas Americans tended to interpret the behavior as being due to the properties of the object alone.

The Intellectual Histories of East Asia and Europe

Why should Asians and Americans perceive causality so differently? Scholars in many fields, including ethnography, history, and philosophy of science, hold that, at least since the 6th century B.C., there has been a very different intellectual tradition in the West than in the East (especially China and those cultures, like the Korean and Japanese, that were heavily influenced by China; Nisbett et al., in press). The ancient Greeks had an *analytic* stance: The focus was on categorizing the object with reference to its attributes and explaining its behavior using rules about its category memberships. The ancient Chinese had a *holistic* stance, meaning that there was an orientation toward the field in which the object was found and a tendency to explain the behavior of the object in terms of its relations with the field.

In support of these propositions, there is substantial evidence that early Greek and Chinese science and mathematics were quite different in their strengths and weaknesses. Greek science looked for universal rules to explain events and was concerned with categorizing objects with respect to their essences. Chinese science (some people would say it was a technology only, though a technology vastly superior to that of the Greeks) was more pragmatic and concrete and was not concerned with foundations or universal laws. The difference between the Greek and Chinese orientations is well captured by Aristotle's physics, which explained the behavior of an object without reference to the field in which it occurs. Thus, a stone sinks into water because it has the property of gravity, and a piece of wood floats because it has the property of levity.

In contrast, the principle that events always occur in some context or field of forces was understood early on in China.

Some writers have suggested that the mentality of East Asians remains more holistic than that of Westerners (e.g., Nakamura, 1960/1988). Thus, modern East Asian laypeople, like the ancient Chinese intelligentsia, are attuned to the field and the overall context in determining events. Western civilization was profoundly shaped by ancient Greece, so one would expect the Greek intellectual stance of object focus to be widespread in the West.

Attention to the Field Versus the Object

If East Asians tend to believe that causality lies in the field, they would be expected to attend to the field. If Westerners are more inclined to believe that causality inheres in the object, they might be expected to pay relatively more attention to the object than to the field. There is substantial evidence that this is the case.

Attention to the field as a whole on the part of East Asians suggests that they might find it relatively difficult to separate the object from the field. This notion rests on the concept of field dependence (Witkin, Dyk, Faterson, Goodenough, & Karp, 1974). Field dependence refers to a relative difficulty in separating objects from the context in which they are located. One way of measuring field dependence is by means of the rod-and-frame test. In this test, participants look into a long rectangular box at the end of which is a rod. The rod and the box frame can be rotated independently of one another, and participants are asked to state when the rod is vertical. Field dependence is indicated by the extent to which the orientation of the frame influences judgments of the verticality of the rod. The judgments of East Asian (mostly Chinese) participants have been shown to be more field dependent than those of American participants (Ji, Peng, & Nisbett, in press).

In a direct test of whether East Asians pay more attention to the field than Westerners do (Masuda & Nisbett, 1999), Japanese and American participants saw under-water scenes that included one or more *focal* fish (i.e., fish that were larger and faster moving than other objects in the scene) among many other objects, including smaller fish, small animals, plants, rocks, and coral. When asked to recall what they had just viewed, the Japanese and American participants reported equivalent amounts of detail about the focal fish, but the Japanese reported far more detail about almost everything else in the background and made many more references to interactions between focal fish and background objects. After watching the scenes, the participants were shown a focal fish either on the original background or on a new one. The ability of the Japanese to recognize a particular focal fish was impaired if the fish was shown on the "wrong" background. Americans' recognition was uninfluenced by this manipulation.

ORIGINS OF THE CULTURAL DIFFERENCE IN CAUSAL COGNITION

Most of the cross-cultural comparisons we have reviewed compared participants who were highly similar with respect to key demographic variables, namely, age, gender, socioeconomic status, and educational level. Differences in cognitive abilities were controlled for or ruled out as potential explanations for the data in studies involving a task (e.g., the rod-and-frame test) that might be affected by such abilities. Moreover, the predicted differences emerged regardless of whether the East Asians were tested in their native languages in East Asian countries or tested in English in the United States. Thus, the lack of obvious alternative explanations, combined with positive evidence from intellectual history and the convergence of the data across a diverse set of studies (conducted in laboratory as well as naturalistic contexts), points to culturally shared causal theories as the most likely explanation for the group differences.

But why might ancient societies have differed in the causal theories they produced and passed down to their contemporary successor cultures? Attempts to answer such questions must, of course, be highly speculative because they involve complex historical and sociological issues. Elsewhere, we have summarized the views of scholars who have suggested that fundamental differences between societies may result from ecological and economic factors (Nisbett et al., in press). In China, people engaged in intensive farming many centuries before Europeans did. Farmers need to be cooperative with one another, and their societies tend to be collectivist in nature. A focus on the social field may generalize to a holistic understanding of the world. Greece is a land where the mountains descend to the sea and large-scale agriculture is not possible. People earned a living by keeping animals, fishing, and trading. These occupations do not require so much intensive cooperation, and the Greeks were in fact highly individualistic. Individualism in turn encourages attending only to the object and one's goals with regard to it. The social field can be ignored with relative impunity, and causal perception can focus, often mistakenly, solely on the object. We speculate that contemporary societies continue to display these mentalities because the social psychological factors that gave rise to them persist to this day.

Several findings by Witkin and his colleagues (e.g., Witkin et al., 1974), at different levels of analysis, support this historical argument that holistic and analytic cognition originated in collectivist and individualist orientations, respectively. Contemporary farmers are more field dependent than hunters and industrialized peoples; American ethnic groups that operate under tighter social constraints are more field dependent than other groups; and individuals who are attuned to social relationships are more field dependent than those who are less focused on social relationships.

FUTURE DIRECTIONS

A number of questions seem particularly interesting for further inquiry. Should educational practices take into account the differing attentional foci and causal theories of members of different cultural groups? Can the cognitive skills characteristic of one cultural group be transferred to another group? To what extent can economic changes transform the sort of cultural-cognitive system we have described? These and other questions about causal cognition will provide fertile ground for research in the years to come.

Recommended Reading

Choi, I., Nisbett, R.E., & Norenzayan, A. (1999). (See References)
Fiske, A., Kitayama, S., Markus, H.R., & Nisbett, R.E. (1998). The cultural matrix of social psychology. In D.T. Gilbert, S.T. Fiske, & G. Lindzey (Eds.), *The handbook of social psychology* (4th ed., Vol. 2, pp. 915–981). Boston: McGraw-Hill.
Lloyd, G.E.R. (1996). Science in antiquity: The Greek and Chinese cases and their relevance to problems of culture and cognition. In D.R. Olson & N. Torrance (Eds.), *Modes of thought: Explorations in culture and cognition* (pp. 15–33). Cambridge, England: Cambridge University Press.
Nisbett, R.E., Peng, K., Choi, I., & Norenzayan, A. (in press). (See References)
Sperber, D., Premack, D., & Premack, A.J. (Eds.). (1995). *Causal cognition: A multidisciplinary debate.* Oxford, England: Oxford University Press.

Note

1. Address correspondence to Richard E. Nisbett, Department of Psychology, University of Michigan, Ann Arbor, MI 48109; e-mail: nisbett@umich.edu.

References

Choi, I., Nisbett, R.E., & Norenzayan, A. (1999). Causal attribution across cultures: Variation and universality. *Psychological Bulletin, 125,* 47–63.
Dweck, C.S., Hong, Y.-Y., & Chiu, C.-Y. (1993). Implicit theories: Individual differences in the likelihood and meaning of dispositional inference. *Personality and Social Psychology Bulletin, 19,* 644–656.
Gardner, H. (1985). *The mind's new science.* New York: Basic Books.
Ji, L., Peng, K., & Nisbett, R.E. (in press). Culture, control, and perception of relationships in the environment. *Journal of Personality and Social Psychology.*
Jones, E.E., & Harris, V.A. (1967). The attribution of attitudes. *Journal of Experimental Social Psychology, 3,* 1–24.
Masuda, T., & Nisbett, R.E. (1999). *Culture and attention to object vs. field.* Unpublished manuscript, University of Michigan, Ann Arbor.
Miller, J.G. (1984). Culture and the development of everyday social explanation. *Journal of Personality and Social Psychology, 46,* 961–978.
Morris, M.W., & Peng, K. (1994). Culture and cause: American and Chinese attributions for social and physical events. *Journal of Personality and Social Psychology, 67,* 949–971.
Nakamura, H. (1988). *The ways of thinking of eastern peoples.* New York: Greenwood Press. (Original work published 1960)
Nisbett, R.E., Peng, K., Choi, I., & Norenzayan, A. (in press). Culture and systems of thought: Holistic vs. analytic cognition. *Psychological Review.*
Norenzayan, A., Choi, I., & Nisbett, R.E. (1999). *Eastern and Western folk psychology and the prediction of behavior.* Unpublished manuscript, University of Michigan, Ann Arbor.
Ross, L. (1977). The intuitive psychologist and his shortcomings. In L. Berkowitz (Ed.), *Advances in experimental social psychology* (Vol. 10, pp. 173–220). New York: Academic Press.
Witkin, H.A., Dyk, R.B., Faterson, H.F., Goodenough, D.R., & Karp, S.A. (1974). *Psychological differentiation.* Potomac, MD: Erlbaum.

Critical Thinking Questions

1. Describe the difference between analytic versus holistic cognition. How do the authors use ancient history of different cultures to explain these types of cognitions?

2. The authors state that for Eastern cultures "causality lies in the field" whereas for Western cultures "causality inheres in the object." Explain what they mean by this and how this relates to the Fundamental Attribution Error.

3. In the article the authors present a fascinating study using *focal fish* as stimuli (Masuda & Nisbett, 1999). Briefly summarize the results of this study and explain how they inform the idea of cultural differences in the Fundamental Attribution Error.

This article has been reprinted as it originally appeared in *Current Directions in Psychological Science*. Citation information for this article as originally published appears above.

The Automaticity of Social Life

John A. Bargh[1] and Erin L. Williams
Yale University

Abstract

Much of social life is experienced through mental processes that are not intended and about which one is fairly oblivious. These processes are automatically triggered by features of the immediate social environment, such as the group memberships of other people, the qualities of their behavior, and features of social situations (e.g., norms, one's relative power). Recent research has shown these nonconscious influences to extend beyond the perception and interpretation of the social world to the actual guidance, over extended time periods, of one's important goal pursuits and social interactions.

Keywords

social cognition; automaticity; unconscious

Automaticity refers to control of one's internal psychological processes by external stimuli and events in one's immediate environment, often without knowledge or awareness of such control; automatic phenomena are usually contrasted with those processes that are consciously or intentionally put into operation. Given the historical focus of social psychology on social problems (e.g., discrimination, aggression), it is important to understand the extent to which such negative outcomes might occur without the person's awareness or despite his or her good intentions.

But just because social psychologists tend to study social problems does not mean that automatic processes produce only negative outcomes. To the contrary, much current automaticity research has focused on how nonconscious processes contribute to successful self-regulation and adaptation. As traditional approaches to self-regulation have emphasized the role of conscious, controlled, or executive processes in overcoming impulsive reactions or bad habits, the potential role of nonconscious self-regulatory processes has been somewhat overlooked until recently. But because only conscious, controlled processes can "time-travel"—when the person remembers the past or anticipates the future—nonconscious processes become essential for keeping the individual grounded adaptively and effectively in the present (Bargh, 1997). In terms of contemporary dual-process approaches to cognition, then, nonconscious processes appear to serve a default, background regulatory function, freeing the conscious mind from the concerns of the immediate environment.

SOCIAL PERCEPTION

Much of the early automaticity research in social psychology focused on social perception—the degree to which people's impressions of others are driven by automatic biases. A widely studied source of such bias has been the accessibility

54

of social-behavior representations (i.e., trait constructs such as "intelligent" or "shy"). The automatic use of a given construct to interpret the meaning of someone else's behavior occurs either when one has frequently used that construct in the past (i.e., chronic accessibility) or when one has recently used that construct in some unrelated context (i.e., priming or temporary accessibility). Priming manipulations typically seek to passively and unobtrusively activate the construct in question by having the participant think about or use it in an early phase of the experiment (e.g., a "language test") that is ostensibly unrelated to what follows.

In general, early automaticity research showed that several different forms of social representations become automatically activated in the course of social perception, triggered by the presence of their corresponding features in the environment. The race-, gender-, or age-related features of another person can automatically trigger group stereotypes associated with them; one's consistent affective reactions toward social objects (specific individuals, groups) can become automatically activated upon the mere perception of those objects; and features of one's significant others (e.g., mother, close friend) can automatically activate the specific mental representations of these individuals (see review in Wegner & Bargh, 1998).

Indeed, most automatic effects on social life are mediated by the nonconscious activation of social representations—either *preconsciously* through direct activation by strongly associated stimuli in the environment (as in racial stereotyping effects) or *postconsciously* through recent, conscious use in an unrelated context (as in most category-priming effects). Given the important mediational role played by these structures, current research has focused on discovering the types of information stored within them (e.g., evaluations, goals, trait concepts), as it is these contents that then automatically guide thought and behavior.

THE PERCEPTION–BEHAVIOR LINK

Under the hypothesis that whatever representations become active in social perception will also tend to directly influence behavior, initial tests of automatic social behavior used the same priming methods as in the prior social-perception research to subtly activate trait constructs. However, instead of being asked for their impressions of a target person, participants were put into a situation in which they had the opportunity to act (or not) in line with the primed construct. In an initial study, participants who had been unobtrusively exposed to (i.e., primed with) instances of the concept "rude" were considerably more likely to interrupt a subsequent conversation than were those primed with the concept "polite" (Bargh, Chen, & Burrows, 1996; see Fig. 1).

The logic of the perception–behavior link is that it should apply to any knowledge structure automatically activated in the course of social perception. Social or group stereotypes are one well-researched example. In the course of social perception, people tend to automatically encode minority-group members in terms of their associated stereotypes. Because stereotypes become automatically activated by the mere perception of group features (e.g., skin color) in an individual, the activated stereotype should produce stereotype-consistent behavioral tendencies. *self-fulfilling prophecy*

55

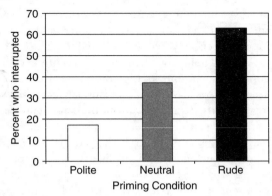

Fig. 1. Percentage of participants primed with the concept "polite," the concept "rude," or a neutral concept who interrupted a conversation between the experimenter and a confederate (Bargh, Chen, & Burrows, 1996, Experiment 1). From "Automaticity of Social Behavior: Direct Effects of Trait Construct and Stereotype Priming on Action," by J.A. Bargh, M. Chen, & L. Burrows, 1996, *Journal of Personality and Social Psychology, 71,* page 235. Copyright 1996 by the American Psychological Association. Reprinted with permission.

Over the past decade, many studies have obtained just this result. Subtle priming of the stereotype of the elderly (which includes the notions that the elderly are forgetful, as well as physically slow and weak) caused college students to walk more slowly when leaving the experimental session (in one study) and to subsequently have poorer memory for the features of a room (in another)—both effects predicted from the content of that stereotype. Stereotypes associated with social roles produce similar effects: Priming the professor stereotype led to students answering a greater number of questions correctly in a trivia game (see review in Dijksterhuis & Bargh, 2001).

NONCONSCIOUS GOAL PURSUIT

Another potential mechanism by which the social environment can directly influence social behavior is through the activation and operation of *goal representations* that have become strongly associated with a particular situation. If an individual repeatedly chooses to pursue a certain goal in a situation, then eventually merely encountering that situation is enough to automatically activate the goal and put it into operation (see Bargh, Gollwitzer, Lee-Chai, Barndollar, & Troetschel, 2001). For example, a parent who chose to forego her own interests and instead pursue her child's best interests, when there was a conflict between the two, eventually would come to act in her child's interests without having to think or consciously decide to; another person who tended to put her own interests first would eventually, over time, automatically pursue her own goals instead of those of her child.

Tests of this model have used the same priming procedures as discussed above to activate a variety of goal representations; the effects of the primed goals are then assessed across a variety of dependent measures. These have included not only cognitive and behavioral consequences of the goal pursuit but also classic qualities of motivational states, such as persistence in the face of obstacles and resumption of interrupted tasks. This research has shown that when a goal is activated outside of the participant's awareness, the same outcomes are obtained as in previous research on conscious goal pursuit. For example, in one study, subliminal priming of a cooperation goal produced the same increase in cooperative behavior as did explicit, conscious instructions to cooperate (Bargh et al., 2001). Importantly, participants showed no signs of being aware either of the activation of the goal or of its operation over time to guide their behavior. In the cooperation-goal study, for example, participants in the conscious-cooperation condition could accurately report on how cooperative they had just been; those in the nonconscious (primed) cooperation condition could not.

APPLICATIONS TO SPHERES OF SOCIAL LIFE

Close Relationships

Much recent work on the automaticity of social life has focused on close relationships. Because of the importance of the goals one typically pursues with close relationship partners (e.g., intimacy, belonging, achievement) and the high frequency of interacting with them, the significant others in one's life are likely to become external triggers of nonconscious goal pursuits. Across five studies, Fitzsimons and Bargh (2003) found that priming the representations of participants' close others (e.g., spouses, parents, colleagues) caused the participants to behave in line with the goals stored within those representations. People waiting at an airport were more likely to donate time to help the experimenter after being asked questions about their friends than they were after being asked about their coworkers; participants in a laboratory study who had earlier indicated having a goal to make their mother proud of them outperformed others on a subsequent verbal task, but only after subliminal priming of the representation of their mother.

Situational Features

Are there automatic influences on social behavior toward people one does not already know well? In general, it is the function of social norms to provide guidelines for how to behave toward strangers and new acquaintances. One is generally expected to act in a mildly positive manner toward strangers, to not harm them, and to assist them to the extent they truly need help and one has the ability to help.

Routine settings and situations also have particularized norms for conduct that are automatically activated when one enters those settings. In harmony with the hypothesis that the mental representation of "library" contains within it action components that automatically guide appropriate action in that setting, Aarts and Dijksterhuis (2003) found that showing participants a picture of a library and instructing them to go to the library after the experimental session caused them to speak more softly during the experiment, compared to control participants.

Social Structure (Power)

Sociostructural variables, such as where one fits in the organizational or power hierarchy of a group, can also have implicit, automatic effects on thought and behavior. Generally, the non-conscious activation of the concept of power seems to produce greater concern with one's own goals and less concern with the outcomes of others, consistent with the traditional lore that "power corrupts." Fortunately, not everyone has such self-centered automatic goals when in positions of power. Chen, Lee-Chai, and Bargh (2001) showed that there are those who instead automatically pursue the goal of helping and advancing the outcomes of those in their charge. Across several experiments, Chen et al. (2001) found that when these communally-oriented people (as determined by their responses to an initial questionnaire taken some months before the experimental session) were primed with power-related stimuli, they became *less* selfish than usual and more concerned with the outcomes of other participants, compared to a control condition.

(NONCONSCIOUSLY) MOTIVATED COGNITION

One burgeoning area of research involving automatic social phenomena is *motivated cognition*—especially self-protective motives. Spencer, Fein, Wolfe, Fong, and Dunn (1998) demonstrated that threatening participants' self-esteem (through false task-failure feedback) automatically caused an increase in their tendency to stereotype others. Apparently (and depressingly), the denigration of others appears to be an automatic and reflexive response to personal failures and threats to one's self-esteem.

But there are grounds for hope. Moskowitz, Gollwitzer, Wasel, and Schaal (1999) showed that automatic stereotype influences can be effectively countered if the individual possesses an automatic goal to be egalitarian and fair toward others. However, egalitarian participants did, however, show the same evidence of stereotype activation as did the other participants. Apparently, then, the stimulus of a minority-group member automatically started two processes at the same time: the activation of the stereotype and the activation of the egalitarian motive, with the latter functioning to shut down or inhibit the former before it could influence judgments. Moskowitz et al. (1999) have thus identified a positive form of automatic motivated cognition and shown how it is possible for chronically good intentions to prevail.

BENEFITS OF NONCONSCIOUS SELF-REGULATION

From Freud onward, scholars of successful adaptation and self-regulation have regarded nonconscious phenomena as mainly problematic—sources of negative outcomes (e.g., psychopathology, bad habits) and certainly not a help to adaptive functioning. However, recent theoretical analyses of intuition have emphasized the importance of immediate, automatic influences on choices and decision making. These have been touted as the mechanisms underlying the "gut feelings" or "hunches" that, far from being random or illusory, do a fairly good job of directing us (see Dijksterhuis & Nordgren, in press; Lieberman, 2000).

In general, the nonconscious nature of these judgment- and behavior-guiding processes makes them a boon to effective self-regulation, because of their immediacy, efficiency, and reliability. It would seem to make good sense for as much guidance of current behavior to occur outside those conscious limits as possible.

CONCLUSIONS AND FUTURE DIRECTIONS

The automatic influences on social life are many and diverse. Other people, their characteristic features, the groups they belong to, the social roles they fill, and whether or not one has a close relationship with them have all been found to be automatic triggers of important psychological and behavioral processes. So too have features of standard situations, which become automatically associated with general norms and rules of conduct, as well as with one's own personal goals when in those situations.

One new line of research concerns how specific emotions such as anger, guilt, and happiness prime (i.e., nonconsciously influence) judgments and behavior (e.g., Lerner, Small, & Loewenstein, 2004). Most people are aware of the powerful influences that emotions can have over immediate behavior and judgments but remain unaware that these influences can carry over into unrelated contexts in which decisions and behavioral choices are made. Indeed, most priming studies depend on the fact that mental representations activated in one context take time to return to a deactivated state and are more likely to have an influence while active than they are at other times. The carry-over effects of recent emotional experiences are likely to prove a common source of automatic influences in everyday life.

Research programs are moving beyond first-generation questions of whether nonconscious influences exist and what forms they might take to second-generation questions of how priming operates in the stimulus-rich real world. For instance, laboratory research has shown that a given priming stimulus can provoke, in parallel, a variety of immediate automatic responses (e.g., in perception, in motivation). But in unconstrained real-world settings, people are bombarded with thousands of such stimuli every day, from advertisements to items in store windows to individuals one passes while walking down a busy street. Which of these will exert nonconscious influences, and which will not?

Another direction for research is determining how the various kinds of automatic effects interact with each other. The responses suggested by nonconscious influences may be in conflict with each other, such that one cannot possibly act on every preconsciously generated behavioral impulse. Models of how these conflicts are resolved, utilizing both nonconscious and conscious means, are now beginning to enter the literature (e.g., Morsella's PRISM model; Morsella, 2005); further research on how these parallel potentialities are transformed into one-at-atime responses by individuals is urgently needed.

Finally, the recent discovery of *mirror neurons* (e.g., Rizzolatti, Fogassi, & Gallese, 2001), and what they have revealed about the hard-wired nature of the perception–behavior link in humans, is a tremendously important development in the history of psychology. These neurons, located in the premotor cortex of higher primates, have the intriguing property of becoming active both when a person watches an action being performed and when the person performs that action him- or herself. Social cognitive neuroscience research has already shown just how deeply and fundamentally—dare we say, automatically—our minds are connected to each other and to the larger social world.

Recommended Reading

Bargh, J.A., & Chartrand, T.L. (1999). The unbearable automaticity of being. *American Psychologist, 54*, 462–479.
Chaiken, S., & Trope, Y. (Eds., 1999). *Dual-process theories in social psychology.* New York: Guilford.
Gladwell, M. (2004). *Blink: The power of thinking without thinking.* New York: Little, Brown.
Myers, D.G. (2002). *Intuition: Its powers and perils.* New Haven, CT: Yale University Press.
Wilson, T.D. (2002). *Strangers to ourselves.* Cambridge, MA: Harvard University Press.

Acknowledgments—Preparation of this manuscript was supported in part by Grant R01-MH60767 from the National Institute of Mental Health (USA). We thank Ap Dijksterhuis and Ezequiel Morsella for comments and advice on an earlier version.

Note

1. Address correspondence to John A. Bargh, Department of Psychology, Yale University, P.O. Box 208205, New Haven, CT 06520; e-mail: john.bargh@yale.edu.

References

Aarts, H., & Dijksterhuis, A. (2003). The silence of the library: Environment, situational norms, and social behavior. *Journal of Personality and Social Psychology, 84*, 18–28.
Bargh, J.A. (1997). The automaticity of everyday life. In R.S. Wyer (Ed.), *Advances in social cognition* (Vol. X, pp. 1–61). Mahwah, NJ: Erlbaum.
Bargh, J.A., Chen, M., & Burrows, L. (1996). Automaticity of social behavior: Direct effects of trait construct and stereotype priming on action. *Journal of Personality and Social Psychology, 71*, 230–244.
Bargh, J.A., Gollwitzer, P.M., Lee-Chai, A.Y., Barndollar, K., & Troetschel, R. (2001). The automated will: Nonconscious activation and pursuit of behavioral goals. *Journal of Personality and Social Psychology, 81*, 1014–1027.
Chen, S., Lee-Chai, A.Y., & Bargh, J.A. (2001). Relationship orientation as a moderator of the effects of social power. *Journal of Personality and Social Psychology, 80*, 173–187.
Dijksterhuis, A., & Nordgren, L.F. (in press). A theory of unconscious thought. *Perspectives on Psychological Science.*
Dijksterhuis, A., & Bargh, J.A. (2001). The perception-behavior expressway: Automatic effects of social perception on social behavior. In M.P. Zanna (Ed.), *Advances in experimental social psychology* (Vol. 33, pp. 1–40). San Diego: Academic Press.
Fitzsimons, G.M., & Bargh, J.A. (2003). Thinking of you: Nonconscious pursuit of interpersonal goals associated with relationship partners. *Journal of Personality and Social Psychology, 84*, 148–164.
Lerner, J.S., Small, D.A., & Loewenstein, G. (2004). Heart strings and purse strings: Carry-over effects of emotions on economic transactions. *Psychological Science, 15*, 337–341.

Lieberman, M.D. (2000). Intuition: A social cognitive neuroscience approach. *Psychological Bulletin, 126,* 109–137.

Morsella, E. (2005). The functions of phenomenal states: Supermodular interaction theory. *Psychological Review, 112,* 1000–1021.

Moskowitz, G.B., Gollwitzer, P.M., Wasel, W., & Schaal, B. (1999). Preconscious control of stereotype activation through chronic egalitarian goals. *Journal of Personality and Social Psychology, 77,* 167–184.

Rizzolatti, G., Fogassi, L., & Gallese, V. (2001). Neurophysiological mechanisms underlying the understanding and imitation of action. *Nature Reviews Neuroscience, 2,* 661–670.

Spencer, S.J., Fein, S., Wolfe, C.T., Fong, C., & Dunn, M.A. (1998). Automatic activation of stereotypes: The role of self-image threat. *Personality and Social Psychology Bulletin, 24,* 1139–1152.

Wegner, D.M., & Bargh, J.A. (1998). Control and automaticity in social life. In D. Gilbert, S. Fiske, & G. Lindzey (Eds.), *Handbook of social psychology* (4th ed, pp. 446–496). Boston: McGraw-Hill.

Critical Thinking Questions

1. Define automaticity and explain how it is related to social perception.

2. Clarify how the concept of automaticity has been applied to the social spheres of close relationships, situational features, and social structure.

3. The authors present research involving automaticity and *motivated cognition.* By defining each, explain why these two concepts are seemingly at odds with each other. Then, explain how the authors integrate them.

This article has been reprinted as it originally appeared in *Current Directions in Psychological Science*. Citation information for this article as originally published appears above.

Section 3: Close Relationships: Attraction, Attachment, and Love

Literature, film, music, and art provide insight into what people value. A casual glance reveals that, throughout the ages and cultures, in various forms and media, close relationships are important to people. In its early years (the 1970s), the scientific study of relationships met with ridicule and disdain, hailed as common sense and scorned as the domain of poets. Fortunately, relationships researchers ignored their critics, and turned their attention to issues such as relationship development, the advantages of close relationships for physical health and psychological well-being, and the evolutionary underpinnings of pair-bonding and sexual interest. Not every finding in the arena of close relationships has supported common sense: married people are not necessarily happier than singles, men fall in love more quickly than women do, and not everyone wants a huge circle of friends. The insights of poets and screenwriters may give insight into what our cultures consider ideals—and provide entertainment and pleasure to aficionados—but what we have learned through the scientific study of relationships fills volumes.

Poets and writers recognize that different individuals can have very different conceptions of the ideal relationship or partner. The insights uniquely provided by relationship researchers are specifications of the origins of these different conceptions, and models of how these different conceptions may predict variations in satisfaction, views of the relationship, or propensities to leave or go. For example, the papers by Mikulincer and Shaver (2006) and by Furman (2003) note that some theorists have speculated that the type of attachment a child develops with a caregiver creates a general model of how relationships operate. A child whose needs are consistently met without being smothered learns to trust the caregiver enough to explore; as adults, people who developed this secure model tend to trust their romantic partners and explore through work and leisure. Mikulincer and Shaver (2006) further demonstrate that empathic responses also are predicted by these different mental models. Secure adults evince empathy and compassion toward others who are suffering, whereas insecure adults either distance themselves psychologically or focus on their own discomfort. Literature and film sometimes trace a character's cold and unfeeling disposition back to his or her childhood, and social science reveals that there indeed is some truth in that.

The recognition of similarities between parent-child relationships and adult romantic relationships is not an effort to equate the two, of course: Compared to healthy adult relationships, healthy parent-child relationships do not include a sexual relationship. The latter usually also involve unidirectional (rather than bidirectional) care-giving. Diamond (2004) argues that the emotional attachment and caregiving that often occurs in romantic relationships is quite distinct from sexual interest. Attachments develop from early relationships with primary caregivers, and then carry over into attachments to peers and romantic partners. Sexual interest, she argues, has a different evolutionary history and purpose. Supporting this view, different portions of the brain are active when adults are viewing photographs of friends versus romantic partners. In the Western ideal, romantic feelings and sexual interest co-occur . . . but they are distinctly different phenomena nonetheless.

Given the importance of the decision regarding the selection of a long-term partner, "trying on" different kinds of relationships certainly has its value. [Indeed, some scholars have suggested that romantic relationships that terminate before marriage ultimately undercut the divorce rate!!] Relationship ideals are put to their initial tests through dating, usually beginning during adolescence. In contemporary Western cultures at least, early romantic relationships may look a good deal like close friendships, with a sexuality component. During this critical time of transition, parents and peers may provide care-giving and support, respectively. Furman (2002) indicates that romantic relationships during the college years (i.e., young adulthood) are especially important for social and emotional support. Thus, relationships in young adulthood seem to include the mutual care-giving found in adult romantic relationships. It bears mention, of course, that some findings about adolescent romantic relationships are bounded by culture and era. In Shakespeare's day, Juliet was of a marriageable age at 12, and she probably had very few (if any) male friends! But the story tells us one thing quite plainly: Sexual interest increases along with the physical changes that occur during adolescence.

Beyond romantic love and sexual attraction, relationships affect the way that people think, feel, and behave. As noted earlier, empathic responses to the suffering of others is predicted by people's primary mental representations of relationships (Mikulincer & Shaver, 2006). Reis and Collins (2004) note a variety of other affective responses that are predicted by relationship satisfaction, mental models of relationships, and the specific kind of relationship that one has: feelings of self-worth, subjective well-being, jealousy, bereavement. Indeed, some emotions are hard to imagine outside the realm of relationships. [One can feel angry that one's computer crashed, bored during a class, or disappointed at a poor grade . . . but its hard to imagine feeling jealous, bereaved, betrayed or guilty without the involvement of a close other.]. How people think and process information about the social world also is influenced by close relationships: people compare newly-encountered individuals to friends and family members, extend their own self-serving biases to close others, and evince better memory for information relevant to people close to them. Finally, relationships influence people's behavior. Beyond compassionate behavior, relationship characteristics influence how people cope with stress, their success at work, and the kinds of activities that they enjoy outside of work.

Given their pervasive impact across life domains, most people view close relationships with their family, friends, lovers, or spouses as the most important part of their lives. What exactly people want from relationships varies across time (e.g., adolescence versus adulthood) and gender, and also varies along individual differences in ideals or attachment styles. Although they can be the source of conflict, relationships also can provide social support and intimacy, sexual gratification, social status and resources. Relationships are as important to study as they are interesting to study. Certainly, there remains ample grist for the mills of relationships researchers, with plenty to spare for the novelists, artists, and poets.

Attachment Security, Compassion, and Altruism

Mario Mikulincer[1]
Bar-Ilan University, Ramat Gan, Israel

Phillip R. Shaver
University of California, Davis

Abstract

Theoretically, people who have the benefits of secure social attachments should find it easier to perceive and respond to other people's suffering, compared with those who have insecure attachments. This is because compassionate reactions are products of what has been called the caregiving behavioral system, the optimal functioning of which depends on its not being inhibited by attachment insecurity (the failure of the attachment behavioral system to attain its own goal, safety and security provided by a caring attachment figure). In a series of recent studies, we have found that compassionate feelings and values, as well as responsive, altruistic behaviors, are promoted by both dispositional and experimentally induced attachment security. These studies and the theoretical ideas that generated them provide guidelines for enhancing compassion and altruism in the real world.

Keywords

attachment; caregiving; compassion; altruism

In a world burdened by international, interethnic, and interpersonal conflict, all people of goodwill wish it were possible to foster compassion and willingness to help others rather than ignore others' needs and exacerbate their suffering. Many have probably entertained the intuitive notion that if only people could feel safer and less threatened, they would have more psychological resources to devote to noticing and reacting favorably to other people's suffering. While conducting research guided by seminal ideas first articulated by John Bowlby (1969/1982) in his books on attachment theory, we have demonstrated the usefulness of enhancing attachment security as a method of fostering compassion and altruism. In this article, we briefly describe some of our recent studies after providing the theoretical essentials necessary to understand them.

ATTACHMENT THEORY: BASIC CONCEPTS

According to Bowlby (1969/1982), human beings are born with an innate psychobiological system (the *attachment behavioral system*) that motivates them to seek proximity to people who will protect them (*attachment figures*) in times of need. The operation of this system is affected by an individual's social experiences, especially with early caregivers, resulting in measurable individual differences in attachment security. Interactions with attachment figures who are available and responsive, especially in times of need, promote optimal functioning of the attachment system, create a core sense of attachment security (a sense based on expectations that key people will be available and supportive in times of need), and result in the formation of positive *working models* (mental representations of self and others). When attachment figures are not supportive, however, a sense of security is not attained, negative working models are formed, and other, secondary strategies for regulating distress are adopted.

These secondary strategies are of two major kinds: *hyperactivation* and *deactivation of the attachment system.* (We reviewed evidence for these strategies in Mikulincer & Shaver, 2003.) Hyperactivation refers to intense efforts to attain proximity to attachment figures and ensure their attention and support. People who rely on hyperactivating strategies compulsively seek proximity and protection, are hypersensitive to signs of possible rejection or abandonment, and are prone to ruminating on personal deficiencies and threats to relationships. Deactivation refers to the inhibition of proximity-seeking inclinations and actions, and the suppression or discounting of any threat that might activate the attachment system. People who rely on these strategies tend to maximize distance from others, experience discomfort with closeness, strive for personal strength and self-reliance, and suppress distressing thoughts and memories.

In studies of adolescents and adults, tests of these theoretical ideas have focused on attachment style—the systematic pattern of relational expectations, emotions, and behaviors that results from a particular history of interactions with attachment figures (Hazan & Shaver, 1987). Attachment styles vary along two dimensions (Brennan, Clark, & Shaver, 1998). One dimension, attachment *avoidance*, reflects the extent to which a person relies on deactivating strategies. The other dimension, attachment *anxiety*, reflects the degree to which a person relies on hyperactivating strategies. People who score relatively low on both dimensions are said to be secure or to have a strong sense of security. Although attachment style is conceptualized as a global orientation toward close relationships, there are theoretical and empirical reasons for believing that an individual's global style is just the top node in a hierarchical network of attachment-related thoughts, some of which apply only to certain kinds of relationships and others of which apply only in certain relational contexts (Mikulincer & Shaver, 2003). These attachment-related thoughts, which can be activated by actual or imagined encounters with supportive or unsupportive people, can be incongruent with a person's global attachment style (e.g., Mikulincer & Shaver, 2001).

THE CAREGIVING SYSTEM AND ITS INTERPLAY WITH THE ATTACHMENT SYSTEM

According to Bowlby (1969/1982), the caregiving behavioral system was crafted by evolution because it provided protection and support to individuals who were either chronically dependent or temporarily in need. "Caregiving" refers to a broad array of behaviors that complement a relationship partner's attachment behaviors or signals of need. In the parent-child relationship—the prototypical relationship in which the caregiving behavioral system is manifested—the goal of the child's attachment system (proximity that fosters protection and provides security) is also the aim of the parent's caregiving system, and signals of increased security on the child's part can reduce the parent's caregiving behaviors. If one extends this conceptualization to the broader realm of compassion and altruism, the aim of the caregiving system is to alter a needy person's situation or condition in order to foster his or her safety, well-being, and security.

Beyond explaining this complementarity between a support seeker's attachment system and a support provider's caregiving system, Bowlby (1969/1982) also discussed the interplay between these two systems within a person as he or she alternates between needing and providing support. According to Bowlby, because of the urgent need to protect oneself from imminent threats, activation of the attachment system inhibits activation of other behavioral systems and thereby interferes with many nonattachment activities, including caregiving. Under conditions of threat, adults generally turn to others for support, rather than thinking first about providing support to others. Only when they feel reasonably secure themselves can people easily direct attention to others' needs and provide support, even in a general context of danger. In threatening situations, possessing greater attachment security may allow people to provide more effective care for others, because the sense of security is closely related to optimistic beliefs and feelings of self-efficacy when coping with one's own or a relationship partner's distress (Mikulincer & Shaver, 2003). This inner sense of security helps to explain why in many emergencies some parents focus first on their children's safety even if it means putting themselves in harm's way.

With this theoretical analysis in mind, we began a program of research on attachment, compassion, and altruism. Our main hypothesis was that people who are dispositionally secure, or whose level of security has been contextually enhanced (e.g., by experimental manipulations, such as reading a story about a supportive person), would be more likely than relatively insecure people to empathize with and provide care for others. We also hypothesized that although both anxious and avoidant people are conceptualized in attachment theory as insecure, different psychological mechanisms would underlie their responses to other people's suffering. In a number of studies, Batson (1991) has shown that lack of empathy or compassion can be due either to lack of prosocial motivation toward other people or to the arousal of what he calls "personal distress," a form of self-focused agitation and discomfort that is not translated into effective helping. We expected that people who scored high on attachment avoidance and pursued deactivating strategies would distance themselves from others' suffering, so that they would have sharply decreased empathy and compassion. In contrast, we expected that people who scored high on attachment anxiety, and were therefore easily distressed in a self-focused way, would react to others' suffering with personal distress.

RECENT STUDIES OF ATTACHMENT, COMPASSION, AND ALTRUISM

Even before we undertook our studies, there were hints in the literature that attachment security would be associated with compassion and altruistic caregiving. Kunce and Shaver (1994), for example, found that secure individuals (as compared with their insecure counterparts) described themselves as more sensitive to their romantic partners' needs and more likely to provide emotional support. In a recent study, Westmaas and Silver (2001) found that higher scores on avoidance and anxiety were associated with less inclination to care for a confederate of the experimenter who had been diagnosed with cancer.

Although such studies consistently revealed an association between attachment security and compassionate behavior, they were correlational in nature and did not necessarily indicate that a sense of attachment security was active while study participants were responding to other people's needs. We therefore adopted an experimental strategy more appropriate for testing causal predictions about the effects of attachment security on compassion and altruism. Using well-validated cognitive techniques—for example, subliminally exposing study participants to security-related words (*love, hug*) or instructing them to imagine a scenario in which they felt safe and secure—we momentarily activated representations of attachment security and then assessed their psychological and behavioral effects.

Overall, these studies demonstrated convincingly that contextual activation of the sense of attachment security leads people to respond more like people who are dispositionally secure. For example, we found that contextual activation of attachment security reduced negative reactions to out-group members (Mikulincer & Shaver, 2001). Compared with a control group, people whose momentary sense of security was heightened were more willing to interact with a member of a potentially threatening out-group (e.g., an Israeli Arab who had written a derogatory essay about the study participants' Israeli Jewish in-group), were less threatened by the social and economic threats aroused by recent Russian Jewish immigrants to Israel, and were less discriminatory toward homosexuals. In these studies, security enhancement strikingly reduced in-group/out-group differences that were evident in control groups and groups of participants who received experimental inductions of positive affect unrelated to attachment (such as through reading a comic story or imagining winning a lottery).

Another experiment examined the effects of attachment security on compassionate responses toward other people's suffering (Mikulincer et al., 2001, Study 1). In this study, dispositional attachment anxiety and avoidance were assessed with the Experience in Close Relationships scale (ECR; Brennan et al., 1998), and the sense of attachment security was activated (primed) by having participants read a story about a student who was in trouble, sought help from his or her parents, and received support, comfort, and reassurance from them. In comparison conditions, participants read a comic story (positive-affect priming) or a neutral story (neutral priming). Following the priming procedure, participants rated their current mood, read a brief story about a student whose parents had been killed in an automobile accident, and then rated how much they experienced compassion-related feelings (e.g., compassion, sympathy, tenderness) and feelings of personal distress (e.g., tension, worry, distress).

As predicted, participants primed with an attachment-security story reported higher levels of compassionate feelings than participants in the positive-affect and neutral conditions, and lower levels of personal distress than participants in the neutral condition (see means in Fig. 1). In addition, dispositional attachment anxiety and avoidance were inversely related to compassion, and attachment anxiety, but not avoidance, was positively related to personal distress. This latter finding supported our idea that personal distress interferes with anxious individuals' compassionate reactions to others' needs. Attachment anxiety seems to encourage

70

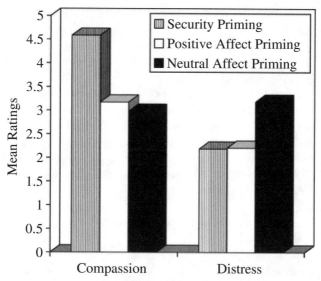

Fig. 1. Means of compassion and personal-distress ratings after reading about a student whose parents had been killed in an automobile accident. Results are shown separately for participants who had previously read an attachment-security story (security priming), a comic story (positive-affect priming), or a neutral story (neutral priming; Mikulincer et al., 2001, Study 1). Ratings were made on a 7-point scale, with higher ratings indicating higher levels of compassion and personal distress.

self-preoccupation and heighten a form of distress that, even if initially triggered in part by empathy, fails to facilitate compassionate responses. The findings were conceptually replicated in four additional studies (Mikulincer et al., 2001, Studies 2–5), using different techniques for heightening security (e.g., asking participants to recall personal memories of supportive care, subliminally exposing them to proximity-related words such as *love* and *hug*) and measuring different dependent variables (e.g., participants' spontaneous descriptions of feelings elicited by others' suffering, accessibility of memories in which participants felt compassion or distress).

These findings also indicated that the effects of security-related priming and attachment-style differences could not be explained in terms of conscious mood. Although the priming of positive affect reduced personal distress, it did not significantly affect compassion, nor did changes in mood mediate the effects of security priming and dispositional attachment security on compassion and personal distress. The effects of attachment security were not the same as the effects of the positive-affect induction and were not explicable in terms of simple mood changes.

Contextual activation of attachment security affects not only compassion toward people in distress, but also broader value orientations. In three experiments (Mikulincer et al., 2003), enhancing attachment security (asking participants to recall personal memories of supportive care or exposing them unobtrusively to a picture of a supportive interaction), as compared with enhancing positive affect or exposing participants to a neutral control condition, strengthened endorsement of two self-transcendent values, benevolence (concern for people who are close to oneself) and universalism (concern for all humanity). Moreover, avoidant attachment, assessed with the ECR, was inversely associated with endorsement of these two prosocial values, supporting our notion that deactivating strategies foster lack of concern for other people's needs.

We (Gillath et al., 2004) have also examined the effects of attachment security on altruistic behavior outside the laboratory. In particular, we assessed engagement in various altruistic activities, such as caring for the elderly or donating blood. We found that avoidant attachment was negatively associated with engaging in such activities. Anxious attachment was not directly related to overall involvement in volunteer activities, but it was associated with egoistic motives for volunteering (e.g., to make oneself feel better, to enjoy a sense of belonging), another indication of anxious individuals' self-focus.

To examine the actual decision to help or not to help a person in distress, we (Mikulincer, Shaver, Gillath, & Nitzberg, 2004, Study 1) created a laboratory situation in which participants could watch a confederate while she performed a series of increasingly aversive tasks. As the study progressed, the confederate became very distressed by the aversive tasks, and the actual participants were given an opportunity to take her place, in effect sacrificing themselves for the welfare of another. Shortly before making the choice, participants were subliminally primed with either representations of attachment security (the name of a security-providing attachment figure) or attachment-unrelated representations (the name of a close person who did not function as an attachment figure or the name of a mere acquaintance). We found that momentary, subliminal activation of the sense of attachment security increased participants' willingness to take the distressed person's place (see Fig. 2). In a second study (Mikulincer et al., 2004, Study 2),

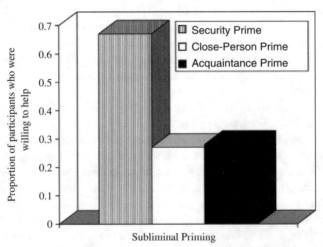

Fig. 2. Proportion of participants who were willing to help a distressed person as a function of priming condition (Mikulincer, Shaver, Gillath, & Nitzberg, 2004, Study 1). Participants were primed subliminally with the name of an attachment figure (security prime), the name of a close person who was not an attachment figure, or the name of an acquaintance.

conscious enhancement of attachment security (asking people to remember experiences of being cared for and supported by others) had the same effect. In both experiments, high avoidance scores were associated with less willingness to help a distressed person, corroborating our study of real-world volunteering.

CONCLUSIONS

Overall, our research suggests that attachment security provides a foundation for compassion and caregiving, whereas two major forms of attachment insecurity interfere with compassionate caregiving. The findings are compatible with our theoretical reasoning that the state of the attachment system affects the operation of the caregiving system. Attachment theory therefore provides a well-validated conceptual framework for further exploration of the developmental and social-relational roots of compassion and altruism, as well as further examination of the processes and mechanisms that underlie compassionate behavior. More research is needed to create better measures of compassion and to determine how the attachment dimensions relate to other measures of prosocial personality and moral development. It would also be interesting to see whether participation in compassionate activities can alleviate attachment insecurity, by bolstering a person's sense of being loved and needed, and by bolstering prosocial working models of self. It will also be important to explore how various experiences and techniques, including psychotherapy, family therapy, skilled meditation, and participation in religious or charitable organizations, might enhance a person's sense of security and thereby foster compassion and altruism. Such procedures, when combined effectively and continued over an extended period of time, might allow human beings to achieve a noble goal: to free all sentient beings from their suffering (Dalai Lama, 2001).

Recommended Reading

Bowlby, J. (1979). *The making and breaking of affectional bonds.* London: Tavistock.
Gilbert, P. (Ed.). (2004). *Compassion: Its nature and use in psychotherapy.* London: Brunner-Routledge.
Mikulincer, M., & Shaver, P.R. (2003). (See References)

Acknowledgments—Preparation of this article was facilitated by grants from the Fetzer Institute and the Positive Psychology Network.

Note

1. Address correspondence to Mario Mikulincer, Department of Psychology, Bar-Ilan University, Ramat Gan 52900, Israel; e-mail: mikulm@mail.biu.ac.il.

References

Batson, C.D. (1991). *The altruism question: Toward a social-psychological answer.* Hillsdale, NJ: Erlbaum.
Bowlby, J. (1982). *Attachment and loss: Vol. 1. Attachment* (2nd ed.). New York: Basic Books. (Original work published 1969)
Brennan, K.A., Clark, C.L., & Shaver, P.R. (1998). Self-report measurement of adult attachment: An integrative overview. In J.A. Simpson & W.S. Rholes (Eds.), *Attachment theory and close relationships* (pp. 46–76). New York: Guilford Press.

Dalai Lama. (2001). *An open heart: Practicing compassion in everyday life* (N. Vreeland, Ed.). Boston: Little, Brown.

Gillath, O., Shaver, P.R., Mikulincer, M., Nitzberg, R.E., Erez, A., & van Ijzendoorn, M.H. (2004). *Attachment, caregiving, and volunteering: Placing volunteerism in an attachment-theoretical framework.* Manuscript submitted for publication.

Hazan, C., & Shaver, P.R. (1987). Romantic love conceptualized as an attachment process. *Journal of Personality and Social Psychology, 52,* 511–524.

Kunce, L.J., & Shaver, P.R. (1994). An attachment-theoretical approach to caregiving in romantic relationships. In K. Bartholomew & D. Perlman (Eds.), *Advances in personal relationships* (Vol. 5, pp. 205–237). London: Kingsley.

Mikulincer, M., Gillath, O., Halevy, V., Avihou, N., Avidan, S., & Eshkoli, N. (2001). Attachment theory and reactions to others' needs: Evidence that activation of the sense of attachment security promotes empathic responses. *Journal of Personality and Social Psychology, 81,* 1205–1224.

Mikulincer, M., Gillath, O., Sapir-Lavid, Y., Yaakobi, E., Arias, K., Tal-Aloni, L., & Bor, G. (2003). Attachment theory and concern for others' welfare: Evidence that activation of the sense of secure base promotes endorsement of self-transcendence values. *Basic and Applied Social Psychology, 25,* 299–312.

Mikulincer, M., & Shaver, P.R. (2001). Attachment theory and intergroup bias: Evidence that priming the secure base schema attenuates negative reactions to out-groups. *Journal of Personality and Social Psychology, 81,* 97–115.

Mikulincer, M., & Shaver, P.R. (2003). The attachment behavioral system in adulthood: Activation, psychodynamics, and interpersonal processes. In M.P. Zanna (Ed.), *Advances in experimental social psychology* (Vol. 35, pp. 53–152). San Diego, CA: Academic Press.

Mikulincer, M., Shaver, P.R., Gillath, O., & Nitzberg, R.E. (2004). *Attachment, caregiving, and altruism: Boosting attachment security increases compassion and helping.* Manuscript submitted for publication.

Westmaas, J.L., & Silver, R.C. (2001). The role of attachment in responses to victims of life crises. *Journal of Personality and Social Psychology, 80,* 425–438.

Critical Thinking Questions

1. The authors hypothesize that secure individuals will be more compassionate and altruistic than insecure individuals. Explain how Bowlby's attachment theory and caregiving system lead the authors to this hypothesis.

2. Describe the research that allows the authors to conclude that "attachment security provides a foundation for compassion and caregiving." Be sure to describe both the methodology and the findings of this research.

3. Explain the relationship behind compassion and caregiving. Speculate on ways in which this research might be used to increase altruism in the real world.

This article has been reprinted as it originally appeared in *Current Directions in Psychological Science*. Citation information for this article as originally published appears above.

Emerging Perspectives on Distinctions Between Romantic Love and Sexual Desire

Lisa M. Diamond[1]
University of Utah

Abstract

Although sexual desire and romantic love are often experienced in concert, they are fundamentally distinct subjective experiences with distinct neurobiological substrates. The basis for these distinctions is the evolutionary origin of each type of experience. The processes underlying sexual desire evolved in the context of sexual mating, whereas the processes underlying romantic love—or pair bonding—originally evolved in the context of infant-caregiver attachment. Consequently, not only can humans experience these feelings separately, but an individual's sexual predisposition for the same sex, the other sex, or both sexes may not circumscribe his or her capacity to fall in love with partners of either gender. Also, the role of oxytocin in both love and desire may contribute to the widely observed phenomenon that women report experiencing greater interconnections between love and desire than do men. Because most research on the neurobiological substrates of sexual desire and affectional bonding has been conducted with animals, a key priority for future research is systematic investigation of the coordinated biological, behavioral, cognitive, and emotional processes that shape experiences of love and desire in humans.

Keywords

attachment; sexual desire; gender; sexual orientation; evolutionary theory

It is a truism that romantic love and sexual desire are not the same thing, but one might be hard pressed to cite empirical evidence to this effect. In recent years, however, researchers in fields ranging from psychology to animal behavior to neurobiology have devoted increasing attention to the experiences, physiological underpinnings, and potential evolutionary origins that distinguish love and desire. The results of these investigations suggest that romantic love and sexual desire are governed by functionally independent social-behavioral systems that evolved for different reasons and that involve different neurochemical substrates. Furthermore, there are gender differences in the interrelationship between love and desire that may have both biological and cultural origins. This emerging body of theory and research has the potential to profoundly reshape the way we conceptualize human sexuality, gender, sexual orientation, and social bonding.

INDEPENDENCE BETWEEN LOVE AND DESIRE

Sexual desire typically denotes a need or drive to seek out sexual objects or to engage in sexual activities, whereas *romantic love* typically denotes the powerful feelings of emotional infatuation and attachment between intimate partners. Furthermore, most researchers acknowledge a distinction between the earlier "passionate" stage of love, sometimes called "limerence" (Tennov, 1979), and the later-developing "companionate" stage of love, called pair bonding or attachment (Fisher, 1998; Hatfield, 1987). Although it may be easy to imagine sexual desire without romantic love, the notion of "pure," "platonic," or "nonsexual" romantic love is somewhat more controversial. Yet empirical evidence indicates that sexual desire is not a prerequisite for romantic love, even in its earliest, passionate stages. Many men and women report having experienced romantic passion in the absence of sexual desire (Tennov, 1979), and even prepubertal children, who have not undergone the hormonal changes responsible for adult levels of sexual motivation, report intense romantic infatuations (Hatfield, Schmitz, Cornelius, & Rapson, 1988).

Furthermore, extensive cross-cultural and historical research shows that individuals often develop feelings of romantic love for partners of the "wrong" gender (i.e., heterosexuals fall in love with same-gender partners and lesbian and gay individuals fall in love with other-gender partners, as reviewed in Diamond, 2003). Although some modern observers have argued that such relationships must involve hidden or suppressed sexual desires, the straightforward written reports of the participants themselves are not consistent with such a blanket characterization. Rather, it seems that individuals are capable of developing intense, enduring, preoccupying affections for one another regardless of either partner's sexual attractiveness or arousal.

MEASURING THE EXPERIENCE AND SUBSTRATES OF LOVE AND DESIRE

Of course, one's interpretation of such data depends on one's confidence in the methods used to assess and contrast love and desire. Whereas sexual arousal can be reliably and validly assessed by monitoring blood flow to the genitals, no definitive test of "true love" exists. Psychologists have, however, identified a constellation of cognitions and behaviors that reliably characterize (and differentiate between) romantic love and passion across different cultures. As summarized by Tennov (1979), passionate love is a temporary state of heightened interest in and preoccupation with a specific individual, characterized by intense desires for proximity and physical contact, resistance to separation, and feelings of excitement and euphoria when receiving the partner's attention. As passionate love transforms into companionate love, desire for proximity and resistance to separation become less urgent, and feelings of security, care, and comfort predominate.

Some of the most provocative and promising research on love and desire focuses on the neurobiological substrates of these distinctive behaviors and cognitions. Although little direct research in this area has been conducted with humans, converging lines of evidence (reviewed by Fisher, 1998) suggest that the marked experiential differences between love and desire may be partially attributable to their distinct neurochemical signatures. Sexual desire, for example, is directly mediated by gonadal estrogens and androgens (see Diamond, 2003; Fisher, 1998), yet these hormones do not mediate the formation of affectional bonds. Rather, animal research indicates that the distinctive feelings and behaviors associated with attachment formation are mediated by the fundamental "reward" circuitry of the mammalian brain, involving the coordinated action of endogenous opioids, catecholamines,[2] and neuropeptides such as oxytocin, which is best known for its role in childbirth and nursing. These neurochemicals regulate a range of emotional, cognitive, behavioral, and biological processes that facilitate social bonding by fostering conditioned associations between specific social partners and intrinsic feelings of reward (reviewed in Carter, 1998).

At the current time, it is not known whether such processes mediate the formation and maintenance of pair bonds between humans, as they have been shown to do in other pair-bonding mammalian species, such as the prairie vole (Carter, 1998). For example, we are only beginning to understand the range of emotional and physical phenomena (other than labor and nursing) that trigger oxytocin release in humans, and whether oxytocin release has consistent effects on subjective experience. Preliminary studies have found fascinating individual differences in the amount of oxytocin released in response to sexual activity, positive emotion, and massage (Carmichael, Warburton, Dixen, & Davidson, 1994; Turner, Altemus, Enos, Cooper, & McGuinness, 1999), and this is a key direction for future research.

Another promising avenue for investigation involves the use of functional magnetic resonance imaging (fMRI) to identify brain regions that are activated during experiences of desire versus infatuation versus attachment. In one preliminary study (Bartels & Zeki, 2000), the brains of individuals who reported being "truly, deeply, and madly in love" were examined under two conditions: while viewing pictures of their beloved and while viewing pictures of other-sex friends. Compared with viewing friends, viewing pictures of loved ones was associated with heightened activation in the middle insula and the anterior cingulate cortex, areas that have been associated in prior research with positive emotion, attention to one's own emotional states, attention to the emotional states of social partners, and even opioid-induced euphoria. Viewing pictures of loved ones was also associated with deactivation in the posterior cingulate gyrus, the amygdala, and the right prefrontal, parietal, and middle temporal cortices, areas that have been associated with sadness, fear, aggression, and depression. Notably, the brain regions that showed distinctive patterns of activity when viewing romantic partners did not overlap with regions typically activated during sexual arousal.

Clearly, much work remains to be done to develop a comprehensive "map" of normative brain activity during both short-term states and longer-term stages of desire, infatuation, and attachment; to examine changes in brain activity as individuals move between these states and stages within specific relationships; and to explore whether inter-individual differences in personality and relationship quality moderate such patterns. Perhaps most important, however, we require a greater understanding of the functional implications of different co-ordinated patterns of activation and deactivation.

THE EVOLUTIONARY ORIGINS OF LOVE AND DESIRE

Given the accumulating evidence that love and desire are, in fact, functionally independent phenomena with distinct neurobiological substrates, a natural question is, *why*? After all, most individuals end up falling in love with partners to whom they are sexually drawn, and this seems to make good evolutionary sense given that pair bonding with one's sexual partner is a good way to ensure that the resulting offspring have two dedicated parents instead of just one. This view assumes, however, that the basic biobehavioral mechanisms underlying affectional bonding evolved for the purpose of reproductive mating, and this may not be the case. Although these processes would clearly have conferred reproductive benefits on early humans, some researchers have argued that they originally evolved for an altogether different purpose: infant-caregiver attachment.

Bowlby (1982) conceptualized attachment as an evolved behavioral system designed to keep infants in close proximity to caregivers (thereby maximizing infants' chances for survival). Attachment establishes an intense affectional bond between infant and caregiver, such that separation elicits feelings of distress and proximity elicits feelings of comfort and security. Other evolutionary theorists have argued that this system was eventually co-opted for the purpose of keeping reproductive partners together to rear offspring (Hazan & Zeifman, 1999). In other words, adult pair bonding may be an *exaptation*—a system that originally evolved for one reason, but comes to serve another. The fundamental correspondence between infant-caregiver attachment and adult pair bonding is supported by extensive research documenting that these phenomena share the same core emotional and behavioral dynamics: heightened desire for proximity, resistance to separation, and utilization of the partner as a preferred target for comfort and security (Hazan & Zeifman, 1999). Even more powerful evidence is provided by the voluminous animal research documenting that these two types of affectional bonding are mediated by the same opioid- and oxytocin-based neural circuitry (Carter, 1998).

This view helps to explain the independence between love and desire, because sexual desire is obviously irrelevant to the process of infant-caregiver bonding. Yet even if one grants that affectional bonding and sexual mating are fundamentally distinct processes that evolved for distinct purposes, the question still remains: Why do the majority of human adults fall in love only with partners to whom they are sexually attracted? One reason is obviously cultural: Most human societies have strong and well-established norms regarding what types of feelings and behaviors are appropriate for different types of adult relationships, and they actively channel adults into the "right" types of relationships through a variety of social practices. Additionally, however, both human and animal data suggest that attachments are most likely to form between individuals that have extensive proximity to and contact with one another over a prolonged period of time (Hazan & Zeifman, 1999). Sexual desire provides a powerful motive for such extended contact, increasing the likelihood that the average adult becomes attached to sexual partners rather than platonic friends.

IMPLICATIONS REGARDING GENDER AND SEXUAL ORIENTATION

Psychologists have long noted that one of the most robust gender differences regarding human sexuality is that women tend to place greater emphasis on relationships as a context for sexual feelings and behaviors than do men (Peplau,

2003). For example, many lesbian and bisexual women report that they were never aware of same-sex desires until after they fell in love with a particular woman (Diamond, 2003). One potential reason for this gender difference is that women appear more likely than men to have their first experiences of sexual arousal in the context of a heterosexual dating relationship, rather than the solitary context of masturbation. Another potential contributor to this gender difference is that historically women have been socialized to restrict their sexual feelings and behaviors to intimate emotional relationships—ideally, marital ties—whereas males have enjoyed more social license regarding casual sexual relations.

Yet our emerging understanding of the neurochemical substrates of love and desire raises the intriguing possibility that biological factors might also contribute to this gender difference. Specifically, several of the neurochemicals that mediate mammalian bonding processes—most notably, oxytocin, vasopressin, and dopamine—also mediate sexual behavior, and these neurochemicals often show hormone-dependent, gender-specific patterns of functioning. For example, female rats have far more extensive oxytocin brain circuits than do male rats, perhaps to facilitate oxytocin-dependent caregiving behaviors, and oxytocin interacts with estrogen to regulate female rats' sexual receptivity (Panksepp, 1998). Among humans, women show greater oxytocin release during sexual activity than do men, and some women show correlations between oxytocin release and orgasm intensity (Carmichael et al., 1994). Such findings raise the provocative possibility that women's greater emphasis on the relational context of sexuality— that is, their greater experience of links between love and desire—may be influenced by oxytocin's joint, gender-specific role in these processes (in addition to culture and socialization).

Furthermore, the fact that women sometimes develop same-sex desires as a result of falling in love with female friends (a phenomenon rarely documented among men) might be interpreted to indicate that oxytocin-mediated links between love and desire make it possible for a woman's affectionally triggered desires to "override" her general sexual orientation. In other words, whereas the fundamental independence between love and desire means that individuals' sexual orientations do not necessarily circumscribe their capacity for affectional bonding, the biobehavioral links between love and desire may make it possible for either experience to trigger the other (Diamond, 2003). Although this might be true for both sexes, it is perhaps more likely for women because of both gender-specific oxytocin-mediated processes and the greater cultural permission for women to develop strong affectional bonds with members of their own sex (for a similar argument regarding same-sex female bonds and gender-differentiated patterns of stress response, see Taylor et al., 2000).

These notions run counter to the conventional notion that lesbians and gay men fall in love only with same-sex partners and heterosexuals fall in love only with other-sex partners. Yet this conventional notion is also contradicted by cross-cultural, historical, and even animal research. For example, given sufficient cohabitation, both male and female prairie voles have been induced to form nonsexual bonds with same-sex partners (DeVries, Johnson, & Carter, 1997), although these bonds form more quickly and are more robust among females. One fascinating area for future research concerns the conditions under which humans form and maintain sexual and affectional relationships that run counter to their established patterns of desire and affection, the implications of such phenomena for later experience and development, and the specific role played by cognitive, behavioral, emotional, and biological mechanisms in regulating such processes.

Historically, it has been assumed that sexual arousal is a more basic, biologically mediated phenomenon than is romantic love, and therefore is more amenable to scientific study. Yet this assumption is outmoded. Research has demonstrated that the distinct behaviors and intense feelings associated with affectional bonds are governed not only by culture and socialization, but also by evolved, neurochemically mediated processes that are a fundamental legacy of our mammalian heritage. Future research on the nature and functioning of these processes in humans will not only provide researchers with novel tools to investigate age-old debates (can you fall in love with two people at once?), but will also make critical contributions to understanding the basic experience of human intimacy and how it is shaped by gender and sexual orientation over the life course.

Recommended Reading

Carter, C.S. (1998). (See References)
Diamond, L.M. (2003). (See References)
Fisher, H.E. (1998). (See References)
Hazan, C., & Zeifman, D. (1999). (See References)

Notes

1. Address correspondence to Lisa M. Diamond, Department of Psychology, University of Utah, 380 South 1530 East, Room 502, Salt Lake City, UT 84112-0251; e-mail: diamond@psych.utah.edu.

2. The release of catecholamines (most notably, dopamine, epinephrine, and norepinephrine) is associated with a variety of physiological responses that prepare the body to "fight or flee" a stressor (e.g., increased heart rate, blood pressure, and blood glucose levels). In contrast, endogenous opioids are known for their role in diminishing endocrine, cardiovascular, and behavioral stress responses, and are particularly well known for blunting the experience of pain. For this reason, they are often called "the body's own pain killers." These neuropeptides also play a role in the subjective experience of pleasure and reward, and facilitate learning and conditioning.

References

Bartels, A., & Zeki, S. (2000). The neural basis of romantic love. *NeuroReport, 11*, 3829–3834.
Bowlby, J. (1982). *Attachment and loss: Vol. 1: Attachment* (2nd ed.). New York: Basic Books.
Carmichael, M.S., Warburton, V.L., Dixen, J., & Davidson, J.M. (1994). Relationships among cardiovascular, muscular, and oxytocin responses during human sexual activity. *Archives of Sexual Behavior, 23*, 59–79.
Carter, C.S. (1998). Neuroendocrine perspectives on social attachment and love. *Psychoneuroendocrinology, 23*, 779–818.
DeVries, A.C., Johnson, C.L., & Carter, C.S. (1997). Familiarity and gender influence social preferences in prairie voles (*Microtus ochrogaster*). *Canadian Journal of Zoology, 75*, 295–301.
Diamond, L.M. (2003). What does sexual orientation orient? A biobehavioral model distinguishing romantic love and sexual desire. *Psychological Review, 110*, 173–192.
Fisher, H.E. (1998). Lust, attraction, and attachment in mammalian reproduction. *Human Nature, 9*, 23–52.

Hatfield, E. (1987). Passionate and companionate love. In R.J. Sternberg & M.L. Barnes (Eds.), *The psychology of love* (pp. 191–217). New Haven, CT: Yale University Press.

Hatfield, E., Schmitz, E., Cornelius, J., & Rapson, R.L. (1988). Passionate love: How early does it begin? *Journal of Psychology and Human Sexuality, 1*, 35–52.

Hazan, C., & Zeifman, D. (1999). Pair-bonds as attachments: Evaluating the evidence. In J. Cassidy & P.R. Shaver (Eds.), *Handbook of attachment theory and research* (pp. 336–354). New York: Guilford.

Panksepp, J. (1998). *Affective neuroscience: The foundations of human and animal emotions.* New York: Cambridge University Press.

Peplau, L.A. (2003). Human sexuality: How do men and women differ? *Current Directions in Psychological Science, 12*, 37–40.

Taylor, S.E., Klein, L.C., Lewis, B.P., Gruenewald, T.L., Gurung, R.A.R., & Updegraff, J.A. (2000). Biobehavioral responses to stress in females: Tend-and-befriend, not fight-or-flight. *Psychological Review, 107*, 411–429.

Tennov, D. (1979). *Love and limerence: The experience of being in love.* New York: Stein and Day.

Turner, R.A., Altemus, M., Enos, T., Cooper, B., & McGuinness, T. (1999). Preliminary research on plasma oxytocin in normal cycling women: Investigating emotion and interpersonal distress. *Psychiatry, 62*, 97–113.

Critical Thinking Questions

1. Critique the author's assertion that "romantic love and sexual desire are not the same thing." Be sure to use cross-cultural, neurobiological, and evolutionary research to support your points.

2. Discuss some of the evolutionary reasons *why* love and desire might function independently.

3. Using both historical and neurobiological evidence explain why women might "place a greater emphasis on relationships as a context for sexual feeling and behaviors than do men."

4. The author presents some fascinating research on the use of fMRIs to examine sexual desire versus romantic attachment. Describe some findings from this research and speculate on the implications of these findings.

This article has been reprinted as it originally appeared in *Current Directions in Psychological Science*. Citation information for this article as originally published appears above.

The Emerging Field of Adolescent Romantic Relationships

Wyndol Furman[1]

Department of Psychology, University of Denver, Denver, Colorado

Abstract

Romantic relationships are central in adolescents' lives. They have the potential to affect development positively, but also place adolescents at risk for problems. Romantic experiences change substantially over the course of adolescence; the peer context plays a critical role as heterosexual adolescents initially interact with the other sex in a group context, then begin group dating, and finally have dyadic romantic relationships. Adolescents' expectations and experiences in romantic relationships are related to their relationships with their peers as well as their parents. Although research on adolescents' romantic relationships has blossomed in the past decade, further work is needed to identify the causes and consequences of romantic experiences, examine the diversity of romantic experiences, and integrate the field with work on sexuality and adult romantic relationships.

Keywords

romantic relationships; attachment; love; friendships; adolescent adjustment

A review of the literature on adolescent romantic relationships a decade ago would have uncovered very little empirical research. The work that had been conducted consisted primarily of descriptive studies on the frequency of dating or other romantic behaviors. A substantial amount of work on sexual behavior had been conducted, but much of that was descriptive as well, and did not say much about the relational context in which the sexual behavior occurred. In other words, the literature contained a lot of information about the proportions of adolescents of different ages or backgrounds who were sexually active, but much less about who their partners were and what their relationships with them were like.

Happily, the field has changed substantially in the past decade. A cadre of social scientists have been studying adolescents' romantic relationships, and the number of articles and conference presentations seems to increase each year. The fields of adolescent romantic relationships and sexual behavior are still not well integrated, but the connections between them are increasing. Most of the work has been done on heterosexual relationships, but research on lesbian, gay, and bisexual relationships is beginning as well.

The increasing interest in adolescents' romantic relationships may partially stem from a recognition that these relationships are not simply trivial flings. As young people move from preadolescence through late adolescence, their romantic relationships become increasingly central in their social world. Preadolescents spend an hour or less a week interacting with the other sex. By the 12th grade, boys spend an average of 5 hr a week with the other sex, and girls spend an average of 10 hr a week. Furthermore, 12th-grade boys and girls spend an additional 5 to 8 hr a week thinking about members of the other sex when not with them (Richards, Crowe, Larson, & Swarr, 1998). Romantic partners are also a major source of support for many adolescents. Among 10th graders, only close friends provide more support. During the college years, romantic relationships are the most supportive relationships for males, and among the most supportive relationships for females (Furman & Buhrmester, 1992).

Romantic relationships may also affect other aspects of adolescents' development. For example, they have been hypothesized to contribute to the development of an identity, the transformation of family relationships, the development of close relationships with peers, the development of sexuality, and scholastic achievement and career planning (Furman & Shaffer, in press). One particularly interesting question is whether adolescent romantic experiences influence subsequent romantic relationships, including marriages. Unfortunately, there is limited empirical data on these possible impacts.

Adolescent romantic relationships are not, however, simple "beds of roses." One fifth of adolescent women are victims of physical or sexual abuse by a dating partner (Silverman, Raj, Mucci, & Hathaway, 2001). Breakups are one of the strongest predictors of depression (Monroe, Rhode, Seeley, & Lewinsohn, 1999). Sexually transmitted diseases and teenage pregnancy are also major risks.

Of course, the benefits and risks of particular romantic experiences vary. Having romantic experience at an early age and having a high number of partners are associated with problems in adjustment (see Zimmer-Gembeck, Siebenbruner, & Collins, 2001), although researchers do not know yet the direction of the influence. That is, the romantic experiences may lead to the difficulties, but it is also possible that adolescents who are not well adjusted are more likely than their better adjusted peers to become prematurely or overly involved in romantic relationships. Moreover, little is known about how the length or qualities of romantic relationships may be linked to adjustment.

DEVELOPMENTAL COURSE

Adolescents vary widely in when they become interested in romantic relationships, and the experiences they have once they begin dating. Accordingly, there is not one normative pattern of development. Some commonalities in the nature and sequence of heterosexual experiences can be seen, however. Prior to adolescence, boys and girls primarily interact with same-sex peers. In early adolescence, they begin to think more about members of the other sex, and then eventually to interact more with them (Richards et al., 1998). Initial interactions typically occur in mixed boy-girl groups; then group dating begins, with several pairs engaging in some activity together; finally, dyadic romantic relationships begin to form (Connolly, Goldberg, & Pepler, 2002). Having a large network of other-sex friends increases the likelihood of developing a romantic relationship with someone (Connolly, Furman, & Konarski, 2000).

The developmental course of romantic experiences for gay, lesbian, and bisexual youths is less charted, but is likely to be somewhat different. Most have some same-sex sexual experience, but relatively few have same-sex romantic relationships because of both the limited opportunities to do so and the social disapproval such relationships may generate from families or heterosexual peers

(Diamond, Savin-Williams, & Dubé, 1999). Many sexual-minority youths date other-sex peers; such experiences can help them clarify their sexual orientation or disguise it from others.

The nature of heterosexual or homosexual romantic relationships changes developmentally. Early relationships do not fulfill many of the functions that adult romantic relationships often do. Early adolescents do not commonly turn to a partner for support or provide such caregiving for a partner. In fact, what may be important is simply having such a relationship, especially if the partner is a popular or desired one.

Eventually, adolescents develop some comfort in these interactions and begin to turn to their partners for specific social and emotional needs. Wehner and I proposed that romantic relationships become important in the functioning of four behavioral systems—affiliation, sex-reproduction, attachment, and caregiving (Furman & Wehner, 1994). The affiliative and sexual-reproductive systems are the first to become salient, as young adolescents spend time with their partners and explore their sexual feelings. The attachment and caretaking systems become more important during late adolescence and early adulthood, as relationships become more long term. Several findings are consistent with our proposal. When asked to describe their romantic relationships, adolescents mention affiliative features more often than attachment or caregiving features (Feiring, 1996). Similarly, in another study, young adults retrospectively described their romances in adolescence in terms of companionship and affiliation, and described their relationships in young adulthood in terms of trust and support (Shulman & Kipnis, 2001).

The work on the developmental course of romantic experiences illustrates several important points. First, these relationships do not occur in isolation. Relationships with peers typically serve as a social context for the emergence of heterosexual relationships, and often are a deterrent for gay and lesbian relationships. Second, adolescents' romantic relationships are more than simple sexual encounters; at the same time, one could not characterize most of them as the full-blown attachment relationships that committed adult relationships become (Shaver & Hazan, 1988). Affiliation, companionship, and friendship seem to be particularly important aspects of most of these relationships. Finally, the developmental changes in these relationships are striking. Although at first they are based on simple interest, in the course of a decade, adolescents go from simply being interested in boys or girls to having significant relationships that are beginning to be characterized by attachment and caregiving. Because the changes are qualitative as well as quantitative, they present challenges for investigators trying to describe them or to compare the experiences of different adolescents. Wehner and I (Furman & Wehner, 1994) have tried to provide a common framework for research by examining adolescents' expectations for and beliefs about these relationships, a point I discuss more extensively in the next section.

LINKS WITH OTHER RELATIONSHIPS

Much of the current research on adult romantic relationships has been guided by attachment theory. More than a decade ago, Shaver and Hazan (1988) proposed that committed romantic relationships could be characterized as attachments, just as relationships between parent and child were. Moreover, they suggested that experiences with parents affect individuals' expectations of romantic relationships. Individuals who had secure relationships with parents would be likely to have secure expectations of romantic relationships and, in fact, would be likely to develop secure romantic attachments, whereas those who had adverse experiences with parents would be expected to develop insecure expectations of romantic relationships.

Although researchers generally emphasized the links between relationships with parents and romantic relationships, Wehner and I suggested that friendships would be related to romantic relationships as well (Furman & Wehner, 1994). Friendships and romantic relationships are both egalitarian relationships characterized by features of affiliation, such as companionship and mutual intimacy. Accordingly, we proposed that adolescents' experiences with friends and expectations concerning these relationships influence their expectations of romantic relationships. Subsequently, several studies using multiple methods of assessment demonstrated links between adolescents' expectations of friendships and romantic relationships (see Furman, Simon, Shaffer, & Bouchey, 2002). In fact, these links were more consistent than those between parent-child relationships and romantic relationships. Interestingly, the latter links were found to strengthen over the course of adolescence. Such a developmental shift may occur as the attachment and caregiving features of romantic relationships become increasingly salient.

These studies were cross-sectional, and thus cannot support inferences about causality. However, the findings again underscore the importance of recognizing that romantic relationships are peer relationships and thus, links with friendships are likely as well.

At the same time, various types of relationships have only moderate effects on one another. Experiences in other relationships may influence romantic relationships, but romantic relationships also present new challenges, and thus past experiences are not likely to be simply replicated. What influence do past romantic relationships have on future romantic relationships? Individuals' perceptions of support and negative interaction in their romantic relationships have been found to be stable over the span of a year, even across different relationships (Connolly et al., 2000), but otherwise researchers know little about what does and does not carry over from one romantic relationship to the next.

CURRENT AND FUTURE DIRECTIONS

The existing literature on romantic relationships has many of the characteristics of initial research on a topic. One such characteristic is the methodologies used to date: Investigators have principally relied on questionnaires, administered at one point in time. Interview and observational studies are now beginning to appear, though, and investigators conducting longitudinal studies have begun to report their results concerning adolescent romantic relationships. For example, Capaldi and Clark (1998) found that having a parent whose behavior is antisocial and who is unskilled in parenting is predictive of antisocial behavior in midadolescence, which in turn is predictive of aggression toward dating partners in late adolescence. Reports from other ongoing longitudinal studies of the childhood precursors of adolescent romantic relationships and the consequences of these relationships for subsequent development should appear shortly.

In this article, I have described some of the common developmental changes characteristic of adolescent romantic relationships and how these relationships may be influenced by relationships with friends and parents. At the same time, the diversity of romantic experiences should be underscored. The links between romantic experiences and adjustment vary as a function of the timing and degree of romantic involvement (Zimmer-Gembeck et al., 2001). Investigators are beginning to examine how romantic experiences may be associated with characteristics of the adolescent, such as antisocial or bullying behavior, health status, or sensitivity to being rejected. To date, most of the work has focused on heterosexual youths from middle-class Euro-American backgrounds, and further work with other groups is certainly needed. Additionally, almost all of the research has been conducted in Western societies, yet romantic development is likely to be quite different in other societies where contacts with the other sex are more constrained, and marriages are arranged.

Efforts to integrate the field with related ones are needed. Just as research on sexual behavior could profit from examining the nature of the relationships between sexual partners, investigators studying romantic relationships need to examine the role of sexual behavior in romantic relationships. Ironically, few investigators have done so, and instead these relationships have been treated as if they were platonic. Similarly, research on adolescent relationships could benefit from the insights of the work on adult romantic relationships, which has a rich empirical and theoretical history. At the same time, investigators studying adult relationships may want to give greater consideration to the developmental changes that occur in these relationships and to their peer context—themes that have been highlighted by adolescence researchers. In sum, research on adolescent romantic relationships has blossomed in the past decade, but a broad, integrative perspective will be needed to fully illuminate their nature.

Recommended Reading

Bouchey, H.A., & Furman, W. (in press). Dating and romantic experiences in adolescence. In G.R. Adams & M. Berzonsky (Eds.), *The Blackwell handbook of adolescence.* Oxford, England: Blackwell.

Florsheim, P. (Ed.). (in press). *Adolescent romantic relations and sexual behavior: Theory, research, and practical implications.* Mahwah, NJ: Erlbaum.

Furman, W., Brown, B.B., & Feiring, C. (Eds.). (1999). *The development of romantic relationships in adolescence.* New York: Cambridge University Press.

Shulman, S., & Collins, W. (Eds.). (1997). *Romantic relationships in adolescence: Developmental perspectives.* San Francisco: Jossey-Bass.

Shulman, S., & Seiffge-Krenke, I. (Eds.). (2001). Adolescent romance: From experiences to relationships [Special issue]. *Journal of Adolescence, 24*(3).

Acknowledgments—Preparation of this manuscript was supported by Grant 50106 from the National Institute of Mental Health.

Note

1. Address correspondence to Wyndol Furman, Department of Psychology, University of Denver, Denver, CO 80208; e-mail: wfurman@nova.psy.du.edu.

References

Capaldi, D.M., & Clark, S. (1998). Prospective family predictors of aggression toward female partners for at-risk young men. *Developmental Psychology, 34*, 1175–1188.

Connolly, J., Furman, W., & Konarski, R. (2000). The role of peers in the emergence of romantic relationships in adolescence. *Child Development, 71*, 1395–1408.

Connolly, J., Goldberg, A., & Pepler, D. (2002). *Romantic development in the peer group in early adolescence.* Manuscript submitted for publication.

Diamond, L.M., Savin-Williams, R.C., & Dubé, E.M. (1999). Sex, dating, passionate friendships, and romance: Intimate peer relations among lesbian, gay, and bisexual adolescents. In W. Furman, B.B. Brown, & C. Feiring (Eds.), *The development of romantic relationships in adolescence* (pp. 175–210). New York: Cambridge University Press.

Feiring, C. (1996). Concepts of romance in 15-year-old adolescents. *Journal of Research on Adolescence, 6*, 181–200.

Furman, W., & Buhrmester, D. (1992). Age and sex differences in perceptions of networks of personal relationships. *Child Development, 63*, 103– 115.

Furman, W., & Shaffer, L. (in press). The role of romantic relationships in adolescent development. In P. Florsheim (Ed.), *Adolescent romantic relations and sexual behavior: Theory, research, and practical implications.* Mahwah, NJ: Erlbaum.

Furman, W., Simon, V.A., Shaffer, L., & Bouchey, H.A. (2002). Adolescents' working models and styles for relationships with parents, friends, and romantic partners. *Child Development, 73*, 241–255.

Furman, W., & Wehner, E.A. (1994). Romantic views: Toward a theory of adolescent romantic relationships. In R. Montemayor, G.R. Adams, & G.P. Gullota (Eds.), *Advances in adolescent development: Vol. 6. Relationships during adolescence* (pp. 168–175). Thousand Oaks, CA: Sage.

Monroe, S.M., Rhode, P., Seeley, J.R., & Lewinsohn, P.M. (1999). Life events and depression in adolescence: Relationship loss as a prospective risk factor for first onset of major depressive disorder. *Journal of Abnormal Psychology, 108*, 606–614.

Richards, M.H., Crowe, P.A., Larson, R., & Swarr, A. (1998). Developmental patterns and gender differences in the experience of peer companionship during adolescence. *Child Development, 69*, 154–163.

Shaver, P., & Hazan, C. (1988). A biased overview of the study of love. *Journal of Social and Personal Relationships, 5*, 473–501.

Shulman, S., & Kipnis, O. (2001). Adolescent romantic relationships: A look from the future. *Journal of Adolescence, 24*, 337–351.

Silverman, J.G., Raj, A., Mucci, L.A., & Hathaway, J.E. (2001). Dating violence against adolescent girls and associated substance use, unhealthy weight control, sexual risk behavior, pregnancy, and suicidality. *Journal of the American Medical Association, 286*, 572–579.

Zimmer-Gembeck, M.J., Siebenbruner, J., & Collins, W.A. (2001). Diverse aspects of dating: Associations with psychosocial functioning from early to middle adolescence. *Journal of Adolescence, 24*, 313–336.

Critical Thinking Questions

1. Describe the typical developmental course of adolescent romantic relationships. Explain how research in this area supports the notion that these relationships develop in a social context.

2. The authors make the argument that peer friendships are related to adolescent romantic relationships. Explain how this statement might be consistent with Shaver and Hazan's attachment theory.

3. One criticism of the research in this area is that it has relied primary on questionnaires given at one point in time. Explain why this is a problem. How can
future researchers overcome this limitation?

**This article has been reprinted as it originally appeared in *Current
Directions in Psychological Science*. Citation information for this article
as originally published appears above.**

Relationships, Human Behavior, and Psychological Science

Harry T. Reis[1]
University of Rochester
W. Andrew Collins
University of Minnesota

Abstract

Extensive evidence attests to the importance of relationships for human well-being, and evolutionary theorizing has increasingly recognized the adaptive significance of relationships. Psychological science, however, has barely begun to consider how relationships influence a broad array of basic social, cognitive, emotional, and behavioral processes. This article discusses contemporary theory and research about the impact of relationship contexts, citing examples from research on social cognition, emotion, and human development. We propose that the validity and usefulness of psychological science will be enhanced by better integration of relationship contexts into theories and research.

Keywords

relationship; social cognition; emotion; development

A recent cartoon in the *New* Yorker depicts a middle-aged, probably long-married couple reading quietly in their living room. The man turns to his wife and says, "I can't remember which one of us is me." This cartoon embodies an idea whose time has come in the psychological sciences: that human behavior varies significantly depending on relationship contexts and the cognitive, emotional, and social mechanisms that have evolved for recognizing, evaluating, and responding to those contexts—who else is present and who else is affected by, or has had an effect on, present circumstances. This idea follows from the uncontroversial but often overlooked fact that most human activity involves coordinating one's actions with the actions of others, and that the relative success or failure of such coordination is a principal determinant of productivity and well-being, whether in families, friendships, organizations, neighborhoods, or societies.

Psychological science rarely integrates relationship contexts into its theories and research. One reason for this gap has been the historical focus of psychology on the behavior of individuals. Another has been a shortage of valid concepts, empirical knowledge, and rigorous methods for introducing relationship processes into mainstream psychological research. Recent advances in relationship science—empirical research on relationship processes and their effects—suggest that this void may soon be filled. A virtual explosion of research has provided analytical and methodological tools that allow most psychological or behavioral processes to be investigated from a relationship perspective. The premise of this article is that such investigations will advance the completeness and accuracy of psychological science.

WHY RELATIONSHIPS MATTER

Abundant evidence attests that associations, often powerful ones, exist between the quality and quantity of relationships and diverse outcomes, including mortality rates, recovery from coronary artery bypass surgery, functioning of the immune system, reactions to stress, psychiatric disturbance, and life satisfaction. These effects do not appear to be artifacts of personality, temperament, behavior, or lifestyles, but instead reflect the direct influence of relationship events on biological processes (e.g., Kiecolt-Glaser & Newton, 2001).

How did the processes by which relationship events affect human biology evolve? Many accounts posit that living and working in small, cooperative groups has been the primary survival strategy for the human species, because social organization buffered early humans from the dangers of the natural environment. Thus, it was adaptive for the human mind to develop a series of mechanisms— Bugental (2000) called them the "algorithms of social life"—for regulating social relations. Social organization is composed of interlocking relationships among individuals within a social network.

Although no definitive list of innate systems for regulating social relations and responding to social circumstances exists, many processes of long-standing interest among behavioral researchers are likely candidates: cooperation and competition, adherence to social norms, coalition formation, attachment, face perception, social inclusion and exclusion, communication of emotion, romantic jealousy, empathy, and commitment, for example. These processes are not applied equally to all of an individual's contacts, but rather are applied selectively, depending on the existing relationship and the particular problem to be solved. People become psychologically attached primarily to caregivers and intimates, and cooperation predominates within in-groups. Social interaction involves determining what sort of relationship exists and therefore which processes are most relevant. Growing evidence that these processes are manifested in nonhuman species and that they are governed to some extent by nonconsciously regulated neurobiological systems suggests that responsiveness to relationship contexts is deeply wired into human architecture.

Relationships may be characterized in terms of the properties that describe the involved parties' interdependence with each other—the manner in which individuals alter their behavior in order to coordinate with others' actions and preferences. Thus, persons in relationships respond (or not) to each other's wishes, concerns, abilities, and emotional expressions; they modify their behavior to be together (or not); they allocate tasks between themselves; they react to each other's behaviors and circumstances, misfortune, and happiness; and they take the fact of their interdependence into account in organizing everyday life and longer-term plans. Central to most conceptualizations of relationship is the idea that these patterns of mutual influence are more informative about relationships than are nominal categories (e.g., spouses, co-workers, friends) or simple static descriptors (e.g., length of acquaintance, nature or degree of affect).

Evidence for differential effects of relationship contexts is available in many areas of research. We next describe three such areas to illustrate the importance of such evidence for psychological science.

SOCIAL COGNITION

Much research has investigated the cognitive processes by which individuals perceive, interpret, and respond to their social environments. In most such studies, no relationship exists between the subjects and the objects of thought, who are often, for example, strangers, hypothetical people described by the experimenter, famous persons, or social groups. Even when a relationship does exist, its possible influence on the results obtained is rarely considered. This approach tacitly implies that the principles governing cognition about people who are familiar or close do not differ materially from the principles governing cognition about acquaintances and strangers (or, for that matter, inanimate objects). Increasingly, theory and research challenge this assumption.

Take, for example, one of the most robust social-cognitive phenomena: the *self-serving attributional bias*, which refers to the fact that people give themselves more credit for success and less responsibility for failure than they give strangers. This bias, reported in virtually every textbook in the field, is not observed when the self is compared with close relationship partners, who are accorded the same attributional generosity as is the self (Sedikides, Campbell, Reeder, & Elliot, 1998). Other phenomena that reflect self-serving biases also vary depending on the closeness of the relationship.

Another example concerns the well-documented *self-referential effect*: the enhancement of memory when information is encoded with reference to the self, rather than, for example, another person. This effect is significantly smaller when the other person is an intimate rather than a stranger or acquaintance (Symons & Johnson, 1997). Partners in close or committed relationships typically adopt an interdependent frame of reference ("we," rather than "you and I"), perhaps because, following the logic of a connectionist model, close relationships entail a greater number of direct connections and overlapping links than distant relationships do (Smith, Coats, & Walling, 1999). Even more suggestive is a recent neural imaging study (Lichty et al., 2004) showing substantial overlap—most strongly, in the right superior frontal gyrus and prefrontal cortex—in the brain regions activated by hearing one's own name and hearing the name of a close friend, but no overlap in the areas of activation associated with hearing one's own name and hearing the name of a familiar (but not close) other person. The degree of overlap in the own-name and close-friend conditions was more pronounced to the extent that the relationship with the other was experienced as a close relationship.

Relationship context may also influence social cognition when the close partner is not present. A long-standing and sophisticated program of experimentation has shown that representations of significant others from one's past may affect one's inferences, recollections, evaluations, and feelings about a new acquaintance when the new acquaintance resembles the significant other (and thereby activates mental schemas associated with the preexisting relationship; Andersen & Chen, 2002).

It has long been recognized that social cognition is designed to facilitate the individual's transit through social life. These and similar studies represent an advance in psychological science, demonstrating that which particular social-cognitive process is activated, and the output of its operation, depends critically on the nature of the ongoing relationship between the cognizer and relevant others. Moreover, Bugental (2000) has argued that evolved brain mechanisms tend to be specialized, perhaps as distinct modules, to fit the varying role requirements of different relationship contexts. If so, humans' extraordinary capacity to quickly recognize (within milliseconds) close friends or even distant acquaintances expedites activation of different cognitive processes with different partners.

EMOTION

Ever since Darwin emphasized the social communicative function of emotion in the survival of species, researchers have recognized that emotions have both evolutionary significance and relevance to social life. It is thus somewhat ironic that "interpersonal functions [of emotion] have generally been given short shrift in comparison to intrapersonal functions . . . [although most researchers] believe that emotions are brought into play most often by the actions of others, and, once aroused, emotions influence the course of interpersonal transactions" (Ekman & Davidson, 1994, p. 139). Although not all interpersonal transactions involve partners in ongoing relationships, many do. Consequently, many researchers now acknowledge that affect should be examined in its relationship context.

Several emotions are intrinsically relationship-specific; they are unlikely to arise outside of relationships (e.g., jealousy, maternal and romantic love, grief over loss). For most other emotions, the likelihood, intensity, and nature of expression typically are influenced by the individual's relationship with the target of the emotion. For example, a rude bus driver likely elicits a weaker and different response than a rude spouse, junior colleague, or teenaged daughter. This observation accords with the definition of emotion as a response to environmental events that have significance for personal well-being. Different relationships necessarily imply different consequences for personal well-being.

Diverse studies demonstrate links between the emotion-eliciting power of situations and their relationship context. For example, the intensity of elicited emotions, particularly the so-called hot emotions, varies with the closeness of a relationship. This pattern can be explained by Berscheid and Ammazzalorso's (2001) emotion-in-relationships model, according to which expectancy violations are the cause of emotion. The more interdependent two persons are, the stronger, more numerous, and more consequential their expectations of each other, and thus, the more intense the emotions they elicit. Moreover, people's willingness to communicate about emotional experience depends on their relationship with the person with whom they are communicating. Studies conducted by the first author and his colleagues indicate that people are more willing to express both positive and negative emotions to the extent that a relationship is intimate, trusting, and communal (i.e., a relationship in which partners are responsive to each other's needs), regardless of whether the emotion was triggered by the partner or someone else. Similarly, emotional displays may be suppressed when the emotion is perceived to have relationship-impairing potential. For example, East Asians are more likely than European Americans to suppress certain emotion displays, perhaps reflecting their greater potential to harm relationships in collectivist than in individualist cultures. Although the tendency to experience emotion is widely believed to be hard-wired, behavioral responses to emotion-eliciting events may be shaped to a significant extent by interactions within close relationships.

A further example of the links between emotion and relationship context is that in communal relationships, relative to less caring ones, individuals are more likely to show empathic compassion for a partner's misfortune, better understand each other's emotions (the occasional instance of motivated misunderstanding notwithstanding), and are more likely to share in each other's emotional experience through such processes as emotional contagion, physiological synchrony, vicarious arousal, and rapport (Clark, Fitness, & Brissette, 2001).

Thus, attention to relationship contexts advances understanding of emotional experience and expression.

RELATIONSHIPS AND DEVELOPMENT

Rudimentary social interaction skills are evident at birth, or soon thereafter. Newborns attend to the faces of members of their species. Other innate mechanisms for relating to others (e.g., attachment, or a proximity-seeking bond between child and caregiver) begin to emerge shortly after birth. Infants contribute to these early relationships by orienting clearly and consistently to their caregivers, and caregivers contribute by attending closely to their infants' behavior and emotions. Patterns of exchange and interdependence are apparent from the early weeks of life. A key sign of the importance of early relationships is that infants reliably turn to caregivers for reassurance and confidence in the face of threatening or stressful circumstances, a phenomenon known as the *secure base*. A critical mass of research now shows that these and other such abilities provide an essential infrastructure for many vital activities (relating to other people, exploring the environment, striving for achievement, solving problems creatively, caring for children and other people in need, engaging in health-promoting behavior) throughout life. Moreover, it is increasingly evident that the development of these abilities (and their underlying psychological traits) depends on the child's early relationships.

Caregiver-child pairs vary in the degree to which their relationships readily and unambiguously provide the secure base and the resulting emergent sense of security. Existing evidence indicates a substantial degree of continuity between early experiences and diverse relationships during childhood, adolescence, and adulthood. Discontinuities between earlier and later relationships typically are related to pronounced disruptions or stressors in the intervening years. Several explanations have been suggested for these temporal links. One possibility is that unsatisfying or restricted early relationships disrupt normal development, in turn affecting later behavior and relationships. Research with nonhuman species and with human children reared in orphanages with inadequate care arrangements has shown that even minor deprivation of contact with responsive individuals results in abnormal development of the brain and hormonal systems that regulate coping with stress (Gunnar, 2000). One researcher (Siegel, 1999) has even proposed that the "mind" develops at the intersection of neurophysiological processes and interpersonal relations. A more limited possibility is that early relationships are key sources of expectations about social relations. These "residues" of early relationships have been found repeatedly to be related to the characteristics of later relationships in childhood, adolescence, and adulthood (Roisman, Madsen, Hennighausen, Sroufe, & Collins, 2001). Little evidence supports one popular alternative hypothesis—that the long-term implications of attachment security are better attributed to individual differences in temperament (Thompson, 1998).

The evidence is compelling that relationships are significant in nearly every domain of activity. From infancy to old age, having friends and relating successfully to other people is associated with desirable outcomes in virtually all human domains: school, work, coping with negative events, adaptation during life transitions, parenthood, self-worth, and emotional well-being (Hartup & Stevens, 1997). This fact underscores the adaptive significance of relationships in human evolution and highlights the need to study development as a process that unfolds in relational contexts.

CONCLUDING COMMENT

Diverse emerging evidence indicates that relationship contexts have the potential to influence a diverse array of cognitive, emotional, and behavioral processes. Important challenges remain if these trends are to be cultivated into a systematic body of knowledge. Chief among these challenges is the necessity for identifying and evaluating the boundaries for relationship-context effects, and articulating their operation in a theoretically integrated way: To what extent do which different interpersonal circumstances affect the operation of which processes? Similarly, which individual differences moderate the degree to which interpersonal circumstances influence relationship outcomes and their behavioral effects? Other key questions for further advances in this area of research concern mechanisms. Although the evidence we have cited is suggestive, it remains to be determined how the external reality of relating is translated into the internal reality of basic cognitive, emotional, and biological processes. Finally, the rudimentary theoretical and methodological tools currently available must be supplemented by additional, even more sophisticated models and techniques. Such work promises to allow psychological science to more fully capitalize on a cherished axiom: that behavior is a product of the interaction between the properties of the person and the properties of the environment. To individuals, few features of the environment have greater salience or impact than whom they are with (or thinking about), and the nature of their relationship with that person. Fuller integration of the role of relationship contexts at all levels of psychological theorizing, research, and application is likely to augment the validity and utility of psychological science.

Recommended Reading

Berscheid, E. (1999). The greening of relationship science. *American Psychologist, 54,* 260–266.
Collins, W.A., & Laursen, B. (Eds.). (1999). *Minnesota Symposium on Child Psychology: Vol. 30. Relationships as developmental contexts.* Mahwah, NJ: Erlbaum.

Hinde, R.A. (1997). *Relationships: A dialectical perspective.* East Sussex, England: Psychology Press.

Kelley, H.H., Berscheid, E., Christensen, A., Harvey, J., Huston, T., Levinger, G., McClintock, E., Peplau, L.A., & Peterson, D. (1983). *Close relationships.* New York: Freeman.

Reis, H.T., Collins, W.A., & Berscheid, E. (2000). The relationship context of human behavior and development. *Psychological Bulletin, 126,* 844–872.

Acknowledgments—We gratefully acknowledge the enormous contributions of Ellen Berscheid to the conceptual framework from which this article emerged.

Note

1. Address correspondence to Harry Reis, Department of Clinical and Social Sciences in Psychology, University of Rochester, Rochester, NY 14627; e-mail: reis@psych.rochester.edu.

References

Andersen, S.M., & Chen, S. (2002). The relational self: An interpersonal social-cognitive theory. *Psychological Review, 109,* 619–645.

Berscheid, E., & Ammazzalorso, H. (2001). Emotional experience in close relationships. In M. Hewstone & M. Brewer (Eds.), *Blackwell handbook of social psychology* (Vol. 2, pp. 308–330). Oxford, England: Blackwell.

Bugental, D. (2000). Acquisition of the algorithms of social life: A domain-based approach. *Psychological Bulletin, 126,* 187–219.

Clark, M., Fitness, J., & Brissette, I. (2001). Understanding people's perceptions of relationships is crucial to understanding their emotional lives. In M. Hewstone & M. Brewer (Eds.), *Blackwell handbook of social psychology* (Vol. 2, pp. 253–278). Oxford, England: Blackwell.

Ekman, P., & Davidson, R. (Eds.). (1994). *The nature of emotion: Fundamental questions.* New York: Oxford.

Gunnar, M.R. (2000). Early adversity and the development of stress reactivity and regulation. In C. Nelson (Ed.), *Minnesota Symposium on Child Psychology: Vol. 31. The effects of adversity on neurobehavioral development* (pp. 163–200). Mahwah, NJ: Erlbaum.

Hartup, W.W., & Stevens, N. (1997). Friendships and adaptation in the life course. *Psychological Bulletin, 121,* 355–370.

Kiecolt-Glaser, J., & Newton, T. (2001). Marriage and health: His and hers. *Psychological Bulletin, 127,* 472–503.

Lichty, W., Chyou, J., Aron, A., Anderson, A., Ghahremani, D., & Gabrieli, J. (2004, October). *Neural correlates of subjective closeness: An fMRI study.* Poster presented at the annual meeting of the Society for Neuroscience, San Diego, CA.

Roisman, G.I., Madsen, S., Hennighausen, K., Sroufe, L.A., & Collins, W.A. (2001). The coherence of dyadic behavior across parent-child and romantic relationships as mediated by the internalized representation of experience. *Attachment & Human Development, 3,* 156–172.

Sedikides, C., Campbell, W., Reeder, G., & Elliot, A. (1998). The self-serving bias in relational context. *Journal of Personality and Social Psychology, 74,* 378–386.

Siegel, D.J. (1999). *The developing mind: Toward a neurobiology of interpersonal experience.* New York: Guilford.

Smith, E.R., Coats, S., & Walling, D. (1999). Overlapping mental representations of self, in-group, and partner: Further response time evidence and a connectionist model. *Personality and Social Psychology Bulletin, 25,* 873–882.

Symons, C., & Johnson, B. (1997). The self-reference effect in memory: A meta-analysis. *Psychological Bulletin, 121,* 371–394.

Thompson, R.A. (1998). Early sociopersonality development. In W. Damon (Series Ed.) & N. Eisenberg (Vol. Ed.), *The handbook of child psychology* (Vol. 3, pp. 25–104). New York: Wiley.

Critical Thinking Questions

1. Describe some of the positive outcomes associated with having relationships. How might evolution explain these associations?

2. Describe the effects of relationship contexts for each of the following areas of research: social cognition, emotion, and development. How does an understanding of relationship contexts advance the knowledge in each of these areas?

3. The central idea of this article is the importance of considering relationship contexts in psychological science, yet the authors never explicitly define this term. What does the term "relationship context" mean to you? Use specific information from the article to support your point.

This article has been reprinted as it originally appeared in *Current Directions in Psychological Science*. Citation information for this article as originally published appears above.

Section 4: The Interpersonal Extremes: Prosocial Behavior and Aggression

Human behavior comprises ponderous contradictions, bizarre puzzles, and almost inconceivable extremes. A human being may sacrifice her own life to save a stranger, or throttle a romantic partner within inches of his life. A human being may suffer indignities at the hands of a stranger, and yet not wish ill upon that stranger. As a social species, humans behave in both prosocial and antisocial ways, helping and hurting, uplifting and undermining.

Besides representing the extremes of human behavior, what do prosocial behavior and aggression have in common? First, a sizable body of each literature historically has derived from biological or evolutionary explanations for human behavior; the trend in other areas of social psychology to recognize biological and evolutionary factors is fairly recent, and can trace the development of this reasoning back to prosocial and aggression research. For example, certain kinds of aggression (e.g., defending territory; obtaining access to mates and resources; maternal aggression) have survival value for a species; studies that focus upon hormones (e.g., testosterone) suggest a strong biological basis for aggression. Conversely, risking one's life for another person would seem, at first blush, to contradict survival instincts. Theorists point out, though, that risking one's life for another is most likely when the other person belongs to one's shared gene pool. From the logic of inclusive fitness, risking one's life for two siblings (who each share 50% of one's genes) is a fair trade, especially if those siblings are likely to reproduce in the future. But even helping outside one's gene pool sometimes is posited to have a biological basis: people experience emotional reactions when perceiving the emotions of others, including others' apparent experience of suffering. That shared experience of emotion—empathy—can underlie efforts to help (cf. Decety & Jackson, 2006).

Many theorists believe that biological perspectives are insufficient to explain why some people risk their lives to help strangers, why they risk their lives to cause harm to strangers, why they choose to donate to charity, or why they steal from their jobs. Instead, they believe that extreme behaviors derive, on the whole or in part, from learning and environmental cues. That is the second recurring theme in the study of prosocial and antisocial behavior. Many types of physical and verbal aggression, for example, are learned vicariously by watching other people; observation allows people to learn how to copy aggressive behaviors, which behaviors are rewarded or punished, and the environmental contexts under which those rewards or punishments are likely. Aggression in the workplace, for instance, sometimes is modeled by supervisors or peers (cf. LeBlanc & Barling, 2004). People may model how their peers tease a new coworker, covertly may retaliate against a supervisor who levied criticisms, or may adopt an organization's passive-aggressive norm in dealing with requests. Prosocial behavior, too, has a strong learned component. Donating to charity and volunteering one's time, for example, are influenced by the behaviors and professed attitudes of family and peers. Batson and Thompson (2001) note that one long-standing explanation of immoral behavior was the failure to learn the moral values and laws of one's society. Their research demonstrates quite keenly that people typically have learned to distinguish right from wrong. However, people do not always act in ways that demonstrate their understanding of the distinction. For instance, if the personal costs of behaving prosocially are too great (e.g., resources are lost, pain is experienced), people may act in ways that contradict their own moral understanding.

A third recurring theme in the research on prosocial behavior and aggression lies in the fact that many of the theories are motivational. The theorists focus on the desires, drives, or goals that encourage a person to behave in a particular way. With Batson and Thompson's (2001) approach to immoral behavior, these motivations are to appear moral and to avoid personal costs. Some other motivational theories of prosocial behavior have focused on motivations to reduce bad moods, to increase pleasant moods, or to obtain rewards and social accolades. Aggression theories similarly reveal a motivational twist, dating as far back as Freud's death instinct. People may behave aggressively in order to obtain revenge or retribution, to obtain resources otherwise unavailable to them, to protect their mates, and to exert power and dominance over others. [Note that motivational approaches therefore can include a biological and/or environmental focus]. In a timely consideration of a unique form of aggression—terrorism—Kruglanski and Fishman (2006) contrast two distinct motivational perspectives. In the "syndrome" view, terrorists are hypothesized to be psychologically disturbed or frustrated into performing aggressive acts; the motivation therefore resembles hostile aggression, that is, hurting others simply for the sake of hurting them. In the "tool" view, to which Kruglanski and Fishman subscribe, terrorism is a form of instrumental aggression. That is, the motivation for terrorism is a means to an end. They further argue that knowing the motivations for terrorism can inform measures for combating it; the same could be said prosocial behavior, and for antisocial behavior in general.

A final recurring theme in each literature is a recognition of personality factors and individual differences. In the area of aggression, personality characteristics such as authoritarianism, Type A personality, and vengefulness have been associated with increased aggressive behavior. For example, individual differences in the tendency to infer hostile intent from others (i.e., the hostile attribution bias) predicts workplace aggression (LeBlanc & Barling, 2004), which can range from destruction of property to the spreading of harmful rumors. In the area of prosocial behavior, researchers have examined personality factors such as self-consciousness, which is a dispositional version of the objective self-awareness that can be created by mirrors (as noted by Batson & Thompson, 2001). Individuals high in self-consciousness (or who are objectively self-aware) are increasingly likely to behave according to moral norms and standards. Dispositional empathy or perspective-taking, which encourage identification with the person who requires help, also is associated with increased levels of helping. Recent work with functional magnetic resonance imaging (fMRI) shows that the same regions of the brain are active when people are experiencing their own suffering as when they are empathizing with the suffering of another person (Decety & Jackson, 2006). Conceivably, the increased levels of helping evinced by individuals high in dispositional empathy derives from their keenly feeling the suffering of others.

Although we will witness countless acts of violent aggression on television and film, and also will watch our screen heroes risk their lives repeatedly to save strangers, most of us rarely will witness these actual behaviors in our daily lives. Thankfully, we also are unlikely to perform the most extreme levels of these extreme behaviors ourselves: we will not commit mass murder or throw ourselves onto a live grenade to save several dozen people. We will, however, regularly experience and perpetrate less dramatic acts of aggression and prosocial behavior. Cheating and charity, vengeance and volunteering are part of daily life. Social scientists show us that these acts are multiply-determined: a complex mixture of biology, learning, personality, and motivation. Human beings may manifest ponderous contradictions, bizarre puzzles, and nearly inconceivable extremes, but these increasingly can be understood through the lens of social psychology.

Why Don't Moral People Act Morally? Motivational Considerations

C. Daniel Batson[1] and Elizabeth R. Thompson

Department of Psychology, University of Kansas, Lawrence, Kansas

Abstract

Failure of moral people to act morally is usually attributed to either learning deficits or situational pressures. We believe that it is also important to consider the nature of moral motivation. Is the goal actually to be moral (moral integrity) or only to appear moral while, if possible, avoiding the cost of being moral (moral hypocrisy)? Do people initially intend to be moral, only to surrender this goal when the costs of being moral become clear (overpowered integrity)? We have found evidence of both moral hypocrisy and overpowered integrity. Each can lead ostensibly moral people to act immorally. These findings raise important questions for future research on the role of moral principles as guides to behavior.

Keywords

morality; integrity; hypocrisy; motivational conflict

Moral people often fail to act morally. One of the most important lessons to be learned from the tragically common atrocities of the past century—the endless procession of religious wars, mass killings, ethnic cleansings, terrorist bombings, and corporate coverups of product dangers—is that horrendous deeds are not done only by monsters. People who sincerely value morality can act in ways that seem to show a blatant disregard for the moral principles held dear. How is this possible?

Answers by psychologists tend to be of two types. Those who approach the problem from a developmental perspective are likely to blame a learning deficit: The moral principles must not have been learned well enough or in the right way. Those who approach the problem from a social-influence perspective are likely to blame situational pressures: Orders from a higher authority (Milgram, 1974) and pressure to conform (Asch, 1956) can lead one to set aside or disengage moral standards (Bandura, 1999).

There is truth in each of these explanations of moral failure. Yet neither, nor the two combined, is the whole truth. Even people who have well-internalized moral principles, and who are in relatively low-pressure situations, can fail to act morally. To understand how, one needs to consider the nature of moral motivation.

MORAL HYPOCRISY

It is often assumed that moral individuals want to be moral, to display *moral integrity*. But our research suggests that at least some individuals want to appear moral while, if possible, avoiding the cost of actually being moral. We call this motive *moral hypocrisy.*

To examine the nature of moral motivation, we have used a simple—but real—moral dilemma. The dilemma involves having research participants assign themselves and another participant (actually fictitious) to different tasks. One task is clearly more desirable; it has positive consequences (the chance to earn raffle tickets). The other task has neutral consequences (no chance to earn raffle tickets) and is described as rather dull and boring. Participants are told that the other participant will not know that they were allowed to assign the tasks; the other participant will think the assignment was made by chance.

Most research participants faced with this simple situation assign themselves the positive-consequences task (70% to 80%, depending on the specific study), even though in retrospect very few (less than 10%) say that this was the moral thing to do. Their actions fail to fit their moral principles (Batson, Kobrynowicz, Dinnerstein, Kampf, & Wilson, 1997).

Adding a Salient Moral Standard . . . and a Coin

Other participants have been confronted with a slightly more complex situation. The written instructions that inform them of the opportunity to assign the tasks include a sentence designed to make the moral standard of fairness salient: "Most participants feel that giving both people an equal chance—by, for example, flipping a coin—is the fairest way to assign themselves and the other participant to the tasks." A coin is provided for participants to flip if they wish. Under these conditions, virtually all participants say in retrospect that either assigning the other participant the positive-consequences task or using a fair method such as the coin flip is the most moral thing to do. Yet only about half choose to flip the coin.

Of those who choose not to flip, most (80% to 90%, depending on the specific study) assign themselves to the positive-consequences task. More interesting and revealing, the same is true of those who flip the coin; most (85% to 90%) assign themselves the positive consequences. In study after study, the proportion who assign themselves the positive-consequences task after flipping the coin has been significantly greater than the 50% that would be expected by chance. This was true even in a study in which the coin was labeled "SELF to POS" on one side and "OTHER to POS" on the other side. Clearly, some participants who flip the coin do not abide by the outcome. To appear fair by flipping the coin, yet still serve self-interest by ignoring the coin and assigning oneself the positive-consequences task, seems to be evidence of moral hypocrisy. Ironically, this hypocrisy pattern was especially strong among persons scoring high on a self-report measure of moral responsibility (Batson et al., 1997; Batson, Thompson, Seuferling, Whitney, & Strongman, 1999).

. . . And a Mirror

Other participants face an even more complex situation. After being provided the fairness standard and coin to flip, they assign the tasks while sitting in front of a mirror. The mirror is used to increase self-awareness and, thereby, pressure to reduce discrepancy between the moral standard of fairness and the task assignment (Wicklund, 1975). In a study that presented participants with this situation, exactly half of those who chose to flip the coin assigned themselves to the positive-consequences task. Apparently, having to face head-on the discrepancy between their avowed moral standard (be fair) and their standard-violating behavior (unfairly ignoring the result of the coin flip) was too much. In front of the mirror, those who wish to appear moral must be moral (Batson et al., 1999).

Taken together, the results of these studies seem to provide considerable evidence of moral hypocrisy. They conform precisely to the pattern we would expect if the goal of at least some research participants is to appear moral yet, if possible, avoid the cost of being moral. To the extent that moral hypocrisy is their motive, it is hardly surprising that ostensibly moral people fail to act morally. Any situational ambiguity that allows them to feign morality yet still serve self-interest—such as we provide by allowing participants to flip the coin—will undermine moral action if their motive is moral hypocrisy.

OVERPOWERED INTEGRITY

Before concluding that the world is full of moral hypocrites, it is important to consider a quite different motivational explanation for the failure of participants in our studies to act morally. Perhaps at least some of those who flip the coin do so with a genuine intent to assign the tasks fairly. Their initial motive is to be moral (moral integrity). But when they discover that the flip has gone against them and their intent to be moral will cost them the positive-consequences task, conflict arises. Self-interest overpowers integrity, with the result that they appear moral by flipping the coin, yet still serve self-interest. The general idea of overpowered integrity is, then, that a person's motivation to be truly moral may be overpowered by stronger self-interested motives when being moral entails personal cost (as it often does). In the words of the oft-quoted biblical phrase, "The spirit is willing, but the flesh is weak" (Matthew 26: 41).

Empirically Differentiating Moral Hypocrisy and Overpowered Integrity

How might one know which motivational process is operating, moral hypocrisy or overpowered integrity? The key difference between the two is the actor's intent when initially faced with a moral dilemma. In the former process, the initial motive is to appear moral yet avoid the cost of being moral; in the latter, the initial motive is to be moral. One factor that should clarify which of these motives is operating when people initially face a moral dilemma is whether they want to maintain control over the outcome of an apparently moral way to resolve the dilemma.

In our task-assignment paradigm, research participants motivated by moral hypocrisy, who intend to give themselves the positive consequences yet also appear moral, should be reluctant to let someone else flip the coin. If a coin is to be flipped, it is important that they be the ones to do so because only then can they rig the outcome. In contrast, participants initially motivated to be moral, who genuinely want to assign the tasks fairly, should have no need to maintain control of the flip. It should make no difference who flips the coin; any fair-minded person will do.

Following this logic, we gave participants an additional decision option: They could allow the task assignment to be determined by the experimenter flipping a coin. Of participants who were faced with this situation (no mirror present) and used a coin flip, 80% chose to have the assignment determined by the experimenter's flip rather than their own. This pattern suggested that many participants' initial motive was moral integrity, not moral hypocrisy (Batson, Tsang, & Thompson, 2000).

Two further studies provided evidence that this integrity could be overpowered. In these studies, we increased the cost of being moral. Instead of being neutral, consequences of the less desirable task were negative. Participants were told that every incorrect response on the negative-consequences task would be punished with a mild but uncomfortable electric shock. Faced with the prospect of receiving shocks, only one fourth of the participants were willing to let the experimenter's flip determine the task assignment. Another fourth flipped the coin themselves; of these, 91% assigned themselves the positive-consequences task, indicating once again a biased coin flip. Almost all of the remaining one half showed clear signs of overpowered integrity. They gave up any pretense of morality and assigned themselves the positive-consequences task without even feigning fairness. They were also quite ready, in retrospect, to admit that the way they assigned the tasks was not morally right.

Cost-Based Justification for Setting Morality Aside

How did these last participants deal with the clear discrepancy between their moral standards and their action? Comments made during debriefing suggest that many considered the relatively high personal cost introduced by the prospect of receiving electric shocks to be sufficient justification for not acting on their principles.

A cost-based justification for setting aside moral principles may seem quite understandable. After all, it is no surprise that participants do not want to receive electric shocks. But a cost-based justification carries ironic and chilling implications. Just think: If personal cost is sufficient to justify setting aside moral principles, then one can set aside morality when deciding whether to stand by or intervene as the perpetrators of hate crimes pursue their victims. One can set aside morality when considering one's own position of wealth while others are in poverty. One can set aside morality when considering whether to recycle newspaper or plastic containers or whether to contribute one's fair share to public television. Yet is it not in precisely such situations that moral principles are supposed to do their most important work as guides to behavior?

If, as is often assumed, the social role of morality is to keep individuals from placing their own interests ahead of the parallel interests of others, then cost-based justification poses a serious problem. A principle that says, "Do not give your own interests priority . . . unless there is personal cost," is tantamount to having no real principle at all. It turns morality into a luxury item—something one might love to have but, given the cost, is content to do without.

CONCLUSION

We have considered the interplay of three different motives: First is self-interest. If the self has no clear stake in a situation, then moral principles are not needed to restrain partiality. Second is moral integrity, motivation to be moral as an end in itself. Third is moral hypocrisy, motivation to appear moral while, if possible, avoiding the cost of actually being moral. We have suggested two motivational explanations for the failure of ostensibly moral people to act morally: moral hypocrisy and overpowered integrity. The latter is the product of a conflict between self-interest and moral integrity: A person sincerely intends to act morally, but once the costs of being moral become clear, this initial intent is over-powered by self-interest. Our research indicates that both moral hypocrisy and overpowered integrity exist, and that each can lead moral people to act immorally. Moreover, our research indicates that the problem is not simply one of inconsistency between attitude and behavior—between saying and doing—produced by failure to think about relevant behavioral standards. Making relevant moral standards salient (e.g., by suggesting that a coin toss would be the fairest way to assign tasks) did little to increase moral behavior. The moral lapses we have observed are, we believe, best understood motivationally.

We have only begun to understand the nature of moral motivation. There are persistent and perplexing questions still to be answered. For example, what socialization experiences stimulate moral integrity and hypocrisy, respectively? To what degree do parents preach the former but teach the latter? How might one structure social environments so that even those individuals motivated by moral hypocrisy or vulnerable to overpowered integrity might be led to act morally? Answers to such intriguing—and challenging—questions may help society avoid the atrocities of the past century in the next.

Recommended Reading

Bandura, A. (1999). (See References)
Batson, C.D., Kobrynowicz, D., Dinnerstein, J.L., Kampf, H.C., & Wilson, A.D. (1997). (See References)
Batson, C.D., Thompson, E.R., Seuferling, G., Whitney, H., & Strongman, J. (1999). (See References)
Bersoff, D.M. (1999). Why good people sometimes do bad things: Motivated reasoning and unethical behavior. *Personality and Social Psychology Bulletin, 25,* 28–39.
Todorov, T. (1996). *Facing the extreme: Moral life in the concentration camps* (A. Denner & A. Pollak, Trans.). New York: Henry Holt.

Note

1. Address correspondence to C. Daniel Batson, Department of Psychology, University of Kansas, Lawrence, KS 66045.

References

Asch, S. (1956). Studies of independence and conformity: A minority of one against a unanimous majority. *Psychological Monographs, 70* (Whole No. 416).

Bandura, A. (1999). Moral disengagement in the perpetration of inhumanities. *Personality and Social Psychology Review, 3,* 193–209.

Batson, C.D., Kobrynowicz, D., Dinnerstein, J.L., Kampf, H.C., & Wilson, A.D. (1997). In a very different voice: Unmasking moral hypocrisy. *Journal of Personality and Social Psychology, 72,* 1335–1348.

Batson, C.D., Thompson, E.R., Seuferling, G., Whitney, H., & Strongman, J. (1999). Moral hypocrisy: Appearing moral to oneself without being so. *Journal of Personality and Social Psychology, 77,* 525–537.

Batson, C.D., Tsang, J., & Thompson, E.R. (2000). *Weakness of will: Counting the cost of being moral.* Unpublished manuscript, University of Kansas, Lawrence.

Milgram, S. (1974). *Obedience to authority: An experimental view.* New York: Harper & Row.

Wicklund, R.A. (1975). Objective self-awareness. In L. Berkowitz (Ed.), *Advances in experimental social psychology* (Vol. 8, pp. 233–275). New York: Academic Press.

Critical Thinking Questions

1. Immoral behavior has typically been addressed by either a developmental or a social influence perspective. Explain each perspective and describe how considering the motivation of immoral behavior goes beyond these two perspectives.

2. Distinguish between moral hypocrisy and overpowered integrity as motives for immoral behavior. Explain how each has been demonstrated experimentally.

3. Discuss the role of salience and self-awareness in moral hypocrisy. Describe the relevant research for each.

4. Describe the idea behind cost-based justification for acting immorally. What are some of the real-life implications for behaving this way?

This article has been reprinted as it originally appeared in *Current Directions in Psychological Science.* Citation information for this article as originally published appears above.

Terrorism Between "Syndrome" and "Tool"

Arie W. Kruglanski[1] and Shira Fishman

University of Maryland, College Park

Abstract

Two psychological views of terrorism are described, approaching it as a "syndrome" and as a "tool" respectively. Research thus far found little support for the syndrome view. The heterogeneity of terrorism's users is consistent with the tool view, affording an analysis of terrorism in terms of goal–means psychology.

Keywords

terrorism; syndrome; tool

Social scientists' interest in terrorism has been growing steadily, in response to the proliferation of terrorism in the world at large. Psychological research is highly relevant to this endeavor. Terrorists' acts of self-immolation and indiscriminate killings of innocent civilians appear horrific and bizarre. They simply cry out for a psychological explanation.

It is possible to discern two divergent psychological approaches that have been taken to terrorism over the years: treating it as a "syndrome" or treating it as a "tool" (that is, as a means to an end). Though never explicitly articulated, the syndrome view is implicit in treatments of terrorism as a monolithic psychological construct with identifiable properties. This view is reflected in often-posed questions such as "Who are the terrorists?" and "What prompts their behavior?" Seeing terrorism as a syndrome prompts the search for its definite internal causes (e.g., personality traits) and/or external causes (e.g., poverty, political oppression). Such a view also suggests that a generic "terrorist group" has a distinct organizational structure and evolutionary trajectory.

The tool approach, in contrast, is rooted in the psychology of goal–means relations (Gollwitzer & Bargh, 1996; Kruglanski et al., 2002). It assumes little about the uniform properties of terrorists or their groups. It views terrorism as a means to an end, a tactic of warfare that anyone could use. It suggests that, like the rocket launcher, the tank, or the AK-47 assault rifle, terrorism may be employed by non-state militias, state-sponsored military, or even lone perpetrators.

TERRORISM AS SYNDROME

It seems fair to say that the syndrome approach has garnered little support thus far. Take terrorists' personality traits and motivations. Early psychological investigations (see Horgan, 2005, for a review) asked whether terrorists are driven by some kind of psychological disturbance. However, painstaking empirical research conducted on various terrorist organizations did not reveal anything distinctive about the psychological make-up of terrorists.

Research seems to have struck out also in the search for situational "root causes" of terrorism. Empirical data yielded no evidence for a relation between poverty or education and terrorism (Krueger and Maleckova, 2002). From the standpoint of psychological theory, there are reasons to doubt a general causal link between either poverty or political repression and terrorism. Presumably, the underlying logic of such a hypothesized relationship is that poverty or oppression foster frustration, fomenting aggression against others. But in scientific psychology the simple frustration–aggression hypothesis has long been questioned. Just because one is frustrated does not necessarily mean one will become a terrorist; instead, one could escape, withdraw, or aggress against oneself rather than against others. Affluent Western democracies such as Germany, Italy, Spain, France, Canada, and the United States have all seen instances of indigenous terrorism, whereas Stalin's Soviet Union, for example, or Hitler's Nazi Germany (repressive regimes by all criteria) saw none.

Root Causes Versus Contributing Factors

It is not that personality traits or situational conditions (such as poverty or oppression) are altogether irrelevant to terrorism. But their role could be one of contributing factors—which is different and admittedly weaker than the role of root causes. The root-cause concept implies a factor that constitutes both a necessary and a sufficient condition for some effect. Psychological theory and empirical evidence alike raise doubts whether any personality trait, need, or situational circumstance would constitute such a condition, inevitably giving rise to terrorism. But if the idea of terrorism were cognitively accessible and normatively acceptable, traits, motivations, and situational conditions might well prompt individuals to embrace it. Hence, under specific circumstances, these psychological factors could be relevant to terrorism.

Psychological research has demonstrated that motivation significantly affects individuals' tendency to embrace beliefs on various topics, and beliefs in the efficacy and justifiability of terrorism are no exception to this rule. Thus, individuals with appropriate motivations (deriving from their stable personality traits or situational pressures) may well be more prone to endorse terrorism under the appropriate circumstances than individuals with different motivations may be. Pyszczynski et al. (in press) found that, in Iran, mortality salience (induced by asking participants to ponder their own death) enhanced support for suicide terrorism, whereas in the United States it enhanced the support for tough antiterrorist measures (on part of the politically conservative participants). Henry, Sidanius, Levin, & Pratto (in press) found that, in Lebanon, right-wing conservatism predicted support for terrorism, whereas in the United States it predicted support for counterterrorism.

Group Structure

Does the terrorist group exhibit a unique manner of functioning? Different terrorist organizations are quite heterogeneous in terms of their size, their organizational structure (e.g., hierarchical vs. broadly based), and their sources of support. Some terrorist organizations draw their main support from the larger communities in which they are embedded (McCauley, in press); others derive support from kindred terrorist organizations, virtual communities on the internet, or terrorism-sponsoring states. Some terrorist organizations are organizationally "tight" (the Hezbollah is often likened to a well-disciplined military), others (present day Al Qaeda, for example) are diffuse. In short, there doesn't seem to exist a unique terrorist group structure any more than there is a unique terrorist personality or a unique situational cause of terrorism.

These observations bode ill for the view of terrorism as a unitary psychological construct. How then can psychology be relevant to the study of terrorism? To seriously ponder this question, it seems necessary to first define what one means by terrorism. Unfortunately, the picture in this department is rather murky.

DEFINING TERRORISM

Schmid and Jongman (1988) list no less than 109 different definitions of terrorism. Why is it so difficult to agree on a definition? The pejorative connotation of the terrorism label may motivate one to set it apart from forms of aggression one wishes to condone. Consider the U.S. Department of State's recent definition of terrorism: "a premeditated, politically motivated violence conducted in times of peace, perpetrated against non-combatant targets by sub-national groups or clandestine state agents, usually intended to influence an audience to advance political ends" (cited in Hoffman, 1998, p. 38).

This demarcates terrorism from (a) state-originated violence at times of war (e.g., the bombings of German or Japanese cities during WWII), (b) incidental killings of noncombatants (so-called "collateral damage"), and (c) underground resistance to occupation—all activities many Americans deem justifiable. It has often been claimed that one person's terrorist is another person's freedom fighter. This claim is an inevitable consequence of allowing one's motivations to dictate one's definitions.

One way out of the definitional quandary reflected in the multiplicity of definitions is to stick to a core element of most definitions of terrorism: the strategic use of fear to advance one's objectives. In this vein, Carr (2003) stated that "terrorism is simply the contemporary name given to, and the modern permutation of, warfare deliberately waged against civilians with the purpose of destroying their will to support either leaders or policies that the agents of such violence find objectionable" (p. 6). Telhami (2004, p. 15) concurred, referring to terrorism as essentially "an 'instrument' . . . a means employed by groups some of which have just causes and some of which don't."

TERRORISM AS A TOOL

Carr (2003) and Telhami (2004; see also Horgan, 2005) view terrorism as a tool, or a means to an end of whatever kind. The tool view requires the realization that in recent history numerous states actually perpetrated "terrorism." Rummel (1996) estimates that during the 20th century, 169,000,000 people (including numerous civilians) were killed by the activities of governments. In this connection, McCauley (in press, p. 2) observed: "Terrorism is principally a state strategy because the state usually has the predominant power of violence . . ." But isolated individuals too can employ terrorism. Ted Kaczynski used terrorism in pristine isolation. So, apparently, did Erik Rudolph, the Atlanta bomber. John Muhammad and Lee Malvo inflicted terror as a pair.

Treating terrorism as a tool has important implications for the kind of psychology one could use to understand what conditions make terrorism more or less likely. Such psychology derives from the classic theory of the motivation–action interface (e.g., Atkinson & Birch, 1970) and from the recent wave of cognitively based research on goals (Gollwitzer & Bargh, 1996; Kruglanski et al., 2002). Basically, the theory and research suggest that a given means will be utilized, or a given action undertaken, when its expected psychological utility is higher than that of other means. In turn, expected utility is determined by how well a given means is seen as contributing to the desired objectives. A given activity may be seen to advance a goal or undermine it. Goal importance and the available mental resources (how much effort and energy one is able and is willing to invest) will determine the extent to which a readily accessible means will be compared with other possible means prior to utilizing it. These notions are highly relevant to the psychology of terrorism.

Discouraging Terrorism

The launching of terrorism (by a group or an individual perpetrator) requires a deliberate decision, based on the belief that it will (a) be instrumental to the perpetrator's objectives, (b) be better than any other means available, and (c) not undermine other salient objectives (e.g., economic welfare, the upholding of moral values). By the same token, discouraging terrorism requires convincing the perpetrator that (a) this means is ineffectual; (b) there exist alternative, better means to the same ends; and (c) it constitutes a hindrance (has negative instrumentality) to other salient objectives.

Though schematically simple, discouraging terrorism in this way is anything but. A major difficulty is that events are subject to construal, often biased by motivations. Throughout much of the second intifada, about 80% of the Palestinian population supported the use of terror tactics (e.g., suicide bombings) against the Israelis, believing this to be an effective tool of struggle. By contrast, the majority of Israelis (85%) viewed Palestinian terror as counterproductive.

Multifinality

Terrorism may be difficult to give up also because, apart from presumably advancing the perpetrators' ideological (political, religious, ethno-nationalistic) objectives, it affords the emotional satisfaction of watching the enemy suffer. In that sense, terrorism is multi-purpose, compounding its appeal by adding to the number of objectives to which it appears instrumental. In other words, terrorism may be seen to advance several different objectives—for instance, ending occupation, securing for oneself the status of a martyr, taking care of one's family's finances (e.g., through grants dispensed to families of suicide bombers), and vengeance against a despised enemy. The cumulative value of such goals may determine the appeal of terrorism to would-be perpetrators.

This analysis has implications for counterterrorism. For instance, blocking the financial rewards to families of suicide bombers may undercut one possible objective attained by terrorism. On the other hand, such activities as ethnic profiling or targeted assassinations, and such outcomes as inadvertent collateral damage, might fuel the terrorists' rage, amplifying the emotional goal of vengeance against the enemy and adding to terrorism's appeal. A recent empirical analysis (Kaplan, Mintz, Mishal, & Samban, 2005) suggests that targeted assassinations by the Israeli forces boosted the estimated recruitment to the "terrorist stock," presumably due to Palestinians' revenge motivation. Thus, whereas targeted hits do hurt and may decrease the perceived efficacy of terrorism, they might also increase the appeal of terrorism by amplifying the intensity of the emotional goal it may serve.

Feasibility of Alternatives to Terrorism

Whereas terrorism's ability to satisfy multiple goals (such as revenge in addition to political liberation) may increase its appeal, perceived availability of alternative (more instrumental, or less costly) means to terrorism's ends may decrease that appeal. For instance, following the election of Mahmud Abbas to presidency of the Palestinian authority, creating a renewed chance for a peace process (i.e. an alternative means potentially instrumental to ending the Israeli occupation), Palestinian support for suicide attacks dipped to a 7-year low, reaching a mere 27%, according to the Palestinian pollster Khalil Shikaki (2005).

Alternative Objectives

Dissuading the users of terrorism from its deployment may involve a rekindling of alternative objectives, incompatible with terrorism. In the Palestinian context, the opposition to suicide attacks (Shikaki, 2005) is particularly pronounced among Palestinians likely to possess the means to alternative, individualistic goals—e.g. professional, family, or material goals. Such opposition reached 71% among holders of a B.A. degree, compared to 61% among those who are illiterate; 75% among employees, compared to 62% among students; and, curiously enough, 74% among individuals willing to buy lottery tickets—i.e. presumably interested in material goals—compared to 64% among those unwilling to buy them.

A Means–Ends Classification of Terrorism Users

The tool view affords a classification of terrorism users in accordance with their commitment to that particular means. Gunaratna (2002) characterized utopian Islamist groups as ones whose "doctrinal principles include no negotiation, no dialogue and no peacemaking" (p. 93). Given such depth of commitment to violence, it is unlikely that anything short of a total defeat will convince such bodies to relinquish its use.

The situation is different for terrorism users for whom it represents one among several available instruments. Hamas, Hezbollah, or Sinn Féin, for example, though not shy of using terrorism, have other means at their disposal (diplomacy, media campaigns) as well as other goals (of a political or social variety). For instance, once the immediate "irritant" of the Israeli occupation was removed with withdrawal of the Israeli forces from Lebanon and with dismantling of the Jewish settlements in Gaza, the respective populations' goals may have shifted toward rebuilding the economic infrastructure in those locales and the resumption of a peaceful life. This may have created a dilemma for terrorist organizations as far as the use of terrorism is concerned and the risk it entails of destroying the rebuilding efforts. In fact, the direct attacks on Israel by the Hezbollah were markedly reduced following the Israeli withdrawal from Lebanon, as were Hamas attacks from Gaza following the Israeli disengagement.

In short, different organizations may differ in their potential for relinquishing the use of terrorism. Whereas negotiation and effecting a shift to alternative goals or means is unlikely to work with terrorists whose commitment to violence is total and unconditional, it might work with terrorist groups who may entertain alternative means and who value alternative goals such as political support by their constituencies, who under certain circumstances may view terrorism as too costly.

CONCLUSION

The tool view offers general guidelines for the struggle against terrorism. This framework can only be helpful, however, if mapped onto the cultural specifics of given terrorism users, their worldviews and belief systems, the rhetoric they find compelling, and the sources they find credible. For instance, Islamist extremists have argued for the efficacy of terrorism against the West by invoking the defeat of the Crusaders by the Muslim warrior Saladin; such metaphor may carry little meaning for non-Islamic (e.g., Marxist or ethno-nationalist) groups. A Palestinian may morally justify terrorism by invoking the right to self-defense, whereas a leftist terrorist may do so by invoking social justice. Arguments designed to counteract a given terrorist worldview need, therefore, to address the particular premises from which it derives. Occasionally, too, such arguments must take the form of resolute military action that "speaks louder than words" and brings home the costs of terrorism to its perpetrators. Indeed, even as terrorism is politics by other means (i.e., armed struggle), so must be counterterrorism.

Recommended Reading

Crenshaw, M. (2000). The psychology of terrorism: An agenda for the 21st Century. *Political Psychology, 21*, 405–420.
Horgan, J. (2005). (See References)
Telhami, S. (2004). (See References)

Note

1. Address correspondence to Arie W. Kruglanski, Department of Psychology, University of Maryland, College Park, Maryland 20742; e-mail: arie@psyc.umd.edu.

References

Atkinson, J.W., & Birch, D. (1970). *The dynamics of action.* New York: Wiley.
Carr, C. (2003). *The lessons of terror: A history of warfare against civilians.* New York: Random House.

Gollwitzer, P.M., & Bargh, J.A. (Eds.) (1996). *The psychology of action: Linking cognition and motivation to behavior.* New York: The Guilford Press.

Gunaratna, R. (2002). *Inside Al Qaeda: Global network of terror.* New York: Columbia University Press.

Henry, P.J., Sidanius, J., Levin, S., & Pratto, F. (in press). Social dominance orientation, right-wing authoritarianism and support for intergroup violence and terrorism in the United States and Lebanon. *Political Psychology.*

Hoffman, B. (1998). *Inside terrorism.* New York: Columbia University Press.

Horgan, J. (2005). *The psychology of terrorism.* London: Routledge.

Kaplan, E.H., Mintz, A., Mishal, S., & Samban, C. (2005). *What happened to suicide bombings in Israel? Insights from a terror stock model.* Unpublished manuscript, Yale University.

Krueger, A.B., & Maleckova, J. (2002, June 24). Does poverty cause terrorism? *The New Republic, 226*(24), 27–33.

Kruglanski, A.W., Shah, J.Y., Fishbach, A., Friedman, R., Chun, W.Y., & Sleeth-Keppler, D. (2002). A theory of goal systems. In Zanna, M.P. (Ed.). *Advances in Experimental Social Psychology* (Vol. 34, pp. 331–378). New York: Academic Press.

McCauley, C. (in press). Psychological issues in understanding terrorism and the response to terrorism. In C. Stout (Ed.), *The Psychology of Terrorism.* Westport, CT: Greenwood Publishing.

Pyszczynski, T., Abdolahi, A., Solomon, S., Greenberg, J., Cohen, F., & Weise, D. (in press). Mortality salience, martyrdom, and military might: The Great Satan versus the Axis of Evil. *Personality and Social Psychology Bulletin.*

Rummel, R.J. (1996). *Death by government.* New Brunswick, NJ: Transaction Publishers.

Schmid, A.P., & Jongman, A.J. (1988). *Political terrorism.* Amsterdam: North Holland Publishing Company.

Shikaki, K. (2005, March 12–15). Poll No. 15. Ramallah, Palestine: Palestinian Center for Policy and Survey Research.

Telhami, S. (2004). *The Stakes: America in the Middle East.* Boulder, CO: Westview Press.

Critical Thinking Questions

1. Compare and contrast the "syndrome" and "tool" approaches to terrorism. Why is one preferable to the other?

2. Speculate on why it is so difficult for researchers to agree on a definition of terrorism. Is it important for researchers to reach a consensual definition? Explain.

3. Using the "terrorism as a tool" approach to support your points, describe some ways to discourage terrorism. Why might this be more difficult than it seems?

This article has been reprinted as it originally appeared in *Current Directions in Psychological Science.* Citation information for this article as originally published appears above.

Workplace Aggression

Manon Mireille LeBlanc and Julian Barling[1]
Queen's School of Business, Queen's University, Kingston, Ontario, Canada

Abstract

The vast majority of workplace aggression is perpetrated by members of the public, or organizational outsiders. Organizational employees (i.e., insiders) seldom kill or physically assault their colleagues. The most frequent manifestations of insider-initiated aggression involve less dramatic acts, such as shouting at and spreading rumors about colleagues. Both individual (e.g., alcohol consumption, hostile attributional bias) and organizational (e.g., overcontrolling supervision, perceived injustice) factors predict which individuals are most likely to engage in insider aggression. Research has shown that victims of insider-initiated aggression experience negative personal (e.g., emotional well-being and physical health) and organizational (e.g., work attitudes) outcomes. Despite increasing research on workplace aggression, significant gaps in our knowledge remain.

Keywords

workplace violence; workplace aggression; employee characteristics; working conditions

December 26, 2000, Wakefield, Massachusetts, United States: Michael McDermott, a 42-year-old employee of Edgewater Technology, shot dead seven of his coworkers; five of his victims worked in the accounting department. McDermott was apparently upset because the accounting department, at the request of the Internal Revenue Service, was preparing to garnish a portion of his wages.

Michael McDermott is not the "typical" workplace killer: Organizational members (i.e., insiders) seldom murder (Peek-Asa, Runyan, & Zwerling, 2001) or physically assault their colleagues (Baron, Neuman, & Geddes, 1999). The vast majority of workplace aggression is perpetrated by members of the public, or organizational outsiders. For example, in 1997, 860 Americans were murdered on the job, and in approximately 85% of the cases, the assailant was an outsider (U.S. Bureau of Labor Statistics, 1998). In a 1995 study examining eight southern California cities, members of the public were responsible for more than 90% of nonfatal workplace assaults (see Peek-Asa et al., 2001).

Workplace aggression has been categorized into four major types based on the assailant's relationship to the victim. In the first type (Type I), the perpetrator has no legitimate relationship with the targeted organization or its employees and enters the work environment to commit a criminal act (e.g., robbery). More employees in America are murdered each year as a result of Type I aggression than from the other three types combined (see Peek-Asa et al., 2001). Individuals who interact and exchange money with the public (e.g., taxicab drivers) are at highest risk of being victims of this type of workplace aggression.

In the second type (Type II), the assailant has a legitimate relationship with the organization and commits an act of violence while being served by the organization. Although perpetrators of Type II aggression rarely kill their victims (Peek-Asa et al., 2001), they are responsible for an estimated 60% of all nonfatal assaults at work (Peek-Asa & Howard, 1999). Employees who provide service, care, advice, or education (e.g., nurses, social workers, teachers) are at increased risk for Type II aggression, especially if their clients, customers, or patients are experiencing frustration, insecurity, or stress.

In the third type of workplace aggression (Type III), the offender is typically a current or former employee of the organization (i.e., an insider) who targets a coworker or supervisor for perceived wrong-doing. Unlike Type I and Type II aggression, Type III aggression does not appear to be more associated with certain occupations or industries than with others. Rather, insider-initiated aggression has been linked to both individual (e.g., alcohol consumption; Greenberg & Barling, 1999) and organizational (e.g., perceived injustice; Baron et al., 1999) factors.

In the fourth type of workplace aggression (Type IV), the perpetrator has an ongoing or previous legitimate relationship with an employee of the organization. This category includes violence by an intimate partner that takes place at work. In the United States in 1997, 5% of homicides on the job were the result of Type IV aggression (see Peek-Asa et al., 2001).

The focus of this article is on insider-initiated aggression. We focus on this category of workplace aggression for three reasons: First, there are myths surrounding insider-initiated aggression that warrant attention. Second, investigators in organizational psychology have conducted more research on insider-perpetrated aggression than on the other three types of workplace aggression. Third, organizations are more likely to be able to manage this type of workplace aggression, because it is often prompted by some factor in the organization itself (e.g., overcontrolling supervision).

CONCEPTUALIZING WORKPLACE AGGRESSION

Workplace aggression includes a variety of behaviors, ranging from psychological acts (e.g., shouting) to physical assault (Dupré & Barling, 2003). Recently, Baron et al. (1999) proposed that aggressive workplace behaviors can be grouped into three different categories, *expressions of hostility* (i.e., hostile verbal or symbolic behaviors, such as "the silent treatment"), *obstructionism* (i.e., behaviors that are designed to hamper the target's performance, such as refusing to provide needed resources), and *overt aggression.* (e.g., assaults, destruction of property). Investigators have demonstrated that the most frequent manifestations of insider-initiated aggression are not acts of overt aggression but less dramatic psychologically aggressive acts, such as spreading rumors about and giving dirty looks to colleagues (e.g., Baron et al., 1999).

PREDICTORS OF INSIDER-INITIATED AGGRESSION

Research on insider-initiated aggression is complex because this phenomenon can have multiple sources, targets, and causes. Assailants can be either employees or managers, aggression can be directed toward one or more of three different targets (i.e., current or former superiors, peers, and subordinates), and factors that predict aggression may vary depending on the target of aggression. For example, workplace surveillance increases the risk of employee aggression toward supervisors, but not subordinates or peers (Greenberg & Barling, 1999).

Both individual and workplace factors are important predictors of Type III aggression, and insider-initiated aggression is likely the result of a complex interaction between the two kinds of factors (Dupré & Barling, 2003). Although several individual (e.g., history of aggression, Type A behavior pattern) and organizational (e.g., downsizing and layoffs, surveillance, increased workplace diversity) variables have been linked to aggression at work, we focus on only two individual factors, alcohol consumption and hostile attributional bias,[2] and two organizational factors, perceptions of injustice and overcontrolling supervision. (For a more extensive review of the literature on predictors of insider-initiated aggression, see Dupré & Barling, 2003).

Recent evidence suggests that alcohol consumption contributes to aggression in organizational settings. Alcohol consumption interacts with employee perceptions of procedural injustice to predict aggression against coworkers and subordinates (Greenberg & Barling, 1999). In other words, when employees perceive that their organizations' procedures are unfair (i.e., perceptions of procedural injustice), amount of alcohol consumed is related to aggression against coworkers and subordinates. In contrast, amount of alcohol consumed is not related to such aggression when employees perceive their organizations' procedures to be fair. Alcohol consumption also interacts with job insecurity to predict aggression against subordinates (Greenberg & Barling, 1999). Simply put, amount of alcohol consumed is related to aggression against subordinates when employees' perceptions of job security are low, but not when perceptions of job security are high. Recent research also suggests that the relationship between alcohol abuse and aggression at work is amplified when employees have strong perceptions of being mistreated by others (Jockin, Arvey, & McGue, 2001).

Research has demonstrated that an individual's cognitive appraisal of an event may predict whether he or she becomes angry and aggressive. For example, Epps and Kendall (1995) found that perceptions of hostile intent, and not actual intent, are associated with subsequent aggressive behavior. Douglas and Martinko (2001) extended these findings to the work context. They asked employees to read hypothetical scenarios of negative workplace events (e.g., "You fail to receive a promotion that you wanted for a long time") and interpret the causes of these events. Employees whose explanations for the events involved higher levels of hostile intent were more likely to report engaging in workplace aggression compared with employees who perceived lower levels of hostile intent.

Although individual factors clearly play a role in workplace aggression, some researchers argue that organizational factors are more important predictors of aggression (e.g., Dupré & Barling, 2003). In a study examining both individual (self-esteem, history of aggressive behavior) and organizational (perceptions of interpersonal injustice, abusive supervision) predictors of supervisor-targeted aggression among moonlighters (i.e., individuals who work two jobs with different supervisors), the organizational factors were found to be better predictors than the individual factors (Inness & Barling, 2002).

Organizational injustice is considered one of the most promising avenues in the study of workplace aggression. Although there are various forms of injustice, interpersonal injustice is considered particularly relevant to insider-initiated aggression. Interpersonal justice is the perception that employees are treated with politeness, dignity, and respect by authorities during the enactment of organizational procedures (e.g., performance evaluations). A recent study found that employee perceptions of interpersonally unfair treatment from supervisors were related to employee-initiated aggression against both supervisors and organizations (Inness & Barling, 2002).

Investigators have found that employees who feel overcontrolled by a supervisor have an increased tendency to engage in supervisor-targeted aggression (Day & Hamblin, 1964; Dupré & Barling, 2002). Use of surveillance methods to monitor employees' behavior (e.g., requiring that employees punch time cards) also predicts supervisor-targeted aggression (Greenberg & Barling, 1999).

There is sufficient evidence to conclude that both individual and organizational factors contribute to insider-initiated aggression. More research is needed, however, to understand the interaction between these two kinds of factors.

OUTCOMES OF INSIDER-INITIATED AGGRESSION

To date, knowledge about the outcomes of workplace aggression derives almost exclusively from (a) studies of outsider-initiated aggression and (b) studies that did not differentiate between outsider- and insider-initiated aggression. It is clear from this literature that experiencing aggression at work can have negative consequences for victims and their organizations. However, it appears that victims of aggression experience differential consequences depending on the source of the aggression (i.e., a member of the public or an insider).

A recent study comparing outcomes of insider-perpetrated aggression and outcomes of outsider-initiated aggression (LeBlanc & Kelloway, 2002) demonstrated that victims of insider-initiated aggression tended to have reduced emotional and physical well-being, as well as low levels of organizational commitment; the latter predicted intentions to find another job. In contrast, victims of outsider-initiated aggression perceived the likelihood of future aggression to be higher than non-victims did, and this perception in turn was associated with fear of future aggression. Being a victim of outsider-initiated aggression was not related to emotional or physical health, although it did predict employee intent to find another job. The results of this study suggest that outsider-initiated aggression and insider-initiated aggression are associated with different outcomes for victims.

Tepper (2000) studied the effects of abusive supervision on employee and organizational outcomes. Abusive supervision was identified by measuring "subordinates' perceptions of the extent to which supervisors engage in the sustained display of hostile verbal and nonverbal behaviors, excluding physical contact" (p. 178). Compared with employees who did not feel their supervisors were abusive, those who did perceive their supervisors to be abusive were more likely to quit their jobs, and if they remained employed at their organizations, they reported lower life satisfaction, as well as greater psychological distress and conflict between the demands of work and family. Perceptions of abusive supervision were also related to lower job satisfaction and organizational commitment. However, among the employees with abusive supervisors, those who perceived that they could find work if they quit their jobs experienced fewer negative outcomes than those who were less confident about their ability to find another job.

In summary, Type III aggression has negative consequences for victims and their organizations. Initial evidence suggests that coworker-initiated aggression has negative effects on employees' emotional and physical well-being, as well as organizational outcomes (e.g., commitment). Clearly, more research on personal and organizational outcomes of Type III workplace aggression is warranted.

FUTURE DIRECTIONS

Despite increasing research on workplace aggression, significant gaps in knowledge remain. For example, it would be important to better understand how employees' reactions to workplace aggression vary depending on their source of the aggression (e.g., supervisors, peers, subordinates, members of the public). Insider-initiated aggression is related to employees' emotional and physical well-being, but outsider-initiated aggression is not (LeBlanc & Kelloway, 2002). Investigators need to determine why there are different reactions to aggression depending on the relationship between the perpetrator and victim. It is possible that individuals who work with the public expect to experience aggression (i.e., they view it as "part of the job"), and that this expectation influences their reactions to aggression. In contrast, employees are unlikely to expect to experience aggression from their colleagues, so insider-initiated aggression may break their trust and lead to feelings of betrayal. Examining aggression in romantic and marital relationships may prove useful in understanding employees' reactions to insider-initiated aggression.

Insider-initiated aggression also appears to lower employees' commitment to their organization, although aggression perpetrated by a member of the public does not (LeBlanc & Kelloway, 2002). Future research could investigate the reasons for this difference. Individuals may expect their organizations to protect them from their peers, sub-ordinates, or supervisors and may hold their organizations accountable for insider-initiated aggression. Victims of outsider-initiated aggression may not perceive their aggressors' actions as being "under the control" of their organizations; hence, such victims may not hold their organizations responsible for the aggression. It is up to future researchers to examine these hypotheses.

Although being a victim of workplace aggression is associated with negative outcomes, few studies have examined the outcomes for witnesses of aggression. It is likely that more employees will witness aggression than fall victim to it. The following are potential questions that could be investigated: Do employees who witness insider-initiated aggression report the incidents? Do subordinates modify their perceptions of their supervisors if they witness them behaving aggressively toward other subordinates? When violence toward an intimate partner spills into an organization, how does this aggression impact the witnesses? Clearly, there are many questions concerning vicariously experienced aggression that could be investigated.

The prevention of workplace aggression warrants further investigation, as well. Many organizations have policies (e.g., zero tolerance for aggression, restrictions on carrying concealed weapons) and procedures (e.g., severe penalties, such as employee termination, for engaging in aggression) related to workplace aggression. To date, no studies have investigated whether these policies are effective. There is also little published data on whether sanctions against aggressive behavior are effective in preventing aggression. The effectiveness of organizational training programs aimed at preventing aggressive behaviors also needs to be determined. Researchers should also conduct studies to examine whether support (e.g., emotional support) from organizational insiders (e.g., peers, supervisors) and outsiders (e.g., family members, friends) might lessen the negative effects of work-place aggression on victims.

The predictors and consequences of workplace aggression among young workers also need to be investigated, because the vast majority of teenagers work part-time while still in school (see Loughlin & Barling, 2001). Further, many young people are employed in retail organizations, such as fast-food restaurants and convenience stores, which put them at risk for outsider-initiated aggression. How does being a victim of workplace aggression at a first job influence a young person's perceptions of future employment? Are the consequences of workplace aggression more severe for young workers than mature individuals? Do teenagers engage in workplace aggression for different reasons than do adults?

Workplace violence against intimate partners also needs to be investigated. To date, no published studies in organizational psychology have examined this phenomenon. Hence, there are many questions that need to be answered: Why do some individuals, but not others, decide to target their victims in the workplace? Are abusers more likely to target their victims at work if they no longer live together? Are individuals less likely to be targeted at work when they are employed at organizations with elaborate security systems (e.g., if identification cards are needed to enter buildings)? What are the outcomes for victims of Type IV aggression?

Although insider-initiated aggression rarely leads to physical injury or death, it occurs frequently and its effects can be devastating for victims. Research conducted to date shows that both individual and organizational factors contribute to this phenomenon. Given the increasing incidence of workplace aggression in today's organizations, researchers must continue to investigate this phenomenon.

Recommended Reading

Greenberg, L., & Barling, J. (1999). (See References)
LeBlanc, M.M., & Kelloway, E.K. (2002). (See References)
O'Leary-Kelly, A.M., Griffin, R.W., & Glew, D.J. (1996). Organization-motivated aggression: A research framework. *Academy of Management Review, 21,* 225–253.

Acknowledgments—Preparation of this article was supported by a Social Sciences and Humanities Research Council of Canada (SSHRC) doctoral fellowship to Manon LeBlanc and by a research grant from SSHRC to Julian Barling. We gratefully acknowledge Kate Dupré and Nick Turner for their comments on an earlier version of this manuscript.

Notes

1. Address correspondence to Julian Barling, School of Business, Queen's University, Kingston, Ontario, Canada K7L 3N6; e-mail: jbarling@business.queensu.ca.
2. Hostile attributional bias is the tendency for some individuals to infer that the actions of another person have a hostile intent even when social cues fail to provide a clear intent (i.e., when intent is ambiguous).

References

Baron, R.A., Neuman, J.H., & Geddes, D. (1999). Social and personal determinants of workplace aggression: Evidence for the impact of perceived injustice and the Type A Behavior Pattern. *Aggressive Behavior, 25*, 281–296.

Day, R.C., & Hamblin, R.L. (1964). Some effects of close and punitive styles of supervision. *The American Journal of Sociology, 69*, 499–510.

Douglas, S.C., & Martinko, M.J. (2001). Exploring the role of individual differences in the prediction of workplace aggression. *Journal of Applied Psychology, 86*, 547–559.

Dupré, K.E., & Barling, J. (2002). *The prediction and prevention of workplace aggression and violence.* Unpublished manuscript, Memorial University, St. John's, Newfoundland, Canada.

Dupré, K.E., & Barling, J. (2003). Workplace aggression. In A. Sagie, S. Stashevsky, & M. Koslowsky (Eds.), *Misbehavior and dysfunctional attitudes in organizations* (pp. 13–32). New York: Palgrave/Macmillan.

Epps, J., & Kendall, P.C. (1995). Hostile attributional bias in adults. *Cognitive Therapy and Research, 19*, 159–178.

Greenberg, L., & Barling, J. (1999). Predicting employee aggression against coworkers, subordinates and supervisors: The roles of person behaviors and perceived workplace factors. *Journal of Organizational Behavior, 20*, 897–913.

Inness, M., & Barling, J. (2002). *Situational specificity and individual differences in the prediction of workplace aggression.* Manuscript submitted for publication.

Jockin, V., Arvey, R.D., & McGue, M. (2001). Perceived victimization moderates self-reports of workplace aggression and conflict. *Journal of Applied Psychology, 86*, 1262–1269.

LeBlanc, M.M., & Kelloway, E.K. (2002). Predictors and outcomes of workplace violence and aggression. *Journal of Applied Psychology, 87*, 444–453.

Loughlin, C.A., & Barling, J. (2001). Young workers' work values, attitudes, and behaviors. *Journal of Occupational and Organizational Psychology, 74*, 543–558.

Peek-Asa, C., & Howard, J. (1999). Workplace-violence investigations by the California Division of Occupational Safety and Health, 1993–1996. *Journal of Occupational and Environmental Medicine, 41*, 647–653.

Peek-Asa, C., Runyan, C.W., & Zwerling, C. (2001). The role of surveillance and evaluation research in the reduction of violence against workers. *American Journal of Preventive Medicine, 20*, 141–148.

Tepper, B.J. (2000). Consequences of abusive supervision. *Academy of Management Journal, 43*, 178–190.

U.S. Bureau of Labor Statistics. (1998). *National census of fatal occupational injuries, 1997* (USDL 98-336). Washington, DC: Department of Labor.

Critical Thinking Questions

1. The authors present four major types of workplace aggression. Describe each type. What do they have in common? How are they different?

2. Discuss two individual factors and two organizational factors that have been linked to aggression at work. How do each of these factors relate to workplace aggression?

3. The authors assert that "outsider-initiated aggression and insider-initiated aggression are associated with different outcomes for victims." Describe the evidence that supports this claim. Speculate on why this difference might exist.

This article has been reprinted as it originally appeared in *Current Directions in Psychological Science*. Citation information for this article as originally published appears above.

A Social-Neuroscience Perspective on Empathy

Jean Decety[1] and Philip L. Jackson

University of Chicago and Université Laval, Québec, Canada

Abstract

In recent years, abundant evidence from behavioral and cognitive studies and functional-imaging experiments has indicated that individuals come to understand the emotional and affective states expressed by others with the help of the neural architecture that produces such states in themselves. Such a mechanism gives rise to shared representations, which constitutes one important aspect of empathy, although not the sole one. We suggest that other components, including people's ability to monitor and regulate cognitive and emotional processes to prevent confusion between self and other, are equally necessary parts of a functional model of empathy. We discuss data from recent functional-imaging studies in support of such a model and highlight the role of specific brain regions, notably the insula, the anterior cingulate cortex, and the right temporo-parietal region. Because this model assumes that empathy relies on dissociable information-processing mechanisms, it predicts a variety of structural or functional dysfunctions, depending on which mechanism is disrupted.

Keywords

empathy; intersubjectivity; affective sharing; perspective taking; emotion regulation

Empathy refers to the capacity to understand and respond to the unique affective experiences of another person. At an experiential level of description, this psychological construct denotes a sense of similarity between one's own feelings and those expressed by another person. At a basic level of description, empathy can be conceived of as an interaction between any two individuals, with one experiencing and sharing the feeling of the other. This sharing of feelings does not necessarily imply that one will act or even feel impelled to act in a supportive or sympathetic way. The social and emotional situations eliciting empathy can be quite complex, depending on the feelings experienced by the observed person (target), the relationship of the target to the observer, and the context in which they socially interact.

In recent years, there has been a growing interest in the cognitive-affective neuroscience of empathy. In this article, we first discuss what the components of this psychological construct are and then present empirical data that can cast some light on the neurocognitive mechanisms subserving empathy, with a special emphasis on the perception of pain in others.

THE MAJOR COMPONENTS OF EMPATHY

Despite the various definitions of empathy, there is broad agreement on three primary components: (a) an affective response to another person, which often, but not always, entails sharing that person's emotional state; (b) a cognitive capacity to take the perspective of the other person; and (c) emotion regulation. Some scholars favor a particular aspect over the others in their definitions. For instance, Hoffman (1981) views empathy as a largely involuntary vicarious response to affective cues from another person, while Batson et al. (1997) emphasize people's intentional role-taking ability, which taps mainly into cognitive resources. These two aspects represent the opposite sides of the same coin: Depending on how empathy is triggered, the automatic tendency to mimic the expressions of others (bottom-up processing) and the capacity for the imaginative transposing of oneself into the feeling and thinking of another (top-down processing) are differentially involved. Moreover, both aspects tap, to some extent, similar neural mechanisms that underpin emotion processing. It is unlikely, however, that the overlap between self- and other representations is absolute. Such a complete overlapping between self and other could lead to personal distress (i.e., a self-focused, aversive response to another's emotional state). This would consequently hamper the ability to toggle between self- and other perspectives and would not constitute an adaptive behavior. Therefore, self-regulatory processes are at play to prevent confusion between self- and other feelings.

Affective Sharing Between Self and Others

A number of theorists have pointed out that empathy involves resonating with another person's unconscious affect and experiencing that person's experience along with him or her while keeping one's own self-integrity intact. Notably, Basch (1983) speculated that, because their respective autonomic nervous systems are genetically programmed to respond in a like fashion, a given affective expression by a member of a particular species sometimes triggers a similar response in other members of that species.

The view that unconscious automatic mimicry of a target generates in the observer the autonomic response associated with that bodily state and facial expression subsequently received empirical support from a variety of studies as well as observations from ethologists (Preston & de Waal, 2002). For instance, viewing facial expressions triggers similar expressions on one's own face, even in the absence of conscious recognition of the stimulus. It was proposed that people may "catch" the emotions of others as a result of feedback generated by elementary motor mimicry of others' expressive behavior, producing a simultaneous matching emotional experience. Interestingly, Levenson and Ruef (1992) found that a perceiver's accuracy in inferring a target's negative emotional states is related to the degree of physiological synchrony between the perceiver and the target. In other words, when the physiological state (e.g., heart rate, muscle activity) of two individuals is more closely matched, they are more accurate at perceiving each other's feelings.

Recently a functional magnetic resonance imaging (fMRI) experiment confirmed these results by showing that when participants are required to observe or to imitate facial expressions of various emotions, increased neurodynamic activity is detected in the brain regions that are implicated in the facial expression of these emotions, including the superior temporal sulcus, the anterior insula, and the amygdala, as well as specific areas of the premotor cortex (Carr, Iacoboni, Dubeau, Mazziotta, & Lenzi, 2003). The similarity between the expression of an emotion and the perception of that emotion has also been demonstrated for disgust. Damage to the insula, a region crucial in monitoring body state, can impair both the experience of disgust and the recognition of social signals (e.g., facial and emotional expression) that convey disgust. Functional neuroimaging studies (see Decety & Jackson, 2004, for review) have later shown that observing facial expressions of disgust and feelings of disgust activated very similar sites in the anterior insula and anterior cingulate cortex (ACC).

Altogether these results point to one basic mechanism for social interaction: the direct link between perception and action. Such a system automatically prompts the observer to resonate with the emotional state of another individual, with the observer emulating the motor representations and associated autonomic and somatic responses of the observed target (Preston & de Waal, 2002). This covert mimicry process is responsible for shared affects and feelings between self and other. Developmental research has demonstrated that motor and affective mimicry are active already in the earliest interactions between infants and caregivers, raising the possibility that these processes are hardwired.

The expression of pain provides a crucial signal that can motivate helping behaviors in others. Finding out how individuals perceive others in pain is thus an interesting way to decipher the underlying neural mechanisms of empathy. Recently, a handful of fMRI studies have indicated that the observation of pain in others is mediated by several brain areas that are implicated in processing the affective and motivational aspects of one's own pain. In one study, participants received painful stimuli and observed signals indicating that their partner, who was present in the same room, had received the same stimuli (Singer et al., 2004). The rostral (or anterior) ACC, the insula, and the cerebellum were active during both conditions. In another study, participants were shown photographs depicting body parts in painful or neutral everyday-life situations, and were asked to imagine the level of pain that these situations would produce (Jackson, Meltzoff, & Decety, 2005). In comparison to neutral situations, painful conditions elicited significant activation in regions involved in the affective aspects of pain processing, notably the ACC and the anterior insula. Moreover, analyses taking into account the behavioral responses of participants revealed that the level of activity within the ACC correlated with ratings of pain that subjects ascribed to the different situations. This finding strongly suggests that this region plays a crucial role in affective modulation, which is triggered by the assessment of painful situations. Altogether, these results lend support to the idea that common neural circuits are involved in representing one's own and others' affective pain-related states (Fig. 1).

Adopting the Perspective of the Other

Humans have the capacity to intentionally adopt the subjective perspective of others by putting themselves into other people's shoes and imagining what they feel. Such a capacity requires that one mentally simulate the other's perspective using one's own neural machinery. In one neuroimaging study, the participants

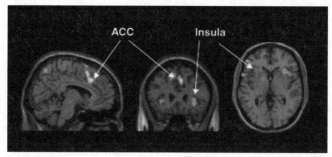

Fig. 1. Sagittal (left), coronal (middle), and horizontal (right) views of activation sites in the anterior cingulate cortex (ACC) and insula elicited in individuals watching pain in others. Physiological research in pain processing indicates that the ACC plays a role in the affective dimension of pain, particularly those related to behavioral responses associated with avoiding or escaping a painful stimulus. This region combines attentional and evaluative functions with that of establishing emotional valence and response priorities. The insula is involved in monitoring the physiological state of the body. It receives direct input from the body's major pain pathway. Interestingly, both the ACC and the insula are found to be activated by the mere sight of pain in others.

were presented with short written sentences that depicted real-life situations likely to induce social emotions (e.g., shame) or other situations that were emotionally neutral (Ruby & Decety, 2004). Participants were each asked to imagine how they would feel if they were in those situations and how their mothers would feel in the same situations. Regardless of the affective content of the situations depicted, when the participants adopted their mothers' perspective, activation was detected in the frontopolar cortex, the ventromedial prefrontal cortex, the medial prefrontal cortex, and the right inferior parietal lobule—congruent with the role of these regions in executive functions associated with the perspective-taking process (Fig. 2). Regions involved in emotional processing, including the amygdala and the temporal poles, were activated in conditions that involved situations that were emotion-laden for both self and other. This study indicates that self- and other-oriented emotional judgments commonly make use of regions implicated in emotion processing, and supports the idea that the imaginative transposing of oneself into the subjective world of another person taps neural circuits shared between people.

In a new fMRI study, participants were shown pictures of people with their hands or feet in painful or nonpainful situations and were instructed to imagine themselves or imagine another individual in the same scenarios. Participants then had to rate the level of perceived pain according to the different perspectives (Jackson, Brunet, Meltzoff, & Decety, 2006). Both the self- and the other perspectives were associated with activation in the neural network involved in pain processing—including the parietal operculum, the ACC, and the anterior insula. However, the self-perspective yielded significantly higher pain ratings and activated the pain matrix more extensively, reaching within the secondary somatosensory cortex, the posterior part of the ACC, and the insula proper—consistent with the pattern of activity detected in firsthand experience of pain.

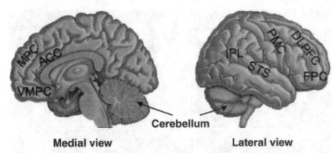

Cerebellum

Medial view   **Lateral view**

Fig. 2. Anatomical and functional regions of the brain mentioned in the text. The superior temporal sulcus (STS) is the most dorsal (highest) region of the temporal lobes located under the fissure that separates the frontal and temporal lobes. The premotor cortex (PMC) is a region of the frontal lobes anterior to the motor cortex on both lateral (side) and medial (inner) surfaces of the brain. The anterior cingulate cortex (ACC), located on the inner surface of the hemispheres, appears to play a role in a variety of autonomic functions, such as regulating heart rate and blood pressure, and is vital to cognitive functions and emotion regulation. Anterior to the PMC is the prefrontal cortex, which is functionally divided into several regions: the dorsolateral (DLPFC), the ventrolateral (referring to the higher and lower portion of the area located on the lateral surface of the brain), and the medial prefrontal cortex (MPC) which is located on the inner surface of the frontal lobes; its lowest portion is often called the ventromedial prefrontal cortex (VMPC). The frontopolar cortex (FPC), the most anterior portion of the frontal lobes, is considered to mediate executive functioning, monitoring and controlling thought and actions—including self-regulation, planning, cognitive flexibility, response inhibition, and resistance to interference. There is increasing evidence to suggest that the right inferior parietal lobule (IPL), the lower part of the parietal lobes, plays a pivotal role in distinguishing the perspectives of the self from those of others, an ability that is relevant to knowing that the contents of other people's minds can be different from one's own.

These studies point out the similarities between self and other regarding neural-network activation during pain perception that are consistent with the shared-representations account of social interaction. However, the findings also highlight important differences between self and other predicted by our model. For instance, while the insula activated when participants imagined the pain of self and others, different nonoverlapping clusters within that region were activated for the two tasks. Likewise, both self- and other perspectives are associated with a common sub-area in the ACC, but self-perspective selectively activated another part of this region, in which neurons coding specifically for pain have been documented.

Self-Agency and Emotion Regulation

Thus, whether one witnesses another individual's emotional state or consciously adopts that person's psychological view, similar neural circuits are activated in the self. These findings fit neatly with the simulation theory, which states that behavior can be simulated by activation of the same neural resources for acting and perceiving (Goldman, 2006). However, a complete overlap between self- and other representations could induce emotional distress or anxiety, which is not the function of empathy. In the experience of empathy, individuals must be able to disentangle themselves from others. This distance is a key characteristic in psychotherapy. Therefore, agency is a crucial aspect of empathy. Affective sharing must be modulated by maintaining a sense of whose feelings belong to whom. It has been proposed that nonoverlapping parts of the neural circuit mediating shared representations (i.e., the areas that are activated for self-processing and not for other processing) generate a specific signal for each form of representation. There is strong evidence from fMRI studies, as well as from lesion studies in neurological patients, that the right temporo-parietal junction plays a critical role for the sense of self-agency (Decety & Sommerville, 2003). It is worth noting that adopting the perspective of another person to imagine his or her emotional reactions (Ruby & Decety, 2004) or to imagine his or her pain (Jackson et al., 2006) was associated with specific increase in the posterior cingulate and precuneus, as well as in the right temporo-parietal junction. These areas are reliably involved in distinguishing the perspective of the self from that of others in a variety of tasks involving actions and emotions. These areas contribute to the sense of agency and self-awareness by comparing self-generated signals to signals from the environment. We argue that this neurocognitive mechanism plays a pivotal role in empathy. Its contribution to social interaction may distinguish emotional contagion, which heavily relies on the automatic link between perception of another person's expressed emotions and one's own experience of the same emotions, and empathy, which necessitates a more detached relationship.

Finally, being aware of one's own emotions and feelings enables one to reflect on them. It has been demonstrated that individuals who can regulate their emotions are more likely to experience empathy and to act in morally desirable ways with others (Eisenberg, Smith, Sadovsky, & Spinrad, 2004). Among various emotion-regulation strategies, reappraisal by denial of relevance (i.e., taking a detached-observer position) by generating an image of the observing self unaffected by the target is known to reduce the subjective experience of anxiety, sympathetic arousal, and pain reactivity. Such a strategy is likely to play an important role in empathy, in order to maintain a detached perspective with the target (for example, a psychotherapist and a client). Recent fMRI studies have identified a limited number of regions in the anterolateral and medial prefrontal cortices that mediate such function (e.g., Kalisch et al., 2005). More research is needed to determine how the neural system subserving emotion regulation modulates (or inhibits) the other components that are involved in empathy, notably the automatic emotional mimicry.

CONCLUSIONS

There is strong evidence that, in the domain of emotion processing and empathic understanding, people use the same neural circuits for themselves and for others. These circuits provide a functional bridge between first-person and third-person information, which paves the way for intersubjective transactions between self and others. These circuits can also be activated when one adopts the perspective of the other. However, were this bridging between self and other absolute, experiencing another's distress state as one's own experience could lead to empathic overarousal, in which the focus would then become one's own feelings of stress rather than the other's need. Self-agency and emotion-regulatory mechanisms thus play a crucial role in maintaining a boundary between self and other.

A better knowledge of the mechanisms involved in empathy will have important implications for the examination and understanding of individuals with social cognitive disorders. Likewise, the absence of empathy in certain neurological and psychiatric disorders, including autism and narcissistic and antisocial personality disorders, may also provide important clues about the relevant brain circuitry underlying affective sharing and empathy. People may indeed lack empathy for various reasons. For instance, emotion sharing or emotion regulation may be impaired in antisocial personality disorder. In contrast, people prone to personal distress may present deficits in self–other distinctiveness. Finding out that these empathy deficits (which are all expressed differently) stem from impairment in distinct neural networks or interaction between them will add to a comprehensive model of empathy and may even guide intervention and treatment strategies in the clinical arena.

Recommended Reading

Decety, J., & Jackson, P.L. (2004). (See References)
Preston, S.D., & de Waal, F.B.M. (2002). (See References)

Note

1. Address correspondence to Jean Decety, Department of Psychology, University of Chicago, 5848 S. University Avenue, Chicago, IL 60637; e-mail: decety@uchicago.edu.

References

Basch, M.F. (1983). Empathic understanding: A review of the concept and some theoretical considerations. *Journal of the American Psychoanalytic Association, 31*, 101–126.
Batson, C.D., Sager, K., Garst, E., Kang, M., Rubchinsky, K., & Dawson, K. (1997). Is empathy-induced helping due to self–other merging? *Journal of Personality & Social Psychology, 73*, 495–509.
Carr, L., Iacoboni, M., Dubeau, M.C., Mazziotta, J.C., & Lenzi, G.L. (2003). Neural mechanisms of empathy in humans: A relay from neural systems for imitation to limbic areas. *Proceedings of National Academy of Sciences, USA, 100*, 5497–5502.
Decety, J., & Jackson, P.L. (2004). The functional architecture of human empathy. *Behavioral and Cognitive Neuroscience Reviews, 3*, 71–100.
Decety, J., & Sommerville, J.A. (2003). Shared representations between self and others: A social cognitive neuroscience view. *Trends in Cognitive Science, 7*, 527–533.
Eisenberg, N., Smith, C.L., Sadovsky, A., & Spinrad, T.L. (2004). Effortful control. In R.F. Baumeister & K.D. Vohs (Eds.), *Handbook of self-regulation* (pp. 259–282). New York: The Guilford Press.
Goldman, A. (2006). *Simulating minds: The philosophy, psychology, and neuroscience of mindreading.* New York: Oxford University Press.
Hoffman, M.L. (1981). Is altruism part of human nature? *Journal of Personality and Social Psychology, 40*, 121–137.
Jackson, P.L., Brunet, E., Meltzoff, A.N., & Decety, J. (2006). Empathy examined through the neural mechanisms involved in imagining how I feel versus how you feel pain: An event-related fMRI study. *Neuropsychologia, 44*, 752–761.

Jackson, P.L., Meltzoff, A.N., & Decety, J. (2005). How do we perceive the pain of others: A window into the neural processes involved in empathy. *NeuroImage, 24,* 771–779.

Kalisch, R., Wiech, K., Critchley, H.D., Seymour, B., O'Doherty, J.P., Oakley, D.A., Allen, P., & Dolan, R.J. (2005). Anxiety reduction through detachment: Subjective, physiological, and neural effects. *Journal of Cognitive Neuroscience, 17,* 874–883.

Levenson, R.W., & Ruef, A.M. (1992). Empathy: A physiological substrate. *Journal of Personality and Social Psychology, 63,* 234–246.

Preston, S.D., & de Waal, F.B.M. (2002). Empathy: Its ultimate and proximate bases. *Behavioral and Brain Sciences, 25,* 1–72.

Ruby, P., & Decety, J. (2004). How would you feel versus how do you think she would feel? A neuroimaging study of perspective taking with social emotions. *Journal of Cognitive Neuroscience, 19,* 988–999.

Singer, T., Seymour, B., O'Doherty, J., Kaube, H., Dolan, R.J., & Frith, C.D. (2004). Empathy for pain involves the affective but not sensory components of pain. *Science, 303,* 1157–1161.

Critical Thinking Questions

1. Explain each of the three components that are included in most definitions of empathy. Speculate on why these three components are so essential to the definition.

2. Explain how fMRI research has supported the finding that the more closely matched individuals are physiologically, the more accurate they are in perceiving each other's feelings.

3. This article represents the union of social psychology and neuroscience. Explain how the authors are taking a traditional social psychological phenomenon (i.e., empathy) and examining it from a neuroscience perspective. What are some of the potential advantages of examining empathy from this perspective? Explain.

This article has been reprinted as it originally appeared in *Current Directions in Psychological Science.* Citation information for this article as originally published appears above.

Section 5: Stereotyping and Prejudice

Humans form social groups with whom they interact regularly, relying upon their own group for necessities that groups especially can provide, such as protection, division of labor, and positive social regard. One's own social groups therefore are extremely important and, given the choice, people would prefer to allocate scarce resources to their own groups, protect their own groups, and render favorable evaluations of their own groups. In the course of ingroup favoritism, other social groups may fare less well by comparison. Prejudice, stereotyping, and discrimination can derive, at least in part, from the interplay between what people desire, value, and know about their own group relative to other groups.

Social psychologists interested in these phenomena distinguish among three inter-related constructs: prejudice, stereotyping, and discrimination. Prejudice is the affective aspect, which includes negative evaluations of an outgroup or outgroup member as well as emotional experiences such as hatred, fear, disdain, or mild disquiet. Stereotypes are the set of beliefs held about group members. Members of group X may be seen as likely to possess particular attributes and may be expected to possess those attributes. As detailed further below, these beliefs and associations among these beliefs vary in their accessibility to conscious awareness. Finally, discrimination comprises negative behaviors expressed toward the out-group or its members. Discrimination can include institutional policies that withhold valued resources, behaviors perpetuated by groups such as ostracism from a popular clique, or behaviors perpetuated by individuals such as expressing ethnic slurs, violent behavior and gaze aversion.

A primary theme that carries through this set of articles is the question of origin: where and why do people develop prejudices and stereotypes, and how do they learn to discriminate. Bigler and Liben (2007) address this question from the perspective of developmental psychology. In their developmental intergroup theory, they argue that children are predisposed to categorize (e.g., initially all four-legged furry creatures may be designated "doggies"), and that the most salient dimensions are likely to form the basis of categorization. Gender, for example, typically is more salient than handedness, particularly when adults frequently use expression such as "boys and girls." Even without explicit labels, repeated pairing of particular attributes with a category is noticed by children as they try to develop a meaningful understanding of the social world. For example, children may notice that all United States Presidents are white men, and thereby may come to infer that visible, powerful leaders are male. This kind of consistent pairing may, in part, underlie the implicit associations discussed by Payne (2006). That is, if Whites in the United States consistently and frequently see Blacks associated with weapons, violence, and crime, then that implicit association can become strong over time. It may be an association whose veracity individuals consciously reject, but at a less conscious level the association may remain intact nonetheless.

The origins of prejudices, stereotypes and discrimination also derive from the broader beliefs and myths of a dominant culture. Those myths are pervasive in popular literature and film, salient examples receive considerable attention in the news (e.g., rags to riches stories), and are implicit in social policies: people grow up with these stories, and these stories become part of an understanding of how the world presumably works. Jost and Hunyady (2005), for instance, discuss the ideologies and myths that help justify the privileged situation of dominant groups. Although contemporary beliefs may not be as explicit as "divine right of kings," those beliefs can be very powerful. Contemporary examples of system-justifying ideologies include the Protestant Work Ethic and the Belief in a Just World. The Protestant Work Ethic, for instance, essentially holds that people are rewarded for hard work: anyone who applies him- or herself can get ahead in life. That set of beliefs implies, then, that people who have power and resources deserve to have them. Conversely, people without resources are seen as too lazy to apply themselves and improve their situations. These beliefs, in turn, influence people's support for policies relevant to equity in employment, education, and housing. Why, for example, would affirmative action policies be necessary if anyone—regardless of gender, ethnicity, socioeconomic background, or religion—can move into positions of authority and status with sufficient hard work and talent? This type of system-justifying belief, focused on dispositional factors such as ability and stable effort, underestimates the role of systemic, historical, and institutional factors in maintaining status differences.

Another broader set of beliefs in contemporary Western culture involves the ideal of marriage as the key to happiness and well-being. Although close relationships undoubtedly are important to well-being, the marital relationship is only one kind of close relationship: relationships among friends and family members also are very important close relationships. Indeed, DePaulo and Morris (2006) note that there is little evidence that married people (or those who were married in the past) are happier than people who always have been single. But they argue that the myth of marital bliss underlies, at least in part, negative stereotypes and discrimination against singles. Again, these myths can be perpetuated by popular literature and film, but also by pressures within social circles ("When are you going to settle down and get married?"). Myths and ideologies are so taken for granted that people may not even notice that they believe them...nor that their behavior is influenced by them. There are many such myths that escape our regular notice. Consider, for example the association between physical attractiveness and morality (i.e., what is beautiful is good). Consciously, most people would reject this association. And yet people recognize good and evil immediately by attractiveness in children's films and Hollywood blockbusters, prefer attractive college applicants to less attractive ones, and even are more lenient toward attractive individuals accused of wrong-doing.

Besides associations derived in childhood and culturally accepted myths, motivational and emotional factors can be the source of prejudice, stereotypes, and discrimination. The system-justifying ideologies discussed by Jost and Hunyady (2005) are, in part, motivation driven. For instance, people especially cling to these ideologies and their general cultural worldviews when they are threatened. Fear of death or intense pain (i.e., mortality salience)—undoubtedly an emotional experience that people are motivated to reduce—can exaggerate endorsement of system-justifying ideologies and increase prejudice-based responses such as ingroup favoritism. Prejudice against individuals who are not heterosexual also may derive in part from threat and anxiety. As Herek (2000) argues, the sexuality of gays and lesbians may be viewed inconsistent with the cultural values and morals endorsed by the dominant culture. These perceived threats to deeply ingrained beliefs may, in turn, underlie discriminatory behavior and prejudiced attitudes.

A secondary theme in this set of articles is the role of conscious awareness. People may be unaware that they possess the kinds of implicit associations described by Payne (2006) and, as he describes, these associations often have only nominal effects on behavior when people are free of time constraints and distractions. Under time pressure or distractions, however, these associations may be a matter of life and death. Even more mundane (but certainly meaningful) outcomes may be influenced by implicit associations. Without consciously intending to do so, the hiring manager or graduate admissions director may show ingroup favoritism if under time pressure or when attempting to multitask. Such effects may be unintended, but also may be guarded against once the risks of their occurring is recognized. Both individuals and institutions wishing to minimize discriminatory responding can create "safeguards" such as sufficient time, mental and personnel resources, and accountability for decisions. Although the less conscious associations may still exist, their negative effects significantly can be attenuated.

Instituting "safeguards" requires some conscious awareness that discrimination is a potential problem. The conscious recognition of potential discrimination varies across target groups. For example, people often acknowledge discrimination based on gender, ethnicity, religion, or sexual orientation. Discrimination against such groups is noticed, scrutinized, and may be cited spontaneously as examples of discrimination. Potential discrimination against certain other groups (e.g., singles; cf. DePaulo & Morris, 2006), however, essentially is off the radar. Although the stereotypes themselves may be accessible (i.e., quickly affecting perceptions and behavior), conscious awareness of their roles may be relatively less accessible. In such instances, people do little to try to inhibit or safeguard against discriminatory behavior. Conversely, people may try to inhibit prejudiced responses if they are consciously aware that discrimination may occur AND if they consider that discrimination to be inappropriate. For example, people are surprisingly comfortable expressing their stereotypic views of elderly people. [Compare with the possible admonishments for making a generalization about an ethnic group]. As another example, people may recognize that society at large condemns prejudiced responding toward a particular group, but may express prejudices within certain smaller subgroups. Thus, although prejudices can affect behavior with or without conscious awareness, conscious awareness appears necessary for undercutting the effect of prejudices upon behavior.

Understanding the origins of prejudice—as well as the role of conscious awareness, culture, and unquestioned assumptions—provides critical insight into a final major theme of these papers: reducing the negative effects of stereotypes and prejudice. Bigler and Liben's (2007) paper would suggest that societies wishing to minimize the development of particular stereotypes should uncouple salient group features and characteristics whenever possible or at least regularly expose children to non-stereotypic models (e.g., women judges, black physicians). DePaulo and Morris's (2006) paper implies that a necessary first step involves recognition by a society that a group is the target of stereotyping, prejudice, and discrimination; Herek's (2000) paper further suggests that recognition is only a first step: to combat stereotyping, prejudice, and discrimination, a society also must feel that the targeted group deserves treatment on par with the dominant group. And, finally, even if a society admonishes stereotyping, prejudice, and discrimination, individual perceivers ultimately have a choice to make. They can try, albeit sometimes unsuccessfully, to minimize the effects of stereotypes and prejudices on their behaviors: allocating sufficient time to tasks where implicit associations may creep into play, acknowledging their biases, and developing skills in cross-group interactions. Prejudices we may always have with us . . . but perhaps in time they may be smaller ones.

Developmental Intergroup Theory: Explaining and Reducing Children's Social Stereotyping and Prejudice

Rebecca S. Bigler[1]

University of Texas at Austin

Lynn S. Liben

The Pennsylvania State University

Abstract

Social stereotyping and prejudice are intriguing phenomena from the standpoint of theory and, in addition, constitute pressing societal problems. Because stereotyping and prejudice emerge in early childhood, developmental research on causal mechanisms is critical for understanding and controlling stereotyping and prejudice. Such work forms the basis of a new theoretical model, developmental intergroup theory (DIT), which addresses the causal ingredients of stereotyping and prejudice. The work suggests that biases may be largely under environmental control and thus might be shaped via educational, social, and legal policies.

Keywords

stereotyping; intergroup; children; prejudice

Young children are often perceived as being untainted by the negative social biases that characterize adults, but many studies reveal that stereotyping and prejudice exist by the age of 4. Contemporary theories explain how cognitive processes predispose children to acquire and maintain social stereotypes and prejudice (see Aboud, 2005; Martin, Ruble, & Szkrybalo, 2002). However, they fail to account for why some dimensions of human variation rather than others (e.g., gender but not handedness) become foundations for social stereotyping and prejudice, and they skirt the issue of whether biases are inevitable and, if not, how they might be prevented. A new theoretical model of social stereotyping and prejudice, *developmental intergroup theory* (DIT; Bigler & Liben, 2006), addresses both these issues. The theory's name reflects its grounding in two complementary theoretical approaches: *intergroup theory*, referring to social identity (Tajfel & Turner, 1986) and self-categorization theories (Turner, Hogg, Oakes, Reicher, & Wetherell, 1987), and *cognitive-developmental theory*, referring to Piagetian and contemporary approaches to cognitive development. We describe empirical foundations and then mechanisms by which children single out groups as targets of stereotyping and prejudice, associate characteristics with groups (i.e., stereotypes), and develop affective responses (i.e., prejudices). Elsewhere (Bigler & Liben, 2006) we focus on how DIT handles developmental differences (e.g., how the development of multiple classification skills during childhood affects stereotyping; see Bigler & Liben, 1992) and individual differences (e.g., the consequences of individual differences in attitudes; see Liben & Signorella, 1980). Here, we focus on how DIT conceptualizes group-level effects.

EMPIRICAL FOUNDATIONS

Causes of stereotypes and prejudice are difficult to study in the everyday world both because messages about social groups are pervasive and because it is impossible or unethical to assign individuals experimentally to most relevant groups (e.g., gender, race, social class). DIT thus draws heavily on research that circumvents these constraints by creating and manipulating *novel* social groups (e.g., Bigler, 1995; Bigler, Jones, & Lobliner, 1997; Bigler, Brown, & Markell, 2001). As in classic intergroup studies, group membership and environmental conditions are experimentally manipulated, permitting conclusions about causal effects of various factors on the development of stereotyping and prejudice.

In a typical study, participants are 6- to 11-year-old summer-school students who are unacquainted with each other when school begins. They are initially given tasks measuring factors (e.g., cognitive-developmental level, self-esteem) hypothesized to affect intergroup attitudes. Novel groups are created, usually by assigning children to wear different colored tee shirts. Characteristics of the groups (e.g., proportional size, purported traits) and their treatment within the classroom (e.g., labeling, segregation) are then manipulated. After several weeks, children's intergroup attitudes are assessed. One study, for example, tested children's intergroup attitudes as a function of adults' labeling and functional use of color groups (Bigler et al., 1997). In experimental classrooms, teachers used color groups to organize classroom desks, bulletin boards, and activities. In control classrooms, teachers ignored the color groups. After several weeks, children completed measures of their perceptions of trait variability within and between color groups, evaluated group competence and performance, and were assessed for behavioral biases and peer preferences. In-group biases developed only in experimental classrooms.

COMPONENT PROCESSES OF DIT

Three core processes (double-bordered rectangles in Fig. 1) are hypothesized to contribute the formation of social stereotyping and prejudice: (a) establishing the psychological salience (EPS) of different person attributes, (b) categorizing encountered individuals by salient dimensions, and (c) developing stereotypes and prejudices (DSP) of salient social groups.

Establishing the Psychological Salience of Person Attributes

Virtually all explanations of social stereotyping rest on categorization. However, there are almost endless bases on which humans might be parsed into groups. How and why are some of the available bases for classification—and not others—used by children to sort individuals? The first component of DIT addresses why some attributes become salient for categorization.

Drawing from constructive theories, we assume that individuals are motivated to understand their physical and social worlds and thus actively seek to determine which of the available bases for classifying people are important. Given the vast diversity of potentially important categories and the complexity of the cues that mark such categories, we reject the idea that evolution "hard

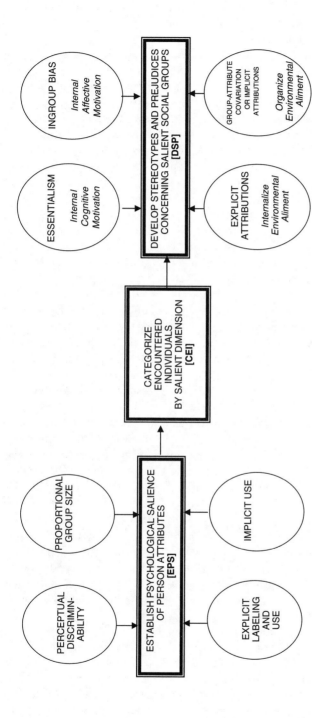

Fig. 1. The key processes involved in the formation of social stereotypes and prejudice in developmental intergroup theory (abbreviated from Bigler & Liben, 2006). Rectangles represent the three key processes contributing to the formation of social stereotyping and prejudice: (a) establishment of the psychological salience of different person attributes, (b) categorization of encountered individuals by salient dimensions, and (c) development of stereotypes and prejudices of salient social groups. Ovals represent the factors that shape the operation of core processes, including four factors that shape the establishment of psychological salience (perceptual discriminability, proportional group size, explicit labeling and use, and implicit use) and four factors that shape the development of stereotypes and prejudice (essentialism, ingroup bias, explicit attributions, and implicit attributions).

wired"specific dimensions as salient bases for classification. We instead suggest that evolution led to a flexible cognitive system that motivates and equips children to infer—from environmental data—which bases of classification are important within a given context.

One relevant factor is the child's tendency to note perceptually salient dimensions of objects and people (Fig. 1., top left oval feeding EPS). Research indicates that young children tend to focus on perceptually salient attributes in person-perception tasks: Perceptually salient features such as race, gender, age, and attractiveness typically become the basis for their social stereotyping, whereas perceptually indistinct features (e.g., some nationalities and political affiliations) typically do not (e.g., Rutland, 1999). Cultural environments may be explicitly structured to make some classification schemes perceptually salient (e.g., requiring Jews to wear yellow stars in Nazi Germany or socializing males and females to wear different hair styles and clothing).

Further, we argue that proportional group size (Fig. 1., top right oval feeding EPS) affects the psychological salience of social groups for children (as for adults; Brewer & Brown, 1998). Proportionally smaller (minority) groups are more distinctive than proportionally larger (majority) groups, thus making minority groups more likely to become the targets of stereotypes and prejudice.

DIT also proposes that the psychological salience of grouping criteria (e.g., gender, color, reading ability) increases when adults label groups or group members, either as a matter of routine (e.g., beginning the day by stating "Good morning girls and boys" [or, "reds and blues"]) or in the service of organizing the environment (e.g., assigning different desks or bulletin boards to each group; Fig. 1., bottom left oval feeding EPS). This outcome holds even when groups are distinguished in a completely neutral (as opposed to stereotypic) manner (e.g., asking children to sit alternately by gender).

We also posit that implicit mechanisms increase the salience of social categories (Fig. 1., bottom right oval feeding EPS). Unlike explicit mechanisms in which categories are directly labeled, implicit mechanisms present some social grouping without explanation, thereby providing a cognitive puzzle for children to solve. One particularly powerful example is de facto segregation. Although segregation has long been linked to stereotyping and prejudice, the explanatory mechanism traditionally offered is unfamiliarity. Under this view, intergroup contact promotes familiarity, thereby increasing intergroup liking (Pettigrew & Tropp, 2000). We propose an additional inferential, constructive process in which children observe the characteristics along which humans are sorted. They notice perceptual similarities among those who live, work, and socialize together and then infer that the social divisions they observe must have been caused by meaningful, inherent differences between groups.

Thus, rather than explaining children's tendency to classify others along some dimension because of reinforcement or imitation, we suggest that children see a dimension used and then construct hypotheses about its importance. Consider a father directing his child to "Ask that lady if we are in the correct line." In traditional social learning theory, this event would not be expected to shape the child's gender stereotyping: The statement involves neither reward nor punishment, nor conveys the father's gender attitudes. In DIT, however, it would be

Table 1. *Key Factors Hypothesized to Affect the Formation of Social Stereotypes and Prejudice in Developmental Intergroup Theory (DIT) and Studies Offering Relevant Empirical Data*

DIT factor	Relevant empirical work	Key manipulations	Major conclusions
Perceptual discriminability	Bigler, 1995; Bigler et al., 1997	Groups were perceptually marked or unmarked.	Higher bias when groups were perceptually marked
Proportional group size	Brown & Bigler, 2002	Groups were equal or unequal in size.	Higher bias when groups were unequal in size
Explicit labeling and use	Bigler et al., 1997, 2001; Patterson & Bigler, 2006	Groups were labeled or ignored by teachers.	Higher bias when groups were labeled by teachers
Implicit use	Bigler, 2004	Groups were segregated or integrated within classrooms.	Higher bias when groups were segregated
Explicit attributions	Patterson, 2007	Groups were labeled as excelling or not at tasks.	Higher bias when groups were linked to positive traits
Implicit attributions	Bigler et al., 2001; Brown & Bigler, 2002	Groups were associated with positive or negative traits via classroom posters.	Higher bias when groups were linked to positive traits

expected to make gender salient, thereby inspiring the child to devise hypotheses about gender's importance. Studies consistent with our hypothesized mechanisms are identified in Table 1.

Categorizing Encountered Individuals by Salient Dimensions

Because children categorize stimuli as they attempt to structure knowledge and reduce cognitive complexity (Mervis & Rosch, 1981), we propose that they will classify encountered individuals into groups using those dimensions that are psychological salient. The degree and way in which the categorization process operates will be affected by the individual child's classification skill (which undergoes age-related change) and environmental experience (e.g., the number of encounters with exemplars). The mere act of categorization triggers processes involved in the construction of social stereotypes.

Developing Stereotypes and Prejudices Concerning Salient Social Groups

The process of categorization is hypothesized to result in constructivist, cognitive-developmental processes (enumerated later) that attach meaning to social groups in the form of beliefs (i.e., stereotypes) and affect (i.e., prejudice). DIT outlines the factors that guide children's acquisition of the content of their social stereotypes and the nature of their affective responses to social groups.

We propose that both internally and externally driven processes lead children to attach meaning to psychologically salient groups. The former are constructive processes through which children actively interpret and recall objects and events in the external world in relation to their current cognitive and affective schemata. Internally driven processes involve the self-generation (rather than passive learning) of links between social categories and (a) attributes (e.g., traits, behaviors, roles) and (b) affect (e.g., liking). In these processes, children go above and beyond the veridical information available in the environment to infer beliefs about the attributes associated with particular social categories. For example, cognitive-developmental psychologists have suggested that some categories, particularly those found in the natural world, are structured by *essentialist* thinking (see Gelman, 2003). Essentialism is the belief that members of a category share important, non-obvious qualities (Fig. 1., top left oval feeding DSP). Thus, children are likely to presume that visible markers of group membership denote other, unseen, inherent qualities (e.g., believing that African Americans and European Americans have different blood types, see Gelman, 2003). Obviously, such beliefs are based not on empirical evidence; instead they reflect the imposition of an internalized group schema onto the world.

With respect to prejudice, the processes are conceptualized as ones in which children actively generate more positive affective links to in-groups than to out-groups. Among adults, the mere act of categorizing individuals into social groups is often sufficient to produce intergroup prejudice and discrimination (Tajfel & Turner, 1986). Children, too, show prejudice within many intergroup contexts, viewing their in-group as superior to out-groups, despite the fact that such beliefs are neither modeled by adults nor objectively true (Fig. 1., top right oval feeding DSP). When stereotype content is acquired via self-generative or constructive processes, children fabricate category–attribute links that favor their own group (Bigler et al., 1997).

Children's cognitive processes are applied to what they encounter in the world. Children are exposed to explicit statements linking social groups to attributes—for example, "African Americans are hostile" and "girls are shy" (Fig. 1., bottom left oval feeding DSP). Explicit remarks are powerful because they operate at two levels simultaneously by employing labels that inherently mark the social groups as important and by providing information about attributes associated with the group. Although public remarks like these have undoubtedly diminished, they still occur, especially among peers. That is, children may "teach" attributions that they have detected (a process described next) or invented, as in the popular children's rhyme: "Girls go to college to get more knowledge; boys go to Jupiter to get more stupider." They may also explicitly teach prejudice without reference to attributes (e.g., "I hate girls").

In addition, children's environments (both macro- and micro-level) are characterized by covariations between social categories and attributes. Illustratively, the occupation of President of the United States shows a perfect correlation to race and gender: All Presidents have been White men. This high-profile correlation is likely to be detected by children, even when it is not explicitly pointed out. The nonverbal behavior that adults direct toward members of social groups or show in response to the presence of group members (e.g., Whites becoming nervous or socially withdrawn in the presence of African Americans) is another source of implicit information likely to cause prejudice. Importantly, these non-verbal behaviors are likely to be unconscious and, as a consequence, adults are unlikely to explain their behaviors to children. We posit that children's attention to such correlations plays a role in shaping the content of stereotypes and, in turn, prejudice (Fig. 1., bottom right oval feeding DSP). Studies providing empirical data relevant to the role of explicit and implicit links in the formation of stereotype content are summarized in Table 1.

The veridical presence of correlations between social categories and some attributes has led some psychologists to claim that stereotypes are accurate generalizations (see Lee, Jussim, & McCauley, 1995). We agree that the detection of group–attribute correlations plays a role in stereotyping, but we view as incomplete approaches holding that stereotypes are *merely* the reflections of true category–attribute relations or that children learn stereotypes *primarily* through environmental models (e.g., via mechanisms described by social-learning theory). Both approaches fail to account for the fact that children and adults typically develop stereotypic views and prejudices concerning groups that are meaningless (and thus uncorrelated with any observable traits or behaviors). Furthermore, such approaches fail to acknowledge that individuals show systematic biases (e.g., illusory correlations) when processing information about social groups (Brewer & Brown, 1998; Martin et al., 2002). In addition, virtually limitless category-to-attribute correlations are available to the child. It seems unlikely that a child could calculate the correlations between (a) each possible social group within an environment and (b) the traits, roles, and activities that co-vary with each of those groups. We think it unlikely, for example, that children calculate the relation between a person's height and the likelihood of being a nurse, between hair color and the likelihood of being gentle, or between religion and the likelihood of using an ironing board. Yet, most children detect the correlation between gender and each of these characteristics, and thus some statistical learning of group-to-attribute relations appears to occur. We argue (as do researchers who study infants' and young children's attention to statistical information in the service of language learning) that some processes must narrow the scope of the problem so that children's attention is directed toward only a subset of possible correlations. DIT suggests such processes, outlining the factors that serve to make some (but not other) attributes the basis for children's social categorization.

IMPLICATIONS

The approach reviewed here implies that certain social policies will affect stereotyping and prejudice formation among children. Specifically, DIT predicts that the psychological salience of particular social groups for children will increase to the extent that societies (a) exaggerate the perceptual discriminability of groups, (b) foster numeric imbalance across multiple contexts, (c) call attention to groups by labeling them or by explicitly and routinely using group membership as a basis for some action, and (d) present conditions (like segregation) that implicitly convey the importance of group membership.

Importantly, most of the factors that serve to make social groups psychologically salient are under social control. Laws, for example, explicitly constrain adults' use of social categories to label children in some ways (e.g., federal law forbids routinely labeling children's race in classrooms) and might be extended to others (e.g., forbidding routine labeling of gender). Laws likewise affect the implicit use of social categories (e.g., by allowing vs. prohibiting single-sex and single-race schools). Once categorization along some particular dimension occurs, stereotyping and prejudice are likely to follow. When groups are labeled, treated, or sorted differently, children come to conceptualize groups as different in meaningful ways and to show preferential bias toward their own in-group. Children are also likely to internalize the stereotypic beliefs explicitly communicated in their environment and to detect covariations between social groups and attributes that would have otherwise gone unnoticed.

Additional research is needed to add to the empirical base for DIT shown in Table 1 and reviewed elsewhere (Bigler & Liben, 2006) and to test means for countering stereotypes and prejudices that have already developed. For example, whereas DIT suggests minimizing attention to group categories to avoid the formation of stereotypes, it might be necessary to actively draw children's attention to groups and to relevant cognitive processes (e.g., reconstructive memory; illusory correlations) when helping children to overcome stereotypes they already harbor. Our hope is that DIT will prove useful not only for understanding the emergence and evolution of stereotypes and prejudices long reported in the social-psychological literature (Brewer & Brown, 1998) but also for developing policies that will reduce their early emergence and their myriad negative consequences.

Recommended Reading

Aboud, F.E. (2005). (See References)
Bigler, R.S., & Liben, L.S. (2006). (See References)
Martin, C.L., Ruble, D.N., & Szkrybalo, J. (2002). (See References)

Note

1. Address correspondence to Rebecca S. Bigler, Department of Psychology, 1 University Station A8000, University of Texas at Austin, Austin, TX 78712; e-mail: bigler@psy.utexas.edu.

References

Aboud, F.E. (2005). The development of prejudice in childhood and adolescence. In J.F. Dovidio, P. Glick, & L.A. Rudman (Eds.), *On the nature of prejudice: Fifty years after Allport* (pp. 310–326). New York: Blackwell.

Bigler, R.S. (1995). The role of classification skill in moderating environmental influences on children's gender stereotyping: A study of the functional use of gender in the classroom. *Child Development, 66,* 1072–1087.

Bigler, R.S. (2004, January). The role of segregation in the formation of children's intergroup attitudes. In S. Levy (Chair), *Integrating developmental and social psychological research on prejudice processes.* Symposium conducted at the 5th annual meeting of the Society for Personality and Social Psychology, Austin, TX.

Bigler, R.S., Brown, C.S., & Markell, M. (2001). When groups are not created equal: Effects of group status on the formation of intergroup attitudes in children. *Child Development, 72,* 1151–1162.

Bigler, R.S., Jones, L.C., & Lobliner, D.B. (1997). Social categorization and the formation of inter-group attitudes in children. *Child Development, 68*, 530–543.

Bigler, R.S., & Liben, L.S. (1992). Cognitive mechanisms in children's gender stereotyping: Theoretical and educational implications of a cognitive-based intervention. *Child Development, 63*, 1351–1363.

Bigler, R.S., & Liben, L.S. (2006). A developmental intergroup theory of social stereotypes and prejudice. In R.V. Kail (Ed.), *Advances in child development and behavior* (Vol. 34, pp. 39–89). San Diego: Elsevier.

Brewer, M.B., & Brown, R.J. (1998). Intergroup relations. In D.T. Gilbert, S.T. Fiske, & G. Lindsey (Eds.), *The handbook of social psychology* (Vol. 2, 4th ed., pp. 554–594). New York: McGraw-Hill.

Brown, C.S., & Bigler, R.S. (2002). Effects of minority status in the classroom on children's inter-group attitudes. *Journal of Experimental Child Psychology, 83*, 77–110.

Gelman, S.A. (2003). *The essential child.* New York: Oxford University Press.

Lee, Y.T., Jussim, L.J., & McCauley, C.R. (Eds.). (1995). *Stereotype accuracy: Toward appreciating group differences.* Washington, DC: American Psychological Association.

Liben, L.S., & Signorella, M.L. (1980). Gender-related schemata and constructive memory in children. *Child Development, 51*, 11–18.

Martin, C.L., Ruble, D.N., & Szkrybalo, J. (2002). Cognitive theories of early gender role development. *Psychological Bulletin, 128*, 903–933.

Mervis, C., & Rosch, E. (1981). Categorization of natural objects. *Annual Review of Psychology, 32*, 89–115.

Patterson, M.M. (2007). *Negotiating (non) normality: Effects of consistency between views of one's self and one's social group.* Unpublished doctoral dissertation, University of Texas at Austin.

Patterson, M.M., & Bigler, R.S. (2006). Preschool children's attention to environmental messages about groups: Social categorization and the origins of intergroup bias. *Child Development, 77*, 847–860.

Pettigrew, T.F., & Tropp, L.R. (2000). Does intergroup contact reduce prejudice?: Recent meta-analytic findings. In S. Oskamp (Ed.), *Reducing prejudice and discrimination* (pp. 93–114). Mahwah, New Jersey: Erlbaum.

Rutland, A. (1999). The development of national prejudice, in-group favouritism and self-stereotypes in British children. *British Journal of Social Psychology, 38*, 55–70.

Tajfel, H., & Turner, J.C. (1986). The social identity theory of intergroup behaviour. In S. Worchel & W.G. Austin (Eds.), *Psychology of intergroup relations* (pp. 7–24). Chicago: Nelson.

Turner, J.C., Hogg, M.A., Oakes, P.J., Reicher, S.D., & Wetherell, M.S. (1987). *Rediscovering the social group: A self-categorization theory.* Oxford: Blackwell.

Critical Thinking Questions

1. Describe the developmental intergroup theory (DIT). Explain how DIT is grounded in intergroup theory and cognitive developmental theory.

2. What is meant by essentialist thinking? How does this concept support DIT?

3. The authors present four implications of DIT. Explain what each implication means. Then elaborate on how each implication derives logically from DIT.

This article has been reprinted as it originally appeared in *Current Directions in Psychological Science*. Citation information for this article as originally published appears above.

Antecedents and Consequences of System-Justifying Ideologies

John T. Jost[1]
New York University

Orsolya Hunyady
Adelphi University

Abstract

According to system justification theory, there is a psychological motive to defend and justify the status quo. There are both dispositional antecedents (e.g., need for closure, openness to experience) and situational antecedents (e.g., system threat, mortality salience) of the tendency to embrace system-justifying ideologies. Consequences of system justification sometimes differ for members of advantaged versus disadvantaged groups, with the former experiencing increased and the latter decreased self-esteem, well-being, and in-group favoritism. In accordance with the palliative function of system justification, endorsement of such ideologies is associated with reduced negative affect for everyone, as well as weakened support for social change and redistribution of resources.

Keywords

system justification; ideology; conservatism; status quo

In the wake of the 2004 U.S. presidential election, the satirical newspaper *The Onion* ran the following headline: "Nation's Poor Win Election for Nation's Rich" (November 11–17, 2004). The accompanying article contained a fictitious quote from the in-credulous winner, President Bush, who observed that "The alliance between the tiny fraction at the top of the pyramid and the teeming masses of mouth-breathers at its enormous base has never been stronger. We have an understanding, them and us. They help us stay rich, and in return, we help them stay poor. No matter what naysayers may think, the system works" (p. 10). For many readers, this parody summarized well the apparent irrationality involved in members of disadvantaged groups' support for conservative ideology and the societal status quo.

The failure of self-interest models to explain ideology and public opinion has led political observers and analysts to search for better explanations. To investigate how and why people accept and maintain the social systems that affect them, we have developed system justification theory (Jost, Banaji, & Nosek, 2004; Jost & Hunyady, 2002). To date, the theory has shed light on such paradoxical phenomena as working-class conservatism (Jost, Glaser, Kruglanski, & Sulloway, 2003), increased commitment to institutional authorities and meritocratic ideology among the poor (Jost, Pelham, Sheldon, & Sullivan, 2003), idealization of the capitalist system (Jost, Blount, Pfeffer, & Hunyady, 2003), and minority-group members' conscious and unconscious preferences for members of majority groups (Jost, Pelham, & Carvallo, 2002).

System justification theory holds that people are motivated to justify and rationalize the way things are, so that existing social, economic, and political arrangements tend to be perceived as fair and legitimate.[2] We postulate that there is, as with virtually all other psychological motives (e.g., self-enhancement, cognitive consistency), both (a) a general motivational tendency to rationalize the status quo and (b) substantial variation in the expression of that tendency due to situational and dispositional factors. Thus, members of disadvantaged as well as advantaged groups would be expected to engage in system justification (at least to some degree) even at considerable cost to themselves and to fellow group members.

TYPES OF SYSTEM-JUSTIFYING IDEOLOGIES

There are a number of ideologies that people adopt to justify the status quo in our society. Over the years, researchers have identified several distinct but related system-justifying ideologies, including the Protestant work ethic, meritocratic ideology, fair market ideology, economic system justification, belief in a just world, power distance, social dominance orientation, opposition to equality, right-wing authoritarianism, and political conservatism. These ideologies are listed and described in Table 1; some focus purely on social and cultural issues, whereas others concern economic matters. The fact that these belief systems reliably correlate with one another—at least in Western capitalist societies— suggests that they may serve a similar ideological function, namely to legitimize existing social arrangements (e.g., Jost, Blount, et al., 2003; Jost & Thompson, 2000; Sidanius & Pratto, 1999). In this article, we will review evidence indicating that these system-justifying ideologies (a) share similar cognitive and motivational antecedents and (b) produce similar consequences for individuals, groups, and systems.

Under a dramatically different socio-economic system than in North America and Western Europe (a system such as communism, for example), the contents of system-justifying ideologies would differ, but the social and psychological processes would be similar. That is, we expect that many of the antecedents of procapitalist ideology in the West would be the same as antecedents of procommunist ideology under a communist regime (see Kossowska & van Hiel, 2003). In both contexts, people tend to anchor on the status quo and are prone to exaggerating the fairness and legitimacy of their own system. Because most of the research to date on the antecedents and consequences of system-justifying ideologies has been conducted in Western, capitalist societies, this is the context that provides the empirical foundation for our conclusions.

ANTECEDENTS AND CONSEQUENCES
OF SYSTEM JUSTIFICATION

Why would people legitimize and support social arrangements that conflict with their own self-interest? There are hedonic benefits to minimizing the unpredictable, unjust, and oppressive aspects of social reality. As Lerner (1980) put it, "People want to and have to believe they live in a just world so that they can go

Table 1. *System-Justifying Ideologies, Their Descriptive Contents, and Illustrative References*

Ideology	Descriptive Content	Sample illustrative reference(s)
Protestant work ethic	People have a moral responsibility to work hard and avoid leisure activities; hard work is a virtue and is its own reward.	Jost & Hunyady (2002)
Meritocratic ideology	The system rewards individual ability and motivation, so success is an indicator of personal deservingness.	Jost, Pelham, et al. (2003)
Fair market ideology	Market-based procedures and outcomes are not only efficient but are inherently fair, legitimate, and just.	Jost, Blount, et al. (2003)
Economic system justification	Economic inequality is natural, inevitable, and legitimate; economic outcomes are fair and deserved.	Jost & Thompson (2000)
Belief in a just world	People typically get what they deserve and deserve what they get; with regard to outcomes, what "is" is what "ought" to be.	Jost & Burgess (2000); Lerner (1980)
Power distance	Inequality is a natural and desirable feature of the social order; large power differences are acceptable and legitimate.	Jost, Blount, et al. (2003)
Social dominance orientation	Some groups are superior to others; group-based hierarchy is a good thing.	Jost & Thompson (2000); Sidanius & Pratto (1999)
Opposition to equality	Increased social and economic equality is unattainable and undesirable; it would be detrimental for society.	Jost & Thompson (2000); Kluegel & Smith (1986)
Right-wing authoritarianism	People should follow conventional traditions and established authorities and stop getting rebellious ideas.	Altemeyer (1998); Jost, Glaser, et al. (2003)
Political conservatism	Traditional institutions in society should be preserved; social and economic inequality is acceptable and natural.	Jost, Glaser, et al. (2003)

about their daily lives with a sense of trust, hope, and confidence in their future" (p. 14). But there are also social and political costs of system justification, insofar as people who rationalize the status quo are less likely to improve upon it. Many people who lived under feudalism, the Crusades, slavery, communism, apartheid, and the Taliban believed that their systems were imperfect but morally defensible and, in many cases, better than the alternatives they could envision. Popular support helped prolong those regimes, much as it helps prolong our current system. In this section, we first consider in greater detail the factors (both dispositional and situational) that make system-justifying ideologies appealing. Then we summarize the ramifications of these ideologies—both favorable and unfavorable— for individuals, groups, and the system as a whole.

Antecedents of System Justification

As with many psychological tendencies, there are both dispositional and situational sources of variation in the expression of system justification. Several are

Table 2. *Some Cognitive-Motivational Antecedents of System-Justifying Ideologies*

Antecedent	Conceptual/operational definition
Needs for order, structure, and closure (+)	Preference for a decision-making environment that is orderly, well structured, and unambiguous; a desire to make decisions quickly and to stick with them
Openness to experience (−)	An orientation that is creative, curious, flexible, and sensation seeking; an affinity for situations involving novelty, diversity, and change
Perception of a dangerous world (+)	Heightened sensitivity to potential dangers in the social environment, including threats of violence, crime, terrorism, and evildoing
Death anxiety/mortality salience (+)	Existential awareness of and fear associated with the prospect of one's own death; anxiety arising from mortality concerns
System instability and threat (+)	Actual or perceived threat to the legitimacy or stability of the social, economic, or political system; an attack (symbolic or material) on the status quo

Note. (+) Indicates that the variable is positively associated with the endorsement of system-justifying ideologies; (−) indicates that it is negatively associated with system justification.

listed in Table 2. People who possess heightened needs to manage uncertainty and threat are especially likely to embrace conservative, system-justifying ideologies (including right-wing authoritarianism, social dominance orientation, and economic system justification). More specifically, uncertainty avoidance; intolerance of ambiguity; needs for order, structure, and closure; perception of a dangerous world; and fear of death are all positively associated with the endorsement of these ideologies. Cognitive complexity and openness to experience are negatively associated with their endorsement (Jost, Glaser, et al., 2003). There is a good match between needs to reduce uncertainty and threat and system justification, because preserving the status quo allows one to maintain what is familiar while rejecting the uncertain prospect of social change. For many people, the devil they know seems less threatening and more legitimate than the devil they don't.

There are other dispositional findings that suggest a motivational basis to system justification. Jost, Blount, et al. (2003) found that self-deception (measured as an individual difference variable) predicts endorsement of fair market ideology and support for capitalism. Scores on the fair market ideology scale— operationally defined as the tendency to believe that market-based procedures and outcomes are inherently fair and legitimate—are moderately to strongly correlated with endorsement of other system-justifying ideologies, including conservatism, opposition to equality, right-wing authoritarianism, belief in a just world, and economic system justification (which also tend to be correlated with one another). The observation that self-deception and feelings of threat are associated with the degree of system justification indicates that there is a motivational (or "hot") component to otherwise "cold" judgments concerning the legitimacy of political and economic institutions.

With regard to situational variables, the appeal of conservative, system-justifying beliefs is enhanced under conditions of high system threat and mortality salience (e.g., Jost, Glaser, et al., 2003; Landau, et al., 2004). Our experiments demonstrate that threats to the legitimacy of the social system lead people to increase their use of stereotypes to justify inequality between groups (e.g., Jost & Hunyady, 2002) and—especially if they are high in self-deception—to defend the capitalist status quo more vigorously (Jost, Blount, et al., 2003). The fact that the 9/11 terrorist attacks simultaneously evoked mortality salience and system threat may help to explain why they precipitated relatively strong increases (among liberals as well as conservatives) in patriotism and support for the Bush administration and its policies. In general, threats to the system—as long as they fall short of toppling the status quo—lead people to bolster existing arrangements by endorsing system-justifying ideologies. Experiments by Kay, Jimenez, and Jost (2002) suggest that, when regime change seems inevitable, people will begin to rationalize the new arrangements almost immediately.

Consequences of System Justification

From a social psychological point of view, there are both advantages and disadvantages of engaging in system justification (see Jost & Hunyady, 2002). In Table 3 we have listed some of the consequences for individuals, for groups, and for the social system as a whole. There is evidence that, at the individual level, system-justifying beliefs and ideologies serve the palliative function of decreasing negative affect and increasing positive affect and satisfaction with one's situation (Jost, Pelham, et al., 2003; Kluegel & Smith, 1986). Studies by Wakslak, Jost, Tyler, and Chen (2005) further demonstrate that endorsement of system justification is associated with reductions in moral outrage, guilt (especially but not exclusively among the advantaged), and frustration (especially but not exclusively among the disadvantaged).

At the same time, however, members of disadvantaged groups are faced with a potential conflict between needs to justify the status quo and competing motives to enhance their own self-esteem and group status. Consequently, members of disadvantaged groups (such as blacks) who reject egalitarian alternatives to the status quo tend to suffer in terms of subjective well-being as indexed by levels of self-esteem and depression (Jost & Thompson, 2000). This conflict is not present for members of advantaged groups, who have no problem reconciling the desire to see the system as fair and just with the desire to see themselves and their fellow group members in favorable terms.

There are also important consequences of system justification for attitudes toward social groups. To the extent that they endorse system-justifying ideologies, members of both advantaged and disadvantaged groups tend to perpetuate the status quo by evaluating the advantaged group more favorably than the disadvantaged group on implicit (unconscious) as well as explicit (conscious) measures. Evidence summarized by Jost et al. (2004) indicates that acceptance of system-justifying ideologies (including the belief in a just world, economic system justification, social dominance orientation, and political conservatism) is associated with (a) increased in-group favoritism among members of advantaged groups (such as whites, Northerners, and heterosexuals), and (b) increased out-group favoritism among members of disadvantaged groups (such as blacks, Southerners, and homosexuals; see Fig. 1).

Table 3. *Several Consequences of Endorsement of System-Justifying Ideologies for Members of Advantaged and Disadvantaged Groups*

Variable	Operational definition(s)	Consequences of system justification for advantaged	Consequences of system justification for disadvantaged
Positive and negative affect	Self-report ratings of (a) happiness, satisfaction, contentment, and general positive affect; and (b) frustration, anger, guilt, shame, discomfort, and general negative affect	Increased positive affect, decreased negative affect	Increased positive affect, decreased negative affect
Self-esteem, subjective well-being	Scores on self-report measures of individual self-esteem, depression, and neuroticism	Increased self-esteem, subjective well-being	Decreased self-esteem, subjective well-being
In-group versus out-group favoritism	Favorability of (implicit and explicit) attitudes toward one's own group relative to the favorability of attitudes toward other groups	Increased in-group favoritism	Increased out-group favoritism (decreased in-group favoritism)
Perceived legitimacy of authorities and institutions	Trust and approval of the government, support for restricting criticism of the government, belief in the fairness of the economic system	Increased perceptions of legitimacy	Increased perceptions of legitimacy
Support for social change and redistribution of resources	Support for policies of redistribution in educational and employment contexts; willingness to support community service programs to help the disadvantaged	Decreased support for social change	Decreased support for social change

In addition, there are clear consequences of system justification for the perceived legitimacy and stability of the over-arching social system. Survey research by Jost, Pelham, et al. (2003) suggests that motives to rationalize the status quo may lead those who suffer the most under current circumstances to defend existing authorities and institutions, to support limitations on rights to criticize the government, and to imbue the economic system with legitimacy. Work by Jost, Blount, et al. (2003) showed that endorsement of fair market ideology was associated with the tendency to minimize the seriousness of ethical scandals involving business corporations.

Finally, Wakslak et al. (2005) found that increased system justification (either in terms of ideological endorsement or the temporary activation of a Horatio Alger "rags to riches" mindset) undermines support for the redistribution of resources and the desire to help the disadvantaged by alleviating negative emotional states. That is, system justification leads to a significant reduction in emotional distress, both in general and with respect to the particular affective

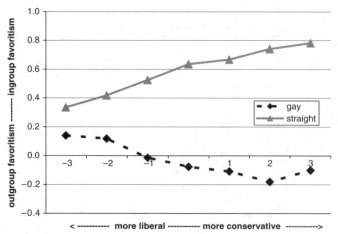

Fig. 1. Implicit in- and out-group favoritism as a function of endorsement of conservative versus liberal ideologies among gay ($n = 3,264$) and straight ($n = 14,038$) respondents. Endorsement of conservative ideology was associated with increased in-group favoritism among straight respondents but with decreased in-group favoritism (and increased out-group favoritism) among gay respondents. Similar results were obtained for explicit measures of favoritism as well as for racial comparisons (black vs. white). Adapted from Jost, Banaji, and Nosek (2004).

states of moral outrage, guilt, and frustration. Because moral outrage inspires efforts to remedy injustice and participate in social change, the lessening of moral outrage triggered by system justification ultimately contributes to a withdrawal of support for social change.

CONCLUSION

The picture that emerges from the research we have summarized is of man as an "ideological animal." Although there are important situational and dispositional sources of variability in the system-justification tendency, most people possess at least some motivation to see the social, economic, and political arrangements that affect them as fair and legitimate. We will end by mentioning some practical implications and directions for future research.

Practical Implications

It is often assumed that liberal and left-wing parties enjoy a "natural advantage" in democratic political systems over conservative, right-wing parties because the poor outnumber the rich. This is derived from the notion that ideologies are rationally adopted according to economic and political self-interest. In this article, we have reviewed evidence that ideological endorsement is a product of motivated social cognition rather than "cold logic." At least two practical consequences follow for political parties and leaders in the U.S. system.

First, although liberals may possess weaker needs for system justification than conservatives in general, even liberals want to feel good about most aspects of their own system. Thus, liberals (as well as conservatives) value patriotism; trust and respect most authorities; and believe that democracy and capitalism are the only acceptable political and economic forms, respectively. However, because liberals are more open than conservatives are to modest change (reform) in the system, they consistently leave themselves open to political charges that they are (a) not supportive enough of the current system (i.e., unpatriotic, nontraditional, unconventional), or (b) the same as conservatives, only weaker (i.e., "Republican lite").

Second, the political advantages associated with conservative, system-justifying agendas may be especially pronounced under conditions of uncertainty and threat. This may be the case even if conservative politicians are themselves responsible for increasing levels of threat. Analysis of public opinion data, for example, indicates that President Bush's approval ratings increased after each incident in which terror alert levels were raised during his first term.

Future Research

In addition to identifying antecedents and consequences of system justification across time and place, we need to make further progress on disentangling the various cognitive and motivational mechanisms involved in justifying the status quo. In this article, we have focused on conscious endorsement of ideologies, but there are unconscious mechanisms as well. Stereotypes, for example, can provide support for existing forms of intergroup relations whether they are consciously endorsed or not. Our research suggests that even incidental exposure to complementary stereotypes—in which members of advantaged and disadvantaged groups are seen as possessing both strengths and weaknesses—increases the perception that society is fair and just. In future work, it would be useful to determine whether the system-justifying potential of specific stereotype contents (e.g., Southerners are "poor but honest," blacks are "aggressive but athletic," and professors are "smart but absentminded") can explain their emergence and popularity.

In this article, we have reviewed evidence suggesting that there are dispositional and situational sources of variability in the individual's need for system justification and that this need may be satisfied through the endorsement of different ideologies (as well as through other means, including stereotyping). These qualities of flexibility and substitutability of means suggest that system justification may operate as a goal. If so, it may exhibit other goal-like properties, such as persistence and resumption following interruption. We expect that the strength of an individual's motivation to restore the system's legitimacy following system threat would steadily increase until the goal is attained and that interruption of goal pursuit would lead people to re-double their system-justification efforts. Experiments directly investigating these possibilities would shed valuable light on the motivational dynamics of system-justification processes.

Recommended Reading

Altemeyer, R.A. (1998). (See References)
Glick, P., & Fiske, S.T. (2001). An ambivalent alliance: Hostile and benevolent sexism as complementary justifications for gender inequality. *American Psychologist, 56,* 109–118.

Jost, J.T., Banaji, M.R., & Nosek, B.A. (2004). (See References)

Jost, J.T., Glaser, J., Kruglanski, A.W., & Sulloway, F. (2003). (See References)

Pratto, F., Sidanius, J., Stallworth, L.M., & Malle, B.F. (1994). Social dominance orientation: A personality variable predicting social and political attitudes. *Journal of Personality and Social Psychology, 67*, 741–763.

Notes

1. Address correspondence to John T. Jost, Department of Psychology, New York University, 6 Washington Place, 5th Floor, New York, NY 10003; e-mail: john.jost@nyu.edu.

2. Unfortunately, space constraints prohibit discussion of how system justification theory differs from cognitive dissonance, just world, social identity, social dominance, and terror management theories, but interested readers are directed elsewhere (esp. Jost et al., 2004, pp. 881–888, 911–912; Jost & Hunyady, 2002, pp. 114–118).

References

Altemeyer, R.A. (1998). The other 'authoritarian personality'. *Advances in Experimental Social Psychology, 30*, 47–91.

Jost, J.T., Banaji, M.R., & Nosek, B.A. (2004). A decade of system justification theory: Accumulated evidence of conscious and unconscious bolstering of the status quo. *Political Psychology, 25*, 881–919.

Jost, J.T., Blount, S., Pfeffer, J., & Hunyady, G. (2003). Fair market ideology: Its cognitive-motivational underpinnings. *Research in Organizational Behavior, 25*, 53–91.

Jost, J.T., & Burgess, D. (2000). Attitudinal ambivalence and the conflict between group and system justification motives in low status groups. *Personality and Social Psychology Bulletin, 26*, 293–305.

Jost, J.T., Glaser, J., Kruglanski, A.W., & Sulloway, F. (2003). Political conservatism as motivated social cognition. *Psychological Bulletin, 129*, 339–375.

Jost, J.T., & Hunyady, O. (2002). The psychology of system justification and the palliative function of ideology. *European Review of Social Psychology, 13*, 111–153.

Jost, J.T., Pelham, B.W., & Carvallo, M. (2002). Non-conscious forms of system justification: Cognitive, affective, and behavioral preferences for higher status groups. *Journal of Experimental Social Psychology, 38*, 586–602.

Jost, J.T., Pelham, B.W., Sheldon, O., & Sullivan, B.N. (2003). Social inequality and the reduction of ideological dissonance on behalf of the system: Evidence of enhanced system justification among the disadvantaged. *European Journal of Social Psychology, 33*, 13–36.

Jost, J.T., & Thompson, E.P. (2000). Group-based dominance and opposition to equality as independent predictors of self-esteem, ethnocentrism, and social policy attitudes among African Americans and European Americans. *Journal of Experimental Social Psychology, 36*, 209–232.

Kay, A., Jimenez, M.C., & Jost, J.T. (2002). Sour grapes, sweet lemons, and the anticipatory rationalization of the status quo. *Personality and Social Psychology Bulletin, 28*, 1300–1312.

Kluegel, J.R., & Smith, E.R. (1986). *Beliefs about inequality.* New York: Aldine de Gruyter.

Kossowska, M., & Van Hiel, A. (2003). The relationship between need for closure and conservative beliefs in Western and Eastern Europe. *Political Psychology, 24*, 501–518.

Landau, M.J., Solomon, S., Greenberg, J., Cohen, F., Pyszczynski, T., Arndt, J., Miller, C.H., Ogilvie, D.M., & Cook, A. (2004). Deliver us from evil: The effects of mortality salience and reminders of 9/11 on support for President George W. Bush. *Personality and Social Psychology Bulletin, 30*, 1136–1150.

Lerner, M.J. (1980). *The belief in a just world.* New York: Plenum.

Nation's poor win election for nation's rich (2004, November 11–17). *The Onion*, pp. 1, 10.

Sidanius, J., & Pratto, F. (1999). *Social dominance.* New York: Cambridge University Press.

Wakslak, C., Jost, J.T., Tyler, T.R., & Chen, E. (2005). *System justification and the alleviation of emotional distress.* Manuscript in preparation.

Critical Thinking Questions

1. Describe the system justification theory. Explain how dispositional and situational antecedents lead to the tendency to embrace system justifying ideologies, even when these ideologies conflict with one's own self interest.

2. Describe some advantages and some disadvantages of engaging in system justification.

3. The authors begin their article quoting a satirical piece from *The Onion*. Clarify how *The Onion* piece explicitly illustrates system justification theory.

This article has been reprinted as it originally appeared in *Current Directions in Psychological Science*. Citation information for this article as originally published appears above.

The Unrecognized Stereotyping and Discrimination Against Singles

Bella M. DePaulo[1]
University of California, Santa Barbara

Wendy L. Morris
McDaniel College

Abstract

A widespread form of bias has slipped under our cultural and academic radar. People who are single are targets of singlism: negative stereotypes and discrimination. Compared to married or coupled people, who are often described in very positive terms, singles are assumed to be immature, maladjusted, and self-centered. Although the perceived differences between people who have and have not married are large, the actual differences are not. Moreover, there is currently scant recognition that singlism exists, and when singlism is acknowledged, it is often accepted as legitimate.

Keywords

singles; stigma; discrimination; stereotypes; relationships

For years, we have been studying what we call *singlism*, the stigmatizing of adults who are single. We have found evidence of singlism in the negative stereotypes and discrimination faced by singles (DePaulo, 2006; DePaulo & Morris, 2005a; DePaulo & Morris, 2005b). Although singlism is a nonviolent, softer form of bigotry than what is often faced by other stigmatized groups such as African Americans or gay men and lesbians, the impact of singlism is far ranging. Unlike more familiar isms such as racism, sexism, or heterosexism, singlism is not often recognized, and when it is pointed out, it is often regarded as legitimate.

WHO IS "SINGLE?"

We can define singles as legally single or socially single, though the two often overlap. According to the U.S. Census Bureau, over 40% of adults are legally single, including people who are divorced or widowed and those who have always been single. In everyday interactions, what matters most often is whether a person is socially single or socially coupled. People who are in sexual partnerships regarded as serious by themselves and others are socially coupled. Impressions of seriousness are shaped by factors such as the length of time the twosome has been together, the regularity and exclusivity with which they see each other, whether they seem to intend to stay together, and whether they live together.

EVIDENCE OF SINGLISM

Negative Stereotypes of the Socially Single

We asked nearly 1,000 undergraduates to list the characteristics that came to mind when they thought about people who were married (in one condition) or single (in the other). Married people were more likely than singles to be described as mature, stable, honest, happy, kind, and loving. Singles were more often called immature, insecure, self-centered, unhappy, lonely, and ugly (but also, on the positive side, independent). The perceived differences between single and married people were often quite large. For example, married people were described as caring, kind, and giving almost 50% of the time, compared to only 2% of the time for singles (Morris, DePaulo, Hertel, & Ritter, 2006).

Next, we wanted to know whether singles are perceived even more negatively after they have passed the age at which most people marry. Groups of undergraduates and community members rated descriptions of single and married people. The targets were described as men or women and as 25 or 40 years old. All groups rated the singles as less socially mature, less well-adjusted, and more self-centered and envious than the married people (though also more independent and career-oriented). As we expected, the differences favoring married people were even greater when the targets were described as 40 years old than when they were described as 25. Still, though, there were significant differences even at the younger age.

Why should 25-year-olds be derogated simply because they are not yet married? As of the year 2004, at least half of all American women, and even more men, had not married by age 25. Maybe, we thought, young adults needed to show that they were at least working at coupling, to avoid getting stigmatized.

In another experiment, undergraduates read profiles describing students who were currently coupled, currently single, previously coupled, or always single. Working at coupling did matter. Students who were described as having current or past relationship experience were regarded as more socially mature, better-adjusted, and less self-centered than the others.

Discrimination Against Singles

Discrimination against single people is often legal. As of 2004, 23 states offered no protections from marital-status discrimination, and others offered only partial protections. Employers can legally subsidize health benefits for spouses of married employees (and sometimes domestic partners), while offering no comparable benefits to a parent, sibling, or friend of their single employees. That amounts to unequal compensation for the same work. Similarly, a married person in need of care can receive it from a spouse who is covered by the Family and Medical Leave Act (FMLA), but singles who need care do not have anyone in their own generation who is eligible for FMLA benefits.

Single men are paid less than their married male colleagues even when they are of similar age and have comparable work experience. Marriage also brings increased tax benefits and social security benefits and discounts on automobile insurance, travel packages, and club memberships (reviewed in DePaulo, 2006).

We have also found experimental evidence of housing discrimination against singles (Morris, Sinclair, & DePaulo, 2006). In three studies, participants read descriptions of three applicants for a rental property and indicated their preferred lessee. Rental agents were much more likely to choose a married couple (60%) over a cohabiting romantic couple (23%) or a pair of friends (17%).

Undergraduates' preference for the married couple was even stronger: 80% chose the married couple, as compared to just 12% choosing the cohabiting couple and 8% who chose the friends. Undergraduates also overwhelmingly favored a married couple (70%) over a single woman (18%) or a single man (12%). The preferences of the rental agents are particularly significant, as they raise the possibility that singles may be at a disadvantage when trying to find housing. Future research should explore this.

Byrne and Carr's (2005) analysis of a nationally representative sample found that people who have always been single and are not cohabiting with a romantic partner are more likely than married people to report experiencing (for example) poorer service in restaurants or condescending attitudes in everyday life. The authors controlled for many factors such as age, race, sexual orientation, and health, making a convincing case that singles really are slighted in their interpersonal experiences. But we still wondered whether singles themselves think they are discriminated against based upon their relationship status.

SINGLISM IS UNACKNOWLEDGED

What is especially interesting about singlism is that most people are unaware that singles are stigmatized at all. When we asked adults to list any groups to which they belonged that might be targets of negative stereotypes or discrimination, only 4% of singles spontaneously mentioned singles as such a category. When explicitly asked whether they thought singles might be a stigmatized group, only 30% of singles and 23% of coupled people said that they were. This level of awareness is low compared to the 100% of gay people, 90% of obese people, 86% of African Americans, and 72% of women who acknowledged their groups' stigma (Morris, 2005).

The practice of singlism is often considered acceptable. While many are outraged by discrimination based on race, gender, or sexual orientation, few people feel any injustice has occurred when a single person is targeted. When participants in an experiment read about housing discrimination against singles, they thought the practice was more legitimate and fair than when they read that the housing discrimination targeted a member of a recognized stigmatized group such as an African American person, a gay person, or an obese person (Morris, Sinclair, & DePaulo, 2006).

WHY ARE SINGLES STIGMATIZED?

Unfounded Stereotypes or Accurate Perceptions?

What if marriage really does transform people, such that they become strikingly happier than they were when they were single and much happier than their peers who have always been single? Then negative perceptions of single people as unhappy would seem more like accurate assessments than like unfair characterizations.

Meta-analytic reviews (summarized by DePaulo & Morris, 2005a) are sometimes said to support the claim that getting married makes people happier, because currently married people score higher on happiness than other groups. But the biggest differences are between the currently married and those who were previously married but are currently divorced or widowed. Getting married cannot account for those differences, because currently married, divorced, and widowed people all got married. The smallest difference ($r = .09$) is between the currently married and those who have always been single.

Nor can it be said that getting married and staying married makes people happy. The meta-analytic reviews summarize studies in which the single, married, and previously married people are all different people. So, the people who stayed married may have been happier than the other people even before they got married. A recent review suggests that happiness may indeed come first in the causal chain leading to other life outcomes (Lyubomirsky, King, & Diener, 2005).

Definitive causal statements about marriage and happiness can never be made, because people cannot be randomly assigned to get married or stay single. Still, longitudinal research can provide an answer to an important question: When people marry, do they become happier than they were when they were single?

An 18-year longitudinal study of thousands of German adults analyzed by Richard Lucas and his colleagues suggests that the long-term answer is no (Lucas, 2005; Lucas, Clark, Georgellis, & Diener, 2003). People who got married and stayed married experienced a small increase in happiness around the year of the wedding, but then their happiness returned to the level it was before. People who married and later divorced were already becoming less happy as the wedding day approached, a trend that did not reverse until the year before the divorce became final. (Their happiness then continued to increase; on the average, though, divorced people did not become as happy as they had been when they were single.)

People who stayed single throughout the study started out slightly less happy (0.2 points on an 11-point scale) than the people who would eventually get married and stay married. However, their mean happiness level was always squarely on the happy end of the scale (never more than 0.6 points lower than the continuously married). It was never as low as that of the divorced people the year before their divorce became official (and it was slightly higher than that of the divorced people for most other years, too). Also, the mean happiness level of the single people was never as low as that of the widowed people right after they were widowed.

The pattern of results is similar for health. People who have always been single are typically just as healthy, or only slightly less healthy, than people who have always been married. When there is a difference related to marital status, it is likely to be the previously married, not the continuously single, who are disadvantaged (DePaulo, 2006; Rook & Zettel, 2005).

Crandall and Warner (2005) argue that negative evaluations are indicative of prejudice, regardless of whether they are accurate. Claims about the transformative power of marriage, though, seem to be grossly exaggerated or just plain wrong. Getting married does not make people lastingly happier or definitively healthier.

Can Singlism Be Explained From an Evolutionary Perspective?

Evolutionary psychologists Pillsworth and Haselton (2005) have noted that we need "adaptations that promote successful mating, such as the basic desire to find a mate and have sex" (p. 98). Thus, people pay attention to whether others are single or coupled because this information is relevant to reproduction. However, the cultural assumption that coupling is the key to happiness is more difficult to explain. As Pillsworth and Haselton note, "the evolutionary perspective does not suggest that coupling will result in a healthier or more satisfying life for any particular individual. . . . In the modern world, coupling does not guarantee an on-average fitness benefit to couple members or their children" (p. 101).

A Cultural Lag in Perceptions?

As recently as the mid-20th century, there were big differences between single and married adults. Then, having sex or children outside of marriage was considered shameful. Women were more dependent on marriage for financial security. Adults married younger, and divorced less often, than they do now. In contrast, Americans today spend more years of their adult lives single than married. Many women earn enough to support themselves and sometimes children, too. Because of advances in birth control and reproductive technology, women can have sex without having children, and they can have children without having sex. Perhaps, then, the negative appraisals of single people are signs of cultural lag: Perceptions of single people have not yet caught up with their rapidly changing place in society (Byrne & Carr, 2005).

Singles as a Threat to Cultural Beliefs

DePaulo (2006) suggests that there is more than just cultural lag at work. In contemporary American society, there is a glorification of marriage and coupling that many single and married people accept uncritically. According to the marital mythology, finding a soul-mate is a transformative experience: Marrying that all-purpose, all-important partner can make a person happy and healthy and fulfill all emotional and social needs. The marital mythology is powerfully attractive, offering as it does a seemingly simple path to a rewarding and meaningful life. Singles—especially those who clearly lead fulfilling lives—challenge that belief system. Singlism serves to maintain cultural beliefs about marriage by derogating those whose lives challenge those beliefs.

THE PARADOX OF SINGLEHOOD

Singles are targeted with stereotyping and discrimination, and married people are glorified. Yet, paradoxically, getting married does not result in lasting improvements in well-being, and people who have always been single are not very different in health or happiness from people who have been continuously married. How is this possible?

Singles often maintain a diversified relationship portfolio, rather than investing so much in just one person. Even in their later years, when others expect them to be lonely and alone, they often enjoy networks of supportive relationships

(Zettel, 2005). Social scientists who study adult relationships have focused over-whelmingly on romantic relationships. Perhaps it is time to give relationships with friends, siblings, and everyone else their due.

Single people who have the resources and opportunities to do so can pursue their passions and excel at work that they love. They can embrace solitude as well as interpersonal engagement. If singles are increasingly living their lives fully, rather than marking time waiting for "the one," then the paradox begins to resolve itself. Maybe singles more often respond to stereotyping and discrimina-tion with resilience than with victimization. Much more research will be needed to know for sure.

FUTURE RESEARCH

In our own work, we found evidence of singlism in the United States and Germany (Hertel, Schütz, DePaulo, Morris, & Stucke, in press). But as Pillsworth and Haselton have noted, "In most cultures around the globe, your spouse is not your best friend, or even your primary social partner" (p. 102). How are singles per-ceived in those cultures? Even within the United States, there is much left to learn about how singlism is shaped by factors such as gender, ethnicity, sexual orientation, and social class.

Reams of research reports have examined marital status as a predictor of well-being. Marital status, though, may be a poor proxy for more important predictors. Do people have the degree of social connectedness that they need and want, whether that is attained by cohabitation, embeddedness in a network of friends, or some other means? Are they living a life that they find engaging and meaningful?

The development of a new field of study offers great promise. Many of the most fundamental questions about singles and singlism have yet to be addressed, or even framed. The answers are likely to have implications for public policy and even for the way people conduct their everyday lives.

Recommended reading

Byrne A., & Carr, D. (2005). (See References)
DePaulo, B. (2006). (See References)
DePaulo, B.M., & Morris, W.L. (2005a). (See References)
DePaulo, B.M., & Morris, W.L. (2005b). (See References)
Gillis, J.R. (1997). The perfect couple. In J.R. Gillis, *A world of their own making* (pp. 133–151). Cambridge, MA: Harvard University Press.

Note

1. Address correspondence to Bella M. DePaulo, P.O. Box 487, Summerland, CA 93067; e-mail: depaulo@psych.ucsb.edu.

References

Byrne, A., & Carr, D. (2005). Caught in the cultural lag: The stigma of singlehood. *Psychological Inquiry, 16*, 84–91.
Crandall, C.S., & Warner, R.H. (2005). How a prejudice is recognized. *Psychological Inquiry, 16*, 137–141.

DePaulo, B. (2006). *Singled out: How singles are stereotyped, stigmatized, and ignored, and still live happily ever after.* New York: St. Martin's Press.

DePaulo, B.M., & Morris, W.L. (2005a). Singles in society and in science. *Psychological Inquiry, 16,* 57–83.

DePaulo, B.M., & Morris, W.L. (2005b). Should singles and the scholars who study them make their mark or stay in their place? *Psychological Inquiry, 16,* 142–149.

Hertel, J., Schütz, A., DePaulo, B.M., Morris, W.L., & Stucke, T.S. (in press). She's single, so what? How are singles perceived compared to people who are married? *Journal of Family Research.*

Lucas, R.E. (2005). Time does not heal all wounds: A longitudinal study of reaction and adaptation to divorce. *Psychological Science, 16,* 945–950.

Lucas, R.E., Clark, A.E., Georgellis, Y., & Diener, E. (2003). Reexamining adaptation and the set point model of happiness: Reactions to changes in marital status. *Journal of Personality and Social Psychology, 84,* 527–539.

Lyubomirsky, S., King, L., & Diener, E. (2005). The benefits of frequent positive affect: Does happiness lead to success? *Psychological Bulletin, 131,* 803–855.

Morris, W.L. (2005). The effects of stigma awareness on the self-esteem of singles (Doctoral dissertation, University of Virginia, 2005). *Dissertation Abstracts International, 66*(03), 1785B.

Morris, W.L., DePaulo, B.M., Hertel, J., & Ritter, L. (2006). *Perception of people who are single: A developmental life tasks model.* Manuscript submitted for publication.

Morris, W.L., Sinclair, S., & DePaulo, B.M. (2006). *The perceived legitimacy of civil status discrimination.* Manuscript submitted for publication.

Pillsworth, E.G., & Haselton, M.G. (2005). The evolution of coupling. *Psychological Inquiry, 16,* 98–104.

Rook, K.S., & Zettel, L.A. (2005). The purported benefits of marriage viewed through the lens of physical health. *Psychological Inquiry, 16,* 116–121.

Zettel, L.A. (2005). Aging alone: Do the social support resources of never-married individuals place them at risk? *Dissertation Abstracts International, 65*(10), 5441B.

Critical Thinking Questions

1. Define singlism. Describe some of the negative stereotypes and discriminatory behaviors singles encounter.

2. Explain the paradox of singlehood. Why do the authors label it a paradox?

3. The authors present singlism as a bias that has "slipped under our cultural and academic radar." Speculate on why this type of bias, as opposed to racism or sexism, might have slipped under the radar. Propose at least one other form of bias that might not be getting the attention it deserves. Explain why you feel that way.

This article has been reprinted as it originally appeared in *Current Directions in Psychological Science*. Citation information for this article as originally published appears above.

The Psychology of Sexual Prejudice

Gregory M. Herek[1]
Department of Psychology, University of California, Davis, California

Abstract

Sexual prejudice refers to negative attitudes toward an individual because of her or his sexual orientation. In this article, the term is used to characterize heterosexuals' negative attitudes toward (a) homosexual behavior, (b) people with a homosexual or bisexual orientation, and (c) communities of gay, lesbian, and bisexual people. Sexual prejudice is a preferable term to *homophobia* because it conveys no assumptions about the motivations underlying negative attitudes, locates the study of attitudes concerning sexual orientation within the broader context of social psychological research on prejudice, and avoids value judgments about such attitudes. Sexual prejudice remains widespread in the United States, although moral condemnation has decreased in the 1990s and opposition to antigay discrimination has increased. The article reviews current knowledge about the prevalence of sexual prejudice, its psychological correlates, its underlying motivations, and its relationship to hate crimes and other antigay behaviors.

Keywords

attitudes; homosexuality; prejudice; homophobia; heterosexism

In a 6-month period beginning late in 1998, Americans were shocked by the brutal murders of Matthew Shepard and Billy Jack Gaither. Shepard, a 21-year-old Wyoming college student, and Gaither, a 39-year-old factory worker in Alabama, had little in common except that each was targeted for attack because he was gay. Unfortunately, their slayings were not isolated events. Lesbians, gay men, and bisexual people—as well as heterosexuals perceived to be gay—routinely experience violence, discrimination, and personal rejection. In all, 1,102 hate crimes based on sexual orientation were tallied by law-enforcement authorities in 1997. Because a substantial proportion of such crimes are never reported to police, that figure represents only the tip of an iceberg (Herek, Gillis, & Cogan, 1999).

People with homosexual or bisexual orientations have long been stigmatized. With the rise of the gay political movement in the late 1960s, however, homosexuality's condemnation as immoral, criminal, and sick came under increasing scrutiny. When the American Psychiatric Association dropped homosexuality as a psychiatric diagnosis in 1973, the question of why some heterosexuals harbor strongly negative attitudes toward homosexuals began to receive serious scientific consideration.

Society's rethinking of sexual orientation was crystallized in the term *homophobia*, which heterosexual psychologist George Weinberg coined in the late 1960s. The word first appeared in print in 1969 and was subsequently discussed at length in a popular book (Weinberg, 1972).[2] Around the same time, *heterosexism* began to be used as a term analogous to sexism and racism, describing an ideological system that casts homosexuality as inferior to heterosexuality.[3] Although usage of the two words has not been uniform, homophobia has typically been employed to describe individual antigay attitudes and behaviors, whereas heterosexism has referred to societal-level ideologies and patterns of institutionalized oppression of nonheterosexual people.

By drawing popular and scientific attention to antigay hostility, the creation of these terms marked a watershed. Of the two, homophobia is probably more widely used and more often criticized. Its critics note that homophobia implicitly suggests that antigay attitudes are best understood as an irrational fear and that they represent a form of individual psychopathology rather than a socially reinforced prejudice. As antigay attitudes have become increasingly central to conservative political and religious ideologies since the 1980s, these limitations have become more problematic. Yet, heterosexism, with its historical macro-level focus on cultural ideologies rather than individual attitudes, is not a satisfactory replacement for homophobia.

Thus, scientific analysis of the psychology of antigay attitudes will be facilitated by a new term. I offer *sexual prejudice* for this purpose. Broadly conceived, sexual prejudice refers to all negative attitudes based on sexual orientation, whether the target is homosexual, bisexual, or heterosexual. Given the current social organization of sexuality, however, such prejudice is almost always directed at people who engage in homosexual behavior or label themselves gay, lesbian, or bisexual. Thus, as used here, the term sexual prejudice encompasses heterosexuals' negative attitudes toward (a) homosexual behavior, (b) people with a homosexual or bisexual orientation, and (c) communities of gay, lesbian, and bisexual people. Like other types of prejudice, sexual prejudice has three principal features: It is an attitude (i.e., an evaluation or judgment); it is directed at a social group and its members; and it is negative, involving hostility or dislike.

Conceptualizing heterosexuals' negative attitudes toward homosexuality and bisexuality as sexual prejudice—rather than homophobia—has several advantages. First, sexual prejudice is a descriptive term. Unlike homophobia, it conveys no a priori assumptions about the origins, dynamics, and underlying motivations of antigay attitudes. Second, the term explicitly links the study of antigay hostility with the rich tradition of social psychological research on prejudice. Third, using the construct of sexual prejudice does not require value judgments that antigay attitudes are inherently irrational or evil.

PREVALENCE

Most adults in the United States hold negative attitudes toward homosexual behavior, regarding it as wrong and unnatural (Herek & Capitanio, 1996; Yang, 1997). Nevertheless, poll data show that attitudes have become more favorable over the past three decades. For example, whereas at least two thirds of respondents to the General Social Survey (GSS) considered homosexual behavior "always wrong" in the 1970s and 1980s, that figure declined noticeably in the 1990s. By 1996, only 56% of GSS respondents regarded it as always wrong (Yang, 1997).

Much of the public also holds negative attitudes toward individuals who are homosexual. In a 1992 national survey, more than half of the heterosexual respondents expressed disgust for lesbians and gay men (Herek, 1994). Respondents to the ongoing American National Election Studies have typically rated lesbians and gay men among the lowest of all groups on a 101-point feeling thermometer, although mean scores increased by approximately 10 points between 1984 and 1996 (Yang, 1997).

Despite these examples of negative attitudes, most Americans believe that a gay person should not be denied employment or basic civil liberties. The public is reluctant to treat homosexuality on a par with heterosexuality, however. Most Americans favor giving same-sex domestic partners limited recognition (e.g., employee health benefits, hospital visitation rights), but most oppose legalizing same-sex marriages. And whereas the public generally supports the employment rights of gay teachers, they do not believe that lesbians and gay men should be able to adopt children (Yang, 1997).

Unfortunately, most studies have not distinguished between lesbians and gay men as targets of prejudice. The available data suggest that attitudes toward gay men are more negative than attitudes toward lesbians, with the difference more pronounced among heterosexual men than women (Herek & Capitanio, 1996; Kite & Whitley, 1998). This pattern may reflect sex differences in the underlying cognitive organization of sexual prejudice (Herek & Capitanio, 1999).

CORRELATES

Laboratory and questionnaire studies have utilized a variety of measures to assess heterosexuals' attitudes toward gay men and lesbians (e.g., Davis, Yarber, Bauserman, Schreer, & Davis, 1998). Consistent with findings from public opinion surveys, they have revealed higher levels of sexual prejudice among individuals who are older, less educated, living in the U.S. South or Midwest, and living in rural areas (Herek, 1994). In survey and laboratory studies alike, heterosexual men generally display higher levels of sexual prejudice than heterosexual women (Herek & Capitanio, 1999; Kite & Whitley, 1998; Yang, 1998).

Sexual prejudice is also reliably correlated with several psychological and social variables. Heterosexuals with high levels of sexual prejudice tend to score higher than others on authoritarianism (Altemeyer, 1996; Haddock & Zanna, 1998). In addition, heterosexuals who identify with a fundamentalist religious denomination and frequently attend religious services typically manifest higher levels of sexual prejudice than do the non-religious and members of liberal denominations (Herek & Capitanio, 1996). Since the 1980s, political ideology and party affiliation have also come to be strongly associated with sexual prejudice, with conservatives and Republicans expressing the highest levels (Yang, 1998).

Sexual prejudice is strongly related to whether or not a heterosexual knows gay people personally. The lowest levels of prejudice are manifested by heterosexuals who have gay friends or family members, describe their relationships with those individuals as close, and report having directly discussed the gay or lesbian person's sexual orientation with him or her. Interpersonal contact and prejudice are reciprocally related. Not only are heterosexuals with gay friends or relatives less prejudiced, but heterosexuals from demographic groups with low levels of sexual prejudice (e.g., women, highly educated people) are more likely to experience personal contact with an openly gay person (Herek & Capitanio, 1996).

Relatively little empirical research has examined racial and ethnic differences. Sexual prejudice may be somewhat greater among heterosexual African Americans than among heterosexual whites, mainly because of white women's relatively favorable attitudes toward lesbians and gay men. The correlates of sexual prejudice may vary by race and ethnicity. Interpersonal contact may be more important in shaping the attitudes of whites than of blacks, for example, whereas the belief that homosexuality is a choice may be a more influential predictor of heterosexual blacks' sexual prejudice (Herek & Capitanio, 1995).

UNDERLYING MOTIVATIONS

Like other forms of prejudice, sexual prejudice has multiple motivations. For some heterosexuals, it results from unpleasant interactions with gay individuals, which are then generalized to attitudes toward the entire group. This explanation probably applies mainly to cases in which interpersonal contact has been superficial and minimal. For other heterosexuals, sexual prejudice is rooted in fears associated with homosexuality, perhaps reflecting discomfort with their own sexual impulses or gender conformity. For still others, sexual prejudice reflects influences of in-group norms that are hostile to homosexual and bisexual people. Yet another source of prejudice is the perception that gay people and the gay community represent values that are directly in conflict with one's personal value system.

These different motivations can be understood as deriving from the psychological functions that sexual prejudice serves, which vary from one individual to another. One heterosexual's sexual prejudice, for example, may reduce the anxiety associated with his fears about sexuality and gender, whereas another heterosexual's prejudice might reinforce a positive sense of herself as a member of the social group "good Christians." Such attitudes are functional only when they are consistent with cultural and situational cues, for example, when homosexuality is defined as inconsistent with a masculine identity or when a religious congregation defines hostility to homosexuality as a criterion for being a good Christian (Herek, 1987).

PREJUDICE AND BEHAVIOR

Hate crimes and discrimination are inevitably influenced by complex situational factors (Franklin, 1998). Nevertheless, sexual prejudice contributes to antigay behaviors. In experimental studies, sexual prejudice correlates with antigay behaviors, although other factors often moderate this relationship (Haddock & Zanna, 1998; Kite & Whitley, 1998). Voting patterns on gay-related ballot measures have been generally consistent with the demographic correlates of sexual prejudice described earlier (Strand, 1998). Recognizing the complex relationship between sexual prejudice and antigay behavior further underscores the value of anchoring this phenomenon in the scientific literature on prejudice, which offers multiple models for understanding the links between attitudes and behavior.

CONCLUSION AND DIRECTIONS FOR RESEARCH

Although more than a quarter century has passed since Weinberg first presented a scholarly discussion of the psychology of homophobia, empirical research on sexual prejudice is still in its early stages. To date, the prevalence and correlates of sexual prejudice have received the most attention. Relatively little research has been devoted to understanding the dynamic cognitive processes associated with antigay attitudes and stereotypes, that is, how heterosexuals think about lesbians and gay men. Nor has extensive systematic inquiry been devoted to the underlying motivations for sexual prejudice or the effectiveness of different interventions for reducing sexual prejudice. These represent promising areas for future research.

In addition, there is a need for descriptive studies of sexual prejudice within different subsets of the population, including ethnic and age groups. Given the tendency for antigay behaviors to be perpetrated by adolescents and young adults, studies of the development of sexual prejudice early in the life span are especially needed. Finally, commonalities and convergences in the psychology of sexual prejudice toward different targets (e.g., men or women, homosexuals or bisexuals) should be studied. Much of the empirical research in this area to date has been limited because it has focused (implicitly or explicitly) on heterosexuals' attitudes toward gay men.

Stigma based on sexual orientation has been commonplace throughout the 20th century. Conceptualizing such hostility as sexual prejudice represents a step toward achieving a scientific understanding of its origins, dynamics, and functions. Perhaps most important, such an understanding may help to prevent the behavioral expression of sexual prejudice through violence, discrimination, and harassment.

Recommended Reading

Herek, G.M. (Ed.). (1998). *Stigma and sexual orientation: Understanding prejudice against lesbians, gay men, and bisexuals.* Newbury Park, CA: Sage.

Herek, G.M., & Berrill, K. (Eds.). (1992). *Hate crimes: Confronting violence against lesbians and gay men.* Thousand Oaks, CA: Sage.

Herek, G.M., Kimmel, D.C., Amaro, H., & Melton, G.B. (1991). Avoiding heterosexist bias in psychological research. *American Psychologist, 46,* 957–963.

Herman, D. (1997). *The antigay agenda: Orthodox vision and the Christian Right.* Chicago: University of Chicago Press.

Rothblum, E., & Bond, L. (Eds.). (1996). *Preventing heterosexism and homophobia.* Thousand Oaks, CA: Sage.

Acknowledgments—Preparation of this article was supported in part by an Independent Scientist Award from the National Institute of Mental Health (K02 MH01455).

Notes

1. Address correspondence to Gregory Herek, Department of Psychology, University of California, Davis, CA 95616-8775.

2. Although Weinberg coined the term homophobia, it was first used in print in 1969 by Jack Nichols and Lige Clarke in their May 23rd column in *Screw* magazine

(J. Nichols, personal communication, November 5, 1998; G. Weinberg, personal communication, October 30, 1998).

3. Heterosexism was used as early as July 10, 1972, in two separate letters printed in the *Great Speckled Bird*, an alternative newspaper published in Atlanta, Georgia. I thank Joanne Despres of the Merriam Webster Company for her kind assistance with researching the origins of this word.

References

Altemeyer, B. (1996). *The authoritarian specter.* Cambridge, MA: Harvard University Press.

Davis, C.M., Yarber, W.L., Bauserman, R., Schreer, G., & Davis, S.L. (Eds.). (1998). *Handbook of sexuality-related measures.* Thousand Oaks, CA: Sage.

Franklin, K. (1998). Unassuming motivations: Contextualizing the narratives of antigay assailants. In G.M. Herek (Ed.), *Stigma and sexual orientation: Understanding prejudice against lesbians, gay men, and bisexuals* (pp. 1–23). Newbury Park, CA: Sage.

Haddock, G., & Zanna, M. (1998). Authoritarianism, values, and the favorability and structure of antigay attitudes. In G.M. Herek (Ed.), *Stigma and sexual orientation: Understanding prejudice against lesbians, gay men, and bisexuals* (pp. 82–107). Newbury Park, CA: Sage.

Herek, G.M. (1987). Can functions be measured? A new perspective on the functional approach to attitudes. *Social Psychology Quarterly, 50,* 285–303.

Herek, G.M. (1994). Assessing attitudes toward lesbians and gay men: A review of empirical research with the ATLG scale. In B. Greene & G.M. Herek (Eds.), *Lesbian and gay psychology* (pp. 206–228). Thousand Oaks, CA: Sage.

Herek, G.M., & Capitanio, J. (1995). Black heterosexuals' attitudes toward lesbians and gay men in the United States. *Journal of Sex Research, 32,* 95–105.

Herek, G.M., & Capitanio, J. (1996). "Some of my best friends": Intergroup contact, concealable stigma, and heterosexuals' attitudes toward gay men and lesbians. *Personality and Social Psychology Bulletin, 22,* 412–424.

Herek, G.M., & Capitanio, J.P. (1999). Sex differences in how heterosexuals think about lesbians and gay men: Evidence from survey context effects. *Journal of Sex Research, 36,* 348–360.

Herek, G.M., Gillis, J., & Cogan, J. (1999). Psychological sequelae of hate crime victimization among lesbian, gay, and bisexual adults. *Journal of Consulting and Clinical Psychology, 67,* 945–951.

Kite, M.E., & Whitley, E., Jr. (1998). Do heterosexual women and men differ in their attitudes toward homosexuality? A conceptual and methodological analysis. In G.M. Herek (Ed.), *Stigma and sexual orientation: Understanding prejudice against lesbians, gay men, and bisexuals* (pp. 39–61). Newbury Park, CA: Sage.

Strand, D. (1998). Civil liberties, civil rights, and stigma: Voter attitudes and behavior in the politics of homosexuality. In G.M. Herek (Ed.), *Stigma and sexual orientation: Understanding prejudice against lesbians, gay men, and bisexuals* (pp. 108–137). Newbury Park, CA: Sage.

Weinberg, G. (1972). *Society and the healthy homosexual.* New York: St. Martin's.

Yang, A. (1997). Trends: Attitudes toward homosexuality. *Public Opinion Quarterly, 61,* 477–507.

Yang, A. (1998). *From wrongs to rights: Public opinion on gay and lesbian Americans moves toward equality.* Washington, DC: National Gay and Lesbian Task Force Policy Institute.

Critical Thinking Questions

1. The author makes the argument that the term homophobia should be replaced with sexual prejudice. Explain the history of this terminology. What are some other examples of terminology that has changed over time in our society? Speculate on why language and terminology are so important to consider.

2. Describe the major reasons the author has for replacing the term homophobia with sexual prejudice. What does he mean when he states that this change

would "anchor [sic] this phenomenon in the scientific literature on prejudice? Why would this be a positive outcome?

3. Describe some of the correlates of sexual prejudice. The author indicates that most of the work on sexual prejudice has focused on these correlates. Speculate on why researchers would have started their work examining these.

This article has been reprinted as it originally appeared in *Current Directions in Psychological Science*. Citation information for this article as originally published appears above.

Weapon Bias: Split-Second Decisions and Unintended Stereotyping

B. Keith Payne[1]
University of North Carolina at Chapel Hill

Abstract

Race stereotypes can lead people to claim to see a weapon where there is none. Split-second decisions magnify the bias by limiting people's ability to control responses. Such a bias could have important consequences for decision making by police officers and other authorities interacting with racial minorities. The bias requires no intentional racial animus, occurring even for those who are actively trying to avoid it. This research thus raises difficult questions about intent and responsibility for racially biased errors.

Keywords

implicit; attitude; stereotyping; prejudice; weapon

The trouble with split-second decisions is that they seem to make themselves. It is not simply that snap decisions are less accurate than "snail" decisions; it is easy to understand why people might make random errors when thinking fast. If you only have 30 seconds, it is probably a bad idea to do your taxes, pick a stock, or solve any problem beginning with "Two trains leave the station . . ." The real puzzle is when snap judgments show systematic biases that differ from our considered decisions. Should I consider those decisions *my* decisions if they differ from my intentions? Who is responsible?

These questions are asked most loudly when decisions have immense consequences, as when a split-second decision has to be made by a surgeon, a soldier, or a police officer. Four New York City police officers had to make that kind of decision while patrolling the Bronx on a February night in 1999. When the officers ordered Amadou Diallo to stop because he matched a suspect's description, Diallo reacted unexpectedly. Rather than raising his hands, he reached for his pocket. The Ghanaian immigrant may have misunderstood the order, or maybe he meant to show his identification. The misunderstanding was mutual: One officer shouted, "Gun!" and the rest opened fire. Only after the shooting stopped was it clear that Diallo held only his wallet.

Many in the public were outraged. Some accused the NYPD of racial bias. Congress introduced legislation. Protests followed the officers' acquittal, in which the defense successfully argued that at the moment of decision, the officers believed their lives were in danger and that they therefore did not have the conscious intent, the *mens rae* (literally, "guilty mind") to commit a crime. The court did not consider the mechanisms that might produce such a belief.

The death of Amadou Diallo dragged into the spotlight some of the disquieting questions that have run through implicit social cognition research for some time. Can stereotypes about race influence such split-second decisions? And can that kind of race bias take place without intent to discriminate? To answer these questions, it is necessary to move away from the particulars of the Diallo case and toward controlled studies in which causes and mechanisms can be identified. What are the psychological factors that would lead a person, in the crucial moment, to shout, "Gun"?

THE WEAPON BIAS

To study these questions, we developed a laboratory task in which participants made visual discriminations between guns and harmless objects (hand tools). A human face flashed just before each object appeared: a black face on some trials, a white face on others (see Fig. 1). The task for participants was to ignore the faces and respond only to the objects (Payne, 2001). There were two versions of the experiment. In one version, participants responded at their own pace. In the other version they had to respond within half a second on each trial. In the self-paced condition, accuracy was very high regardless of race. However, participants detected guns faster in the presence of a black face. This suggested that the black face readied people to detect a gun but did not distort their decisions.

In the snap-judgment condition, race shaped people's mistakes. They falsely claimed to see a gun more often when the face was black than when it was white (Fig. 2). Under the pressure of a split-second decision, the readiness to see a weapon became an actual false claim of seeing a weapon.

These effects are not bound to the details of a particular experimental paradigm. Several independent lab groups have reported strikingly similar results using a variety of different procedures. For example, one procedure presented photos of black and white men who appeared on a computer screen holding a

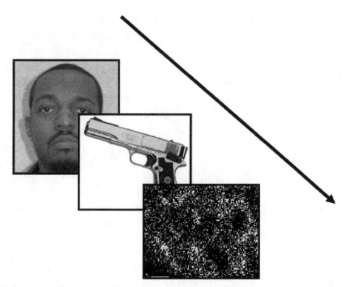

Fig. 1. Schematic illustration of weapons-priming procedure. On each trial, a white or black face appears first, followed by a gun or hand tool, followed by a visual mask. Participants' task is to indicate, as quickly as possible, whether they saw a gun or a tool.

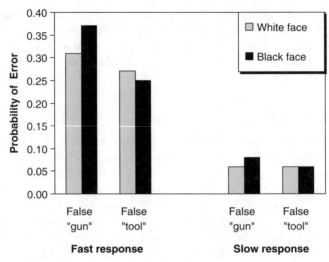

Fig. 2. Probability of falsely identifying a "gun" or "tool" depending on the race of the person shown prior to the object and whether participants were under time pressure to respond. Data adapted from Payne (2001).

variety of objects such as guns, bottles, or cell phones (Correll, Park, Judd, & Wittenbrink, 2002). Participants were told to "shoot" any armed person by pressing one button, and to "not shoot" unarmed persons by pressing a different button. Another procedure presented pictures of white and black men popping out from behind obstacles, again holding either guns or harmless objects (Greenwald, Oakes, & Hoffman, 2002). During some phases of the study, participants were instructed to shoot if a white person, but not a black person, was armed. In other phases, the instructions were reversed. All of these procedures have provided evidence of race bias in both response times and errors. Although the samples in these studies have often been convenience samples, the data suggest that the bias is widespread. Responses made by African American participants in one study were indistinguishable from those of European American participants: both groups were biased toward claiming weapons in black hands more than in white hands (Correll et al., 2002).

Though participants did not need to use race to make their judgments, these studies provide no proof that the bias is unintentional in the strong sense of happening despite intentions to the contrary. Another study tested whether intentional use of race was necessary to produce bias (Payne, Lambert, & Jacoby, 2002). In a baseline condition, participants completed the weapon task under instructions to ignore the faces altogether. A second group was told that the faces might bias them and was instructed to try to avoid being influenced by race. Finally, a third group was also told about the biasing potential of the faces but was instructed to intentionally use the race of the faces as a cue to help them identify guns.

Results showed that although participants' goals affected their self-reported intentions, such goals did not improve their performance. Reliable race bias emerged in all three conditions and was in fact greater in both the "avoid race bias" and the "use race bias" conditions than in the baseline condition. Ironically, directing attention to race had exactly the same effect whether participants attended to race with the intent to discriminate or with the intent to avoid discrimination. In this and other studies, the weapon bias seems largely independent of intent. This is important because it means that the bias can coexist with conscious intentions to be fair and unbiased.

WHAT DRIVES THE WEAPON BIAS?

Why is it that people use stereotypes in their decisions both when they intend to and when they intend not to? And if we are not to turn intelligent people into caricatures or automatons, shouldn't intentions play a role somewhere? Integrating intentional and unintentional aspects of behavior is the job of dual-process theories, which attempt to explain when, how, and why behavior is driven by automatic versus intentionally controlled aspects of thought. My collaborators and I have proposed a particular dual-process theory to account for both intentional control over decisions and the patterns of unintended bias seen in snap judgments (Payne, 2001; Payne, 2005; Payne, Lambert, & Jacoby, 2002).

The first factor is a stereotypic association that, for some people, links African Americans to violence and weapons. These stereotypic links can include both purely semantic associations and emotions such as fear or anger. These associations serve as an impulse that automatically drives responses whenever a person is unable to control a response. The second factor is the degree of intentional control participants have over how they respond (see Fig. 3). To predict whether someone will show the weapon bias, it is critical to know the answers to two questions. First, what is the person's automatic impulse that will drive responses when behavioral control fails? Second, how likely is it that control will fail? Research using a variety of behavioral and neuroscience methods has provided support for the key claims.

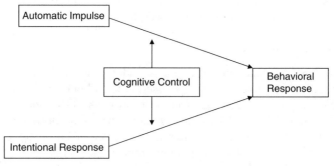

Fig. 3. A dual-process model of weapon bias. When people have full control of their behavior, they respond as intended. When control is impaired, automatic impulse drives responses.

Behavioral Evidence

Evidence for the role of stereotypic associations comes from studies of individual differences. One study found that individuals with more negative self-reported attitudes toward blacks showed greater race bias in their weapon claims (Payne, 2001). In another study, weapon bias correlated with individual differences in perceptions of cultural stereotypes about African Americans (Correll et al., 2002). To avoid the limitations of self-reports, a recent study had participants complete two popular implicit-attitude measures in addition to the weapons task (Payne, 2005). Because implicit measures assess attitudes indirectly, without asking for a self-report, they avoid problems of introspection and social-desirability bias that affect explicit or self-report measures. Individuals with more negative implicit attitudes toward Blacks showed greater weapon bias. Finding consistent correlations using multiple measures provides converging evidence for the important role of stereotypic associations.

The finding that people with stronger stereotypes tend to show greater weapon bias is deceptively simple. It is deceptive because it tempts us to conclude that automatic stereotyping is all there is to the story. But that conclusion leaves out the important factor of how much intentional control people have over their responses. In the first studies described above, there was only one key difference between the snap-judgment and the slow-judgment conditions: how much time participants had to respond. Snap judgments didn't change people's stereotypes. Snap judgments allowed those stereotypes to spill out into overt behavioral errors.

Time pressure is only one way to limit control over responses. Govorun and Payne (2006) showed similar effects as a result of self-regulation depletion. When people are required to self-regulate in one way, they are less likely to control themselves in other ways (Muraven & Baumeister, 2000). We depleted resources for one group of participants by requiring them to persist for several hundred trials on the tedious Stroop color-naming task. The Stroop task presents color words (e.g., *red, green*) in font colors that are either congruent or incongruent with the word meanings. When participants name the font color, incongruent word meanings interfere, requiring cognitive control. A nondepleted group saw a few trials of the Stroop task but did not exert sustained effort. The depleted group showed greater weapon bias, a result of reduced control over their responses.

Neuroscience Evidence

Several studies have examined the neural underpinnings of the weapon bias. Event related potentials (ERP) are more useful than other methods such as functional magnetic resonance imaging or positron emission tomography for this split-second effect because ERPs have greater temporal resolution. ERP studies examine fluctuations in electrical brain activity as a person processes information. Because different ERP components reflect specific cognitive functions, researchers can use those components to reveal processes underlying behavior.

One informative study examined an ERP component called error-related negativity (ERN), which is associated with detecting conflicts between goals and ongoing mental activity (Amodio et al., 2004). Conflict detection is a critical part of mental control because detecting a conflict between current and intended states is necessary for implementing self-control. Individuals showing the greatest ERN activity showed the fewest false weapon claims, and this effect was mediated by the ability to control responses.

A second study using ERP methods found several additional ERP components associated with weapon biases (Correll, Urland, & Ito, 2006). Of particular interest were two components, known as the P200 and the N200. The P200 is associated with emotional reactions to threatening stimuli, whereas the N200 is associated with conflict detection and cognitive control—similar to what was found with the ERN. Consistent with the two-factor theory, participants with greater P200 responses to black individuals, and those with lesser N200 responses, showed greater race bias.

Modeling the Weapon Bias

The evidence reviewed here converges to suggest that both automatic stereotype activation and failures of control are important in the weapon bias. Dual-process theories are commonly tested by comparing implicit and explicit tests, on the assumption that implicit tests measure only automatic responses and explicit tests measure only controlled responses. That assumption is not likely to be realistic, however, as virtually any task reflects a combination of automatic and controlled components (Jacoby, 1991). An alternative approach is to use a formal model to separate component processes within the same task. The value in this approach is that each component process can be studied individually without confounding underlying processes with different test formats.

My collaborators and I have used the process-dissociation procedure (Jacoby, 1991) as a tool to model automatic and controlled factors in the weapon bias. By that model, if a process is automatic, it influences responses regardless of whether it is consistent with intent or inconsistent with intent. In contrast, when a process is controlled, it influences responses only when intended, but not otherwise. When a black face precedes a gun, stereotypes and intent are in concert. Responding based on either will lead to the correct response. When a black face precedes a harmless object, stereotypes and intent are in opposition. The relationships among intentional control, automatic stereotyping, and behavioral responses can be formalized using algebraic equations (Jacoby, 1991; Payne, 2001). We can then decompose responses into numeric estimates of two processes: automatic stereotyping and cognitive control.

Applying the model to the studies just reviewed sheds light on the factors driving the weapon bias. For example, time pressure (Payne, 2001) and self-regulation depletion (Govorun & Payne, 2006) affected only the controlled component but not the automatic component. In other cases, differences in automatic stereotype activation were key. For example, implicit measures of race attitudes correlated with the automatic but not the controlled component (Payne, 2005). The evidence from these studies supports the two-factor account of the weapon bias and provides a means of measuring the underlying factors. The utility of modeling the underlying processes becomes apparent when considering strategies to reduce the race bias.

REDUCING WEAPON BIAS

Bias-reduction strategies might take either of two approaches. On one hand, they can try to change the automatic impulse. On the other hand, they can try to maximize behavioral control. One intriguing study compared police officers and civilians drawn from the same communities and found that both groups showed weapon bias, though officers showed somewhat less bias than civilians (Correll, Park, Judd, Wittenbrink, Sadler, & Keesee, 2006). Even more important, the officers with the most firearms training showed the least race bias. This finding suggests that the routine training that officers receive may effectively reduce weapon bias. There is evidence that practice in identifying weapons may have beneficial effects on both controlled and automatic components of responses and that these benefits extend to police officer volunteers (Plant & Peruche, 2005; Plant, Peruche, & Butz, 2005).

Finally, a recent study shows that although people cannot simply will the weapon bias away, certain specific strategies may be able to eliminate the automatic component of the bias. Stewart and Payne (2006) had participants form simple plans that linked racial categories to specific counterstereotypic thoughts (Gollwitzer, 1999). For example, participants made the plan, "when I see a black face I will think 'safe.'" Unlike participants who simply tried to avoid bias, those who formed specific plans showed no automatic race bias. Together, these studies offer clues to how and why specific strategies may succeed or fail.

IMPLICATIONS AND FUTURE DIRECTIONS

Research on the weapon bias has been consistent in answering several basic questions. Race can bias snap judgments of whether a gun is present, and that bias can coexist with fair-minded intentions. Although overt hostility toward African Americans is probably sufficient to produce this bias, it is not necessary. The bias happens not just because of racial animus but because of stereotypical associations that drive responses when people are unable to fully control them.

The answers to these questions suggest many more questions. One question is how well, and under what conditions, these findings generalize to the decisions police and other authorities make. Samples of police officers provide some evidence that the effect generalizes to a critical population. However, all of the existing studies have used computer tasks, even the most realistic of which do not capture the complexity facing an actual police officer. Future studies might incorporate manipulations of suspects' race into real-time, three-dimensional simulations of the sort that are used in police firearms training.

A second question concerns the mechanisms underlying the weapon bias. Evidence suggests that both emotional responses to and semantic associations with race play a role (Correll, Urland, & Ito, 2006; Judd, Blair, & Chapleau, 2004). But it is unknown under what conditions one or the other is likely to be influential. Do emotional and semantic responses act in identical ways, or do they have different consequences? And do the mechanisms of control differ for emotional versus semantic responses?

Another important question concerns how people attribute responsibility for biases that demonstrably contradict intent. I received two letters shortly after the first paper on the topic was published. A retired police officer rejected the conclusion that race may bias weapon decisions, concerned that the research might lead to unjustified allegations that police, who must make the best decisions they can under terrible conditions, are prejudiced. A second letter writer objected to the conclusion that the weapon bias may happen without intent, concerned that the research might be used to excuse race bias among police officers rather than holding them accountable for their decisions. It is difficult to dismiss the worries of either writer, though they are polar opposites. Each expresses some of the thorny possibilities that may reasonably follow from a complex situation. Do ordinary people consider this a case of diminished capacity and therefore diminished responsibility? Or do they perceive the bias to reflect hidden malice? Are their judgments biased by their own racial attitudes or their attitudes toward police?

Empirical research will not settle the hard normative questions of ethics and responsibility. But it can shed light on how ordinary people actually reason about such unintended biases. Because juries and other decision-making bodies are made up of these same people, the answers are important for how social and political institutions will treat unintended race biases. Understanding the psychology of the weapon bias is a prelude to a better-informed conversation about the hard questions.

Recommended Reading

Payne, B.K. (2001). Prejudice and perception: The role of automatic and controlled processes in misperceiving a weapon. *Journal of Personality Social Psychology, 81,* 181–192.

Payne, B.K., Jacoby, L.L., & Lambert, A.J. (2005). Attitudes as accessibility bias: Dissociating automatic and controlled components. In R. Hassin, J. Bargh, & J. Uleman (Eds.), *The new unconscious.* Oxford, England: Oxford University Press.

Note

1. Address correspondence to Keith Payne, Department of Psychology, University of North Carolina, Chapel Hill, Campus Box 3270, Chapel Hill, NC 27599; e-mail: payne@unc.edu.

References

Amodio, D.M., Harmon-Jones, E., Devine, P.G., Curtin, J.J., Hartley, S.L., & Covert, A.E. (2004). Neural signals for the detection of unintentional race bias. *Psychological Science, 15,* 225–232.

Correll, J., Park, B., Judd, C.M., & Wittenbrink, B. (2002). The police officer's dilemma: Using race to disambiguate potentially threatening individuals. *Journal of Personality and Social Psychology, 83,* 1314–1329.

Correll, J., Park, B., Judd, C.M., Wittenbrink, B., Sadler, M.S., & Keesee, T. (2006). *Across the thin blue line: Police officers and racial bias in the decision to shoot.* Unpublished manuscript, University of Chicago.

Correll, J., Urland, G.L., & Ito, T.A. (2006). Event-related potentials and the decision to shoot: The role of threat perception and cognitive control. *Journal of Experimental Social Psychology, 42,* 120–128.

Gollwitzer, P.M. (1999). Implementation intentions: Strong effects of simple plans. *American Psychologist, 54*, 493–503.

Govorun, O., & Payne, B.K. (2006). Ego depletion and prejudice: Separating automatic and controlled components. *Social Cognition, 24*, 111–136.

Greenwald, A.G., Oakes, M.A., & Hoffman, H.G. (2002). Targets of discrimination: Effects of race on responses to weapon holders. *Journal of Experimental Social Psychology, 39*, 399–405.

Jacoby, L.L. (1991). A process dissociation framework: Separating automatic from intentional uses of memory. *Journal of Memory and Language, 30*, 513–541.

Judd, C.M., Blair, I.V., & Chapleau, K.M. (2004). Automatic stereotypes vs. automatic prejudice: Sorting out the possibilities in the Payne, 2001 weapon paradigm. *Journal of Experimental Social Psychology, 40*, 75–81.

Muraven, M., & Baumeister, R.F. (2000). Self-regulation and depletion of limited resources: Does self-control resemble a muscle? *Psychological Bulletin, 126*, 247–259.

Payne, B.K. (2001). Prejudice and perception: The role of automatic and controlled processes in misperceiving a weapon. *Journal of Personality Social Psychology, 81*, 181–192.

Payne, B.K. (2005). Conceptualizing control in social cognition: How Executive Functioning Modulates the Expression of Automatic Stereotyping. *Journal of Personality and Social Psychology, 89*, 488–503.

Payne, B.K., Lambert, A.J., & Jacoby, L.L. (2002). Best laid plans: Effects of goals on accessibility bias and cognitive control in race-based misperceptions of weapons. *Journal of Experimental Social Psychology, 38*, 384–396.

Plant, E.A., & Peruche, B.M. (2005). The consequences of race for police officers' responses to criminal suspects. *Psychological Science, 16*, 180–183.

Plant, E.A., Peruche, B.M., & Butz, D.A. (2005). Eliminating automatic racial bias: Making race non-diagnostic for responses to criminal suspects. *Journal of Experimental Social Psychology, 41*, 141–156.

Stewart, B.D., & Payne, B.K. (2006). *Counterstereotypical thought plans reduce automatic stereotyping.* Unpublished manuscript, Ohio State University.

Critical Thinking Questions

1. Can stereotypes about race influence split second decisions? Use specific research from the article to defend your response. Be sure to include both research methodology and findings in your discussion.

2. Describe the dual-process theory proposed by the author to account for the weapons bias. Explain how both factors contribute to this bias.

3. Discuss the influence of time pressure and self-regulation depletion on the weapons bias. Propose at least one other factor that might influence one's ability to make accurate split-second decisions.

This article has been reprinted as it originally appeared in *Current Directions in Psychological Science*. Citation information for this article as originally published appears above.

Section 6: Stress, Coping, Health and Well-Being

Stress—a reaction to environmental threats and challenges—is a negative experience with which everyone is familiar. People who are experiencing stress show unpleasant affective reactions (e.g., reductions in subjective well-being, irritability, anxiety), unwelcome cognitive reactions (e.g., difficulty concentrating, motivational deficits), and undesirable physical reactions (e.g., increased susceptibility to illness). Although theorists occasionally discuss "good" stress (i.e., eustress), typically stress connotes a negative experience that people are motivated to reduce. Indeed, the environmental factors that produce stress (i.e., stressors) that are most easily brought to mind are those factors that are negative and aversive: death of a loved one, mounting credit card debt, a quarrel with one's neighbor, or an exam for which one is ill-prepared. But stressors also can be environmental factors that people often construe as positive or desirable events and activities. For example, planning a wedding, beginning a new job, leaving for vacation, or having a baby often are viewed as positive life events, but they also can cause negative stress.

Research on the relations among stress, coping, health, and well-being covers the gamut of potential stressors: chronic and acute, minor and major. For example, researchers might examine post-traumatic stress disorder and reduced cognitive functioning among war veterans, academic and achievement patterns among youth in regions affected by natural disasters, or coping among victims of sexual assault. Other researchers might examine coping strategies of people undergoing treatment for cancer, HIV, or cardiovascular illness, as well as the coping strategies of people close to them. They may examine the effects of stressors that have distinct time boundaries (e.g., preparing for and taking CPA, bar exams, or exams used by post- baccalaureate admissions units), or the daily hassles that most people will experience throughout their lives (e.g., traffic delays or computer crashes). The articles selected for this final section cover this broad spectrum of stressors. Bonanno's (2005) paper focuses on traumas, such as natural disaster and death of a family member. Taylor's (2006) article focuses on the stressor of insufficient social contact and social separation. Cohen and Pressman's (2006) article examines susceptibility to both major (e.g., coronary disease) and minor (e.g., the common cold) illnesses, as well as other health-related stressors (e.g., infertility). Finally, Almeida (2005) examines daily stressors—both major and minor—such as conflicts at home or at work, loss of money, illness, and loss of employment.

This set of papers also reflects the ingenuity of social scientists to tailor their method to the research question. Almeida (2005), for example, notes that the cumulative effects of frequently-occurring minor stressors on health and well-being likely is substantial, perhaps more than the cumulative effects of rare but major events. A relatively new technique—the daily diary method—is especially appropriate for studying the effects of frequent minor stressors. Using fairly sophisticated statistical procedures, researchers can look at naturally occurring patterns within individuals, as well as differences across individuals and groups. For example, imagine that Jane reports a fight with her romantic partner on days 2, 4, and 7 of the study, but no conflicts at work; Liz reports a mild conflict with her romantic partner of day 3, and a conflict at work on day 6. Further imagine that the researcher wants to know a.) the relation between the stressor of conflict and experienced stress on the subsequent day b.) whether that relation is the same depending on the source of conflict, and c.) whether variability in reactions to stress is similar for men and women. In traditional research designs (e.g., most studies reported in your textbook), the two participants—and all of the other participants in the study—would need to have experience the same types of conflicts the same number of times on the same days. [Obviously, this doesn't happen in the real world, so without the diary method, a different question would be addressed such as "Does number of conflicts predict average experiences of stress?"]

The methodologies described by Taylor (2006) also are relatively recent additions to the social psychologist's toolbox, although researchers in fields such as medical science and animal learning have used them for quite some time. The research questions discussed her paper center around the role of hormones in stress and affiliation. In the human research, the hormone oxytocin typically is derived from plasma, and is predicted by naturally-occurring factors such as gaps in relationship support or experimentally-created factors such as social threat (i.e., oxytocin is treated as a dependent variable). To better understand the proposed pathways, researchers using this strategy concurrently turn to animal models (e.g., to manipulate whether the presence of oxytocin aids wound-healing among isolated animals). Researchers' interest in how stress affects the body encompasses more than hormones, of course. Social psychologists also may use psychoimmunological indicators (e.g., killer T-cells, antibodies) or measures of cardiovascular reactivity to answer related questions.

These newer techniques live side-by-side with more traditional methods of examining the effects of stress. Studies conducted by Cohen and his colleagues (as described in Cohen & Pressman, 2006), for example, use more classic methods. In one study, after assessing personality characteristics, individuals were exposed to cold viruses. Objective indicators of illness (e.g., congestion) were less pronounced among people high in positive affectivity (i.e., who regularly experience high levels of positive emotions). These authors as well as Bonanno (2005) also describe research findings from classic longitudinal research studies. In longitudinal studies, participants are followed over time, even across decades. Some of this research is prospective, meaning that the indicators are measured before a particular stressor is evident; other research is retrospective, meaning that after a stressor is present, participants respond about their recollections of the stressful event and about factors presumed not to have been changed by that event (e.g., many personality factors). Researchers then examine how these factors predict coping and health.

Through these various methodologies, researchers also demonstrate quite clearly that individuals vary considerably with respect to their coping strategies and susceptibility to stressors. Some of this variation is dispositional, such as the findings relating low negative affectivity and high positive affectivity to better health outcomes (Cohen & Pressman, 2006) or traits associated with resilience to trauma (Bonanno, 2005). Other sources of variation have a more situational aspect, including the presence and quality of social support (Bonanno, 2005; Cohen & Pressman, 2006; Taylor, 2006). It bears mention, of course, that more dispositional and more situational factors are not necessarily independent: the general extraverted behavior of people high in positive affectivity, for example, can lead them to solicit social support and to foster the kinds of relationships that include social support as a benefit.

Ben Franklin is credited with the observation that "nothing is certain but death and taxes." With apologies to this great thinker, "stressors" easily could be included in this adage or simply could substitute for "death and taxes." A human society without at least frequently-occurring minor stressors such interpersonal disagreements, allergies and bruises, and frustrations is difficult to imagine. How stressors affect health and happiness, as well as how effective coping can be fostered and facilitated, likely will remain an important topic in social psychology for many years to come.

Resilience and Vulnerability to Daily Stressors Assessed via Diary Methods

David M. Almeida[1]
The Pennsylvania State University

Abstract

Stressors encountered in daily life, such as family arguments or work deadlines, may play an important role in individual health and well-being. This article presents a framework for understanding how characteristics of individuals and their environments limit or increase exposure and reactivity to daily stressors. Research on daily stressors has benefited from diary methods that obtain repeated measurements from individuals during their daily lives. These methods improve ecological validity, reduce memory distortions, and permit the assessment of within-person processes. Findings from the National Study of Daily Experiences, which used a telephone-diary design, highlight how people's age, gender, and education and the presence or absence of chronic stressors in their lives predict their exposure and reactivity to daily stressors. Finally, future directions for research designs that combine laboratory-based assessment of stress physiology with daily-diary methods are discussed.

Keywords

daily hassles; diary designs; well-being

Any idiot can handle a crisis—it's this day-to-day living that wears you out.

—Anton Chekhov

Anyone who has recently experienced a crisis such as job loss, marital disruption, or the death of a loved one would certainly disagree with Chekhov's contention. Indeed, these major life stressors require significant adjustment on the part of the individual and adversely affect psychological and physical health (Brown & Harris, 1989). Major life events, however, are relatively rare, and thus their cumulative effect on health and well-being may not be as great as that of minor yet frequent stressors, such as work deadlines and family arguments (Lazarus, 1999; Zautra, 2003). Daily stressors are defined as routine challenges of day-to-day living, such as the everyday concerns of work, caring for other people, and commuting between work and home. They may also refer to more unexpected small occurrences—such as arguments with children, unexpected work deadlines, and malfunctioning computers—that disrupt daily life.

Tangible, albeit minor, interruptions like these may have a more immediate effect on well-being than major life events. Major life events may be associated with prolonged physiological arousal, whereas daily hassles may be associated with spikes in arousal or psychological distress confined to a single day. Yet minor daily stressors affect well-being not only by having separate, immediate, and direct effects on emotional and physical functioning, but also by piling up over a series of days to create persistent irritations, frustrations, and overloads that may result in more serious stress reactions such as anxiety and depression (Lazarus, 1999; Zautra, 2003).

VULNERABILITY AND RESILIENCE
TO DAILY STRESSORS

Some stressors are unhealthier than other stressors, and some individuals are more prone to the effects of stressors than other individuals. Recent improvements in the measurement of daily stressors and in study design have allowed researchers to address (a) how different types of stressors and personal meanings attached to these stressors affect well-being and (b) how sociodemographic factors and personal characteristics account for group and individual differences in daily-stress processes. Figure 1 provides a model for these two areas of inquiry.

The right side of the figure represents daily-stress processes that occur within the individual. To understand these processes, one must consider both the objective characteristics of daily stressors and individuals' subjective appraisal of

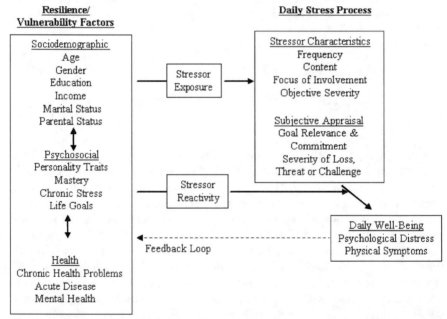

Fig. 1. Model showing how individual resilience or vulnerability factors affect daily-stress processes and well-being. Such factors include socioeconomic, psychosocial, and health characteristics; these influence the likelihood of being exposed to different kinds of stressors and the way individuals appraise stressors. Objective stressor characteristics and stressors' subjective appraisal by individuals in turn influences individuals' psychological and physical well-being. In addition to influencing stressor exposure, resilience or vulnerability factors influence individuals' reactivity to stressors—that is, their likelihood of reacting emotionally or physically. The feedback loop indicates that aspects of stressors and well-being will have subsequent effects on the vulnerability and resilience factors.

stressors. Objective characteristics of daily stressors include their frequency, type (e.g., interpersonal tension, being overloaded or overwhelmed at work), focus of involvement (e.g., whether the stressor involves other persons, such as a sick family member), and objective severity (e.g., degree of unpleasantness and disruption for an average person). Individuals appraise stressors in terms of their perceived severity and in terms of how much they are perceived as disrupting daily goals and commitments. Both objective and subjective components of daily stressors affect daily well-being (Cohen, Kessler, & Gordon, 1997). The objective characteristics of a stressor may play an important role in how that stressor is appraised, which in turn may influence how much distress it causes. Integrating the objective characteristics of stressors with their subjective appraisal allows researchers to investigate whether different kinds of daily stressors elicit different appraisal processes and affect well-being differently.

The left side of Figure 1 represents sociodemographic, psychosocial, and health factors that contribute to individuals' resilience or vulnerability to stress. Resilience and vulnerability factors affect individuals' *exposure* and *reactivity* to daily stressors and, thereby, their daily well-being. Exposure is the likelihood that an individual will experience a daily stressor, given his or her resilience or vulnerability factors. Although daily stressors may be unpredictable, more often they arise out of the routine circumstances of everyday life. The stressor-exposure path illustrates that an individual's sociodemographic, psychosocial, and health characteristics are likely to play a role in determining what kinds of stressors that individual experiences and how he or she appraises them (right side of Fig. 1). Reactivity is the likelihood that an individual will react emotionally or physically to daily stressors and depends on the individual's resilience or vulnerability (Bolger & Zuckerman, 1995). The stressor-reactivity path illustrates that sociodemographic, psychosocial, and health factors modify how daily stressors affect daily well-being. Individuals' personal resources (e.g., their education, income, feelings of mastery and control over their environment, and physical health) and environmental resources (e.g., social support) affect how they can cope with daily experiences (Lazarus, 1999). Finally, the feedback-loop path (dotted arrow from the right to the left of the figure) shows how aspects of stressors and well-being will have subsequent effects on the resilience and vulnerability factors.

DAILY-DIARY METHODOLOGY

The understanding of daily stressors has benefited from the development of diary methods that obtain repeated measurements from individuals during their daily lives. In this method, individuals report the stressors they experienced over the course of several days, as well as their behaviors, physical symptoms, and emotional states on these days. The use of paper-and-pencil diaries has been criticized because some participants may not complete their entries at scheduled times (Stone, Shiffman, Schwartz, Broderick, & Hufford, 2002). However, recent diary methods in which participants respond over the telephone, with personal digital assistants, and on Internet Web pages provide more control over compliance and make it possible to obtain more in-depth information by allowing subjects to skip irrelevant questions and go into greater detail on those that are more relevant to them, for instance by describing experiences in their own words. Diary methods have a number of virtues (Bolger, Davis, & Rafaeli, 2003). By obtaining information about individuals' actual daily stressors over short-term intervals, daily diaries circumvent concerns about ecological validity (applicability to real life) that constrain findings from laboratory research. Further, diary methods alleviate memory distortions that can occur in more traditional questionnaire and interview methods that require respondents to recall experiences over longer time frames.

Perhaps the most valuable feature of diary methods is that they allow assessment of within-person processes. This feature entails a shift from assessing mean levels of stressors and well-being in a group of individuals to charting the day-to-day fluctuations in stress and well-being within an individual, as well as to identifying predictors, correlates, and consequences of these fluctuations (Reis & Gamble, 2000).

Stress is a process that occurs within the individual, and research designs need to reflect this fact. For example, instead of asking whether individuals who encounter many stressors at work experience more distress than individuals with less stressful jobs, a researcher can ask whether a worker experiences more distress on days when he or she has too many deadlines (or is reprimanded) than on days when work has been stress free. This within-person approach allows the researcher to rule out personality and environmental variables that are stable over time as explanations for the relationship between stressors and well-being. In addition, the intensive longitudinal aspect of this design permits researchers to examine how stressors are associated with changes in a person's well-being from one day to the next. By establishing within-person, through-time associations between daily stressors and well-being, researchers can more precisely establish the short-term effects of concrete daily experiences (Bolger et al., 2003; Larson & Almeida, 1999).

EMPIRICAL FINDINGS FROM THE NATIONAL STUDY OF DAILY EXPERIENCES

A recent project called the National Study of Daily Experiences (NSDE) is aimed to investigate the sources of vulnerability and resilience to daily stressors. The NSDE is a telephone-diary study of a U.S. national sample of 1,483 adults ranging in age from 25 to 74 years. Interviews occurred over eight consecutive nights, resulting in 11,578 days of information. Although past research advanced the understanding of daily-stress processes, there are important limitations in these studies that are overcome in the NSDE. First, previous diary studies of daily stressors relied on small and often unrepresentative samples that limited the generalizability of findings. In contrast, the NSDE data come from a representative subsample of adults surveyed in a nationwide study on Midlife in the United States (MIDUS). Second, previous studies of individual differences in vulnerability to stress have typically examined only one source of variability, such as neuroticism (i.e., whether a person is dispositionally anxious). The NSDE, in contrast, uses data on a wide array of personality variables and sociodemographic characteristics collected in the MIDUS survey. Third, previous studies typically have relied on self-administered checklists of daily stressors that only indicate whether or not a given stressor has occurred. The NSDE uses a semistructured telephone interview to measure several aspects of daily stressors, including their objective characteristics as rated by expert coders (e.g., content, severity) and their subjective appraisals by study participants.

Prevalence of Daily Stressors

Respondents reported experiencing on average at least one stressor on 40% of the study days and multiple stressors on 10% of the study days (Almeida, Wethington, & Kessler, 2002). Table 1 provides a breakdown by various stressor categories. The most common stressors for both men and women were interpersonal arguments and tensions, which accounted for half of all the stressors. Gender differences were also evident. Women were more likely than men to report network stressors—stressors involving their network of relatives or close friends—whereas men were more likely than women to report stressors at work or at school. On average, the respondents subjectively rated stressors as having medium severity, whereas objective coders rated the stressors as having low severity. It is interesting that objective and subjective severity were only moderately correlated ($r = .36$). As

Table 1. *Results from the National Study of Daily Experiences: Measures of Stressors*

	Total	Men	Women
	($N = 1,031$)	($n = 469$)	($n = 562$)
Stressor content (% of events)[a]			
Interpersonal tensions	50.0%	49.1%	50.3%
Work or school	13.2	15.7	11.2*
Home	8.2	8.0	8.3
Health care	2.2	1.6	2.7
Network[b]	15.4	12.5	17.8*
Miscellaneous	3.5	4.4	2.7
Type of threat posed by stressor (% of events)			
Loss	29.7	29.9	29.5
Danger	36.2	35.7	36.6
Disappointment	4.2	4.0	4.4
Frustration	27.4	28.3	26.6
Stressor severity (mean)[c]			
Objective assessment	1.8	1.7	1.9
Subjective assessment	2.7	2.5	2.9*
Domain of life potentially disrupted (mean)[d]			
Daily routine	2.3	2.3	2.3
Financial situation	1.3	1.4	1.2*
Way feel about self	1.5	1.4	1.5
Way others feel about you	1.4	1.3	1.4*
Physical health or safety	1.3	1.3	1.3
Health/well-being of someone you care about	1.5	1.5	1.5
Plans for the future	1.4	1.4	1.3

[a]Seven percent of events could not be placed into these content classifications.
[b]Events that happen to other people.
[c]Range: 1–4 (not at all stressful to very stressful).
[d]Range: 1–4 (no risk to a lot of risk).
*Asterisks indicate a significant gender difference, $p < .01$.

appraised by respondents, daily stressors more commonly posed a threat to respondents' daily routines than to other domains of their lives (e.g., their finances, health, and safety). The threat dimensions refer to stressful implications for the respondent. Approximately 30% of the reported stressors involved some sort of loss (e.g., of money), nearly 37% posed danger (e.g., potential for future loss), and 27% were frustrations or events over which the respondent felt he or she had no control.

Daily stressors also had implications for well-being. Respondents were more likely to report psychological distress and physical symptoms on days when they experienced stressors than on stress-free days. Certain types of daily stressors, such as interpersonal tensions and network stressors, were more predictive of psychological distress and physical symptoms than other types of stressors. Furthermore, severe stressors that disrupted daily routines or posed a risk to physical health and self-concept were particularly distressing.

Group and Individual Differences in Daily Stressors

As previously mentioned, demographic and psychological characteristics affect how resilient or vulnerable individuals are to daily stressors (see Fig. 1). Horn and I initially investigated this issue by assessing age differences in exposure and reactivity to daily stressors (Almeida & Horn, 2004). Young (25–39 years) and middle-aged (40–59 years) individuals reported a greater daily frequency of stressors than did older individuals (60–74 years). Compared with older adults, younger and midlife adults also perceived their stressors as more severe and as more likely to affect how other people felt about them. Overloads (i.e., having too little time or other resources) and demands (i.e., having too much to do) were a greater source of daily stressors for younger and midlife adults than for older adults, although the focus of the demands tended to differ by gender. Younger men's daily stressors were more likely than those of older men to revolve around demands and overloads as well as interactions with coworkers. Women in midlife reported the same percentage of overloads as younger women but had a greater proportion of network stressors. Although overloads were not a common type of stressor for older adults, these respondents had the greatest proportion of network stressors (stressors that happen to other people) and spouse-related stressors.

Socioeconomic factors may also help or hinder individuals in facing daily stressors. Consistent with research on socioeconomic inequalities in health, our analyses indicated that, on any given day, better-educated adults reported fewer physical symptoms and less psychological distress than less-educated adults (Grzywacz, Almeida, Neupert, & Ettner, 2004). In contrast to studies of life-event stressors, this study found that college-educated individuals reported more daily stressors than those with no more than high-school education. However, college-educated respondents were less reactive to stressors, which indicates that socioeconomic differentials in daily health could be attributed to differential reactivity to stressors rather than to differential exposure to stressors.

Finally, it is important to acknowledge that ongoing difficulties in a person's life (e.g., caring for a sick spouse, poor working conditions) not only may expose him or her to stressors, but also may increase his or her reactivity to daily stressors by depleting resources. Participants who experienced chronic stressors were more likely than those who did not to report psychological distress on days when they experienced daily stressors (Serido, Almeida, & Wethington, 2004). For women, the interaction of home hassles and chronic stressors was significant; for men, it was the interaction of work hassles and chronic stressors that was significant.

FUTURE DIRECTIONS: PHYSIOLOGICAL INDICATORS OF WELL-BEING

Most research on resilience and vulnerability to daily stressors has relied on self-reported well-being. Results have had to be qualified by discussions of possible biases in study participants' responses and questions concerning the validity of self-reported well-being measures. Thus, questions regarding the direct relation between daily stressors and physiological functioning remain. One promising avenue for future research concerns *allostatic load*, the biological cost of adapting to stresssors. Allostatic load is commonly measured by indicators of the body's response to physiological dysregulation—responses such as high cholesterol levels or lowered blood-clotting ability—and has been found to be predictive of decline in physical health (McEwen, 1998). Ironically, researchers have conceptualized allostatic load as physical vulnerability caused by the body having to adjust repeatedly to stressors, yet few studies have examined allostatic load in conjunction with individuals' daily accounts of stressors. The combination of daily-stressor data from diaries and data from laboratory tests of physiological reactivity would provide an opportunity to examine how daily stressors map onto physiological indicators of allostatic load.

In conclusion, the study of daily stress provides a unique window into the ebb and flow of day-to-day frustrations and irritations that are often missed by research on major life events. The focus on naturally occurring minor stressors assessed on a daily basis offers an exciting opportunity to understand how people adapt to the challenges of life. Adaptation occurs within an individual, so understanding adaptation requires consideration both of stressors themselves and of the persons they affect. Because daily stressors are real-life issues that require immediate attention, daily-diary study of stressors can provide the micro-level data needed to understand the immediate relationships between stressors and how individuals respond to and interpret them. It is true that day-to-day living can wear you out; however certain days are better than others, and certain people are better equipped to handle stressors than other people are.

Recommended Reading

Affleck, G., Zautra, A., Tennen, H., & Armeli, S. (1999). Multilevel daily process designs for consulting and clinical psychology: A preface for the perplexed. *Journal of Consulting and Clinical Psychology, 67,* 746–754.
Almeida, D.M., Wethington, E., & Kessler, R.C. (2002). (See References)
Bolger, N., Davis, A., & Rafaeli, E. (2003). (See References)
Lazarus, R.S. (1999). (See References)
Zautra, A.J. (2003). (See References)

Acknowledgments—The research reported in this article was supported by the MacArthur Foundation Research Network on Successful Midlife Development and by National Institute on Aging Grants AG19239 and AG0210166.

Note

1. David M. Almeida, Department of Human Development and Family Studies, The Pennsylvania State University, 105 White Building, University Park, PA 16802; e-mail: dalmeida@psu.edu.

References

Almeida, D.M., & Horn, M.C. (2004). Is daily life more stressful during middle adulthood? In O.G. Brim, C.D. Ryff, & R.C. Kessler (Eds.), *How healthy are we? A national study of well-being at midlife* (pp. 425–451). Chicago: University of Chicago Press.

Almeida, D.M., Wethington, E., & Kessler, R.C. (2002). The Daily Inventory of Stressful Experiences (DISE): An interview-based approach for measuring daily stressors. *Assessment, 9,* 41–55.

Bolger, N., Davis, A., & Rafaeli, E. (2003). Diary methods: Capturing life as it is lived. *Annual Review of Psychology, 54,* 579–616.

Bolger, N., & Zuckerman, A. (1995). A framework for studying personality in the stress process. *Journal of Personality and Social Psychology, 69,* 890–902.

Brown, G.W., & Harris, T.O. (1989). *Life events and illness.* New York: Guilford.

Cohen, S., Kessler, R.C., & Gordon, L. (1997). Strategies for measuring stress in studies of psychiatric and physical disorders. In S. Cohen, R.C. Kessler, & L. Gordon (Eds.), *Measuring stress: A guide for health and social scientists* (pp. 3–26). New York: Oxford University Press.

Grzywacz, J.G., Almeida, D.M., Neupert, S.D., & Ettner, S.L. (2004). Stress and socioeconomic differentials in physical and mental health: A daily diary approach. *Journal of Health and Social Behavior, 45,* 1–16.

Larson, R., & Almeida, D.M. (1999). Emotional transmission in the daily lives of families: A new paradigm for studying family processes. *Journal of Marriage and the Family, 61,* 5–20.

Lazarus, R.S. (1999). *Stress and emotion: A new synthesis.* New York: Springer.

McEwen, B.S. (1998). Protective and damaging effects of stress mediators. *New England Journal of Medicine, 338,* 171–179.

Reis, H.T., & Gable, S.L. (2000). Event-sampling and other methods for studying everyday experience. In H.T. Reis & C.M. Judd (Eds.), *Handbook of research methods in social and personality psychology* (pp. 190–222). New York: Cambridge University Press.

Serido, J., Almeida, D.M., & Wethington, E. (2004). Conceptual and empirical distinctions between chronic stressors and daily hassles. *Journal of Health and Social Behavior, 45,* 17–33.

Stone, A.A., Shiffman, S., Schwartz, J.E., Broderick, J.E., & Hufford, M.R. (2002). Patient noncompliance with paper diaries. *British Medical Journal, 324,* 1193–1194.

Zautra, A.J. (2003). *Emotions, stress, and health.* New York: Oxford University Press.

Critical Thinking Questions

1. Describe the daily-diary methodology and explain how this relatively new methodology has improved psychological research. What is another area in social psychology that would benefit from the use of the methodology? Explain your response.

2. Summarize the findings regarding the prevalence, age differences, and socioeconomic factors in daily stressors. Based on these findings, propose one practical suggestion for dealing with daily stress. Be sure your suggestion is clearly linked a specific research finding.

3. Compare and contrast major life events and daily stressors. Is it important for researchers to distinguish between the two? Why or why not? Use specific information from the article to back up your points.

This article has been reprinted as it originally appeared in *Current Directions in Psychological Science*. Citation information for this article as originally published appears above.

Tend and Befriend: Biobehavioral Bases of Affiliation Under Stress

Shelley E. Taylor[1]
University of California, Los Angeles

Abstract

In addition to fight-or-flight, humans demonstrate tending and befriending responses to stress—responses underpinned by the hormone oxytocin, by opioids, and by dopaminergic pathways. A working model of affiliation under stress suggests that oxytocin may be a biomarker of social distress that accompanies gaps or problems with social relationships and that may provide an impetus for affiliation. Oxytocin is implicated in the seeking of affiliative contact in response to stress, and, in conjunction with opioids, it also modulates stress responses. Specifically, in conjunction with positive affiliative contacts, oxytocin attenuates psychological and biological stress responses, but in conjunction with hostile and unsupportive contacts, oxytocin may exacerbate psychological and biological stress responses. Although significant paradoxes remain to be resolved, a mechanism that may underlie oxytocin's relation to the health benefits of social support may be in view.

Keywords

oxytocin; opioids; tending; befriending; affiliation

The dominant conception of biobehavioral responses to stress has been the fight-or-flight response. In response to threat, humans or animals can become aggressive and confront a stressor or flee either literally or metaphorically, as through avoidant coping. Fight-or-flight responses depend on two interacting stress systems, the sympathetic nervous system (SNS) and the hypothalamic-pituitary-adrenocortical (HPA) axis, which mobilize the organism for concerted efforts to combat or escape from threat. In important respects, fight-or-flight provides a good characterization of responses to stress. However, from the standpoint of human beings, this analysis is incomplete. One of the most striking aspects of the human stress response is the tendency to affiliate—that is, to come together in groups to provide and receive joint protection in threatening times (Baumeister & Leary, 1995; Taylor, 2002).

Our laboratory has explored a biobehavioral model that characterizes these affiliative behaviors. From animal studies and our own data, we infer that there is an affiliative neurocircuitry that prompts affiliation, especially in response to stress. We suggest that this system regulates social-approach behavior and does so in much the same way as occurs for other appetitive needs. That is, just as people have basic needs such as hunger, thirst, sexual drives, and other appetites, they also need to maintain an adequate level of protective and rewarding social relationships.

As occurs for these other appetites, we suggest there is a biological signaling system that comes into play if one's affiliations fall below an adequate level (see Fig. 1). Once signaled, the appetitive need is met through purposeful social

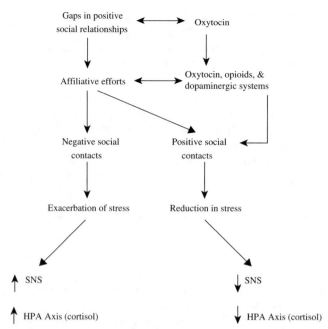

Fig. 1. A model of affiliative responses to stress. Elevations in plasma oxytocin accompany gaps in positive social relationships and are believed to prompt affiliative efforts aimed at restoring positive social contacts; engagement of opioid and dopaminergic systems coupled with oxytocin may lead to a reduction in stress responses, including those of the sympathetic nervous system (SNS) and the hypothalamic-pituitary-adrenocortical (HPA) axis. However, negative social contacts exacerbate stress, leading to an increase in these same biological stress responses.

behavior. If social contacts are hostile or unsupportive, then psychological and biological stress responses are heightened. If social contacts are supportive and comforting, stress responses decline. Positive contacts, in turn, lead to a decline in the need and, in the context of stress, a decline in stress responses. The fact that affiliation may look like other appetitive needs is not coincidental. Because biological neurocircuitries tend to be efficient, the dopamine and opioid systems that are recruited for other reward-based systems may well be recruited for the satisfaction of affiliative needs as well (see Depue & Morrone-Strupinksy, 2005).

In characterizing these social responses to stress we have used the metaphor "tend and befriend" (Taylor, 2002; Taylor et al., 2000). Our position is that under conditions of stress, tending to offspring and affiliating with others ("befriending") are at least as common responses to stress in humans as fight-or-flight. In building our model, we have focused heavily on the hormone oxytocin (see Fig. 1). We maintain that oxytocin is released in response to (at least some) stressors, especially those that may trigger affiliative needs; oxytocin prompts affiliative behavior in response to stress, in conjunction with dopaminergic and opioid systems. This affiliative activity may serve tending needs, including protective responses toward offspring, and/or it may take the form of befriending, namely seeking social contact for one's own protection and solace. Oxytocin, in conjunction with positive social contacts, attenuates biological stress responses (SNS, HPA axis) that can arise in response to social threats. In the sections that follow, we detail the elements in Figure 1, which is used as an organizational as well as a conceptual device.

It is important to note that oxytocin has been implicated in a broad array of social relationships and social activities, including peer bonding, sexual activity, and affiliative preferences under nonstressful circumstances (Carter, 1998; Insel, 1997). Thus, the model to be characterized in the subsequent sections primarily elucidates social behavior under stress and does not address larger issues concerning how oxytocin may be implicated in social activity in nonstressful times.

RELATIONSHIP GAPS AND SEPARATION DISTRESS

Affiliation is vital to the survival of human beings; accordingly, there are likely to be biobehavioral mechanisms that are sensitive to social threats or loss of social contact. Evidence for such an assertion comes from research on separation distress. When young are separated from their mothers, separation distress in offspring can result, leading to distress vocalizations that may prompt the return of the caregiver. This system appears to be dependent, in part, on oxytocin and brain opioids. Evidence consistent with the existence of such a system includes the facts that brain opioids reduce separation distress and that drugs suchas morphine reduce distress vocalizations in animals (Panksepp, 1998).

Adults experience separation distress as well, but until recently the biological underpinnings of adult relationship gaps were not explored. To address this issue, we examined the relation of plasma oxytocin levels to reports of relationship distress in adult women (Taylor et al., 2006). We found that women who were experiencing gaps in their social relationships had elevated levels of oxytocin. Specifically, women with high levels of oxytocin were more likely to report reduced contact with their mothers, their best friends, their pets, and social groups to which they belonged. In addition, those with significant others were more likely to report that their partners were not supportive, did not understand the way they felt about things, and did not care for them. Poor quality of the marital relationship and infrequent display of affection by the partner were also associated with higher levels of plasma oxytocin. Thus, oxytocin appears to signal relationship distress, at least in women.

Plasma oxytocin was not related to general psychological distress, only to gaps or problems in positive relationships; and whereas oxytocin appeared to signal gaps in relationships, levels of the stress hormone cortisol were not similarly elevated. These points suggest that oxytocin may be distinctively related to relationship distress. Similar findings have been reported by Turner, Altemus, Enos, Cooper, and McGuinness (1999), who found that elevated plasma oxytocin was associated with anxiety over relationships, perceived coldness or intrusiveness in relationships, and not being in a primary romantic relationship. Thus, the relation of oxytocin to relationship distress has been confirmed in two independent laboratories.

RELATION OF OXYTOCIN TO AFFILIATION

If oxytocin is related to social distress, then as an affiliative hormone, oxytocin may provide an impetus for social contact to ameliorate stress. There is manifold evidence that oxytocin, indeed, promotes affiliation, most of which has come from animal studies (e.g., Panksepp, Nelson, & Bekkedal, 1999; see Insel, 1997, for a review). Exogenously administered oxytocin has been related to increases in physical proximity, increased maternal behavior, grooming, and preferences for conspecifics in whose presence elevated oxytocin was experienced (see Panksepp, 1998; Taylor, 2002, for reviews). Oxytocin is also thought to underlie affiliative activities in humans as well, including maternal behavior and social bonding more generally (e.g., Carter, 1998; Carter, Lederhendler, & Kirkpatrick, 1999; Taylor, 2002). Thus, it appears that a fairly broad array of affiliative behaviors may be subserved by oxytocin.

RELATIONSHIP OF OXYTOCIN TO STRESS RESPONSES

The next link in the model relates oxytocin to stress responses. Animal studies have shown that exogenous administration of oxytocin or stimulation of oxytocin secretion decreases sympathetic reactivity, blood pressure, pain sensitivity, and corticosteroid levels, among other findings suggestive of a reduced stress response (e.g., Carter, 1998; Insel, 1997). A more modest literature in humans suggests similar effects. For example, among breastfeeding women who have high levels of oxytocin (Light et al., 2000), among women reporting more frequent hugs from partners (Light, Grewen, & Amico, 2005), and among men receiving exogenous oxytocin (Heinrichs, Baumgartner, Kirshbaum, & Ehlert, 2003), psychological and biological stress responses are lower. Overall, the evidence that high levels of or exogenously administered oxytocin attenuate stress responses is strong in animals and suggestive in human studies.

As our model maintains, however, if affiliative efforts are unrequited or negative, heightened stress responses may occur. In a study consistent with this point (Taylor et al., 2006), women participated in a socially threatening laboratory challenge task and their responses were assessed. Those with low levels of plasma oxytocin showed an increase in cortisol in response to the social threat and a decrease during recovery. By contrast, women with initially high plasma oxytocin levels had significantly higher cortisol levels initially, which decreased early on in the laboratory procedures but then again became elevated during the threat tasks. These findings suggest that women with high levels of oxytocin may be especially attuned to social features of the environment and that their levels of stress may be especially exacerbated by unsupportive social contacts. Thus, quality of social contacts during stressful times may be a pivotal variable for understanding the relation of oxytocin to stress responses.

The fact that high levels of oxytocin can be associated both with relationship distress and with reduced stress responses appears inconsistent. One hypothesis is that bursts of oxytocin, as may occur in response to anticipated or actual social contact or exogenous administration of oxytocin, reduce stress responses but that elevated oxytocin in plasma, which likely represents trace evidence of some preceding process, is associated with relationship distress (Turner et al., 1999; but see Grewen, Girdler, Amico, & Light, 2005). Another possible resolution stems from the fact that most studies documenting the stress-reducing qualities of oxytocin have not disentangled the effects of oxytocin from affiliation itself or its anticipation. Oxytocin increases the sensitivity of brain opioid systems, and at least some of the stress-reducing properties of oxytocin appear to be mediated by an opioid pathway and also, as noted earlier, by dopaminergic pathways. It is possible that a need for social contact that is unrequited does not implicate these downstream stress-reducing effects of oxytocin that appear to occur in the context of actual or anticipated affiliative contact.

BENEFITS OF TENDING UNDER STRESS

Why would humans (and some animals) have a biologically regulated affiliative system? Looking at the affiliative system from the standpoint of evolutionary theory suggests that there would be clear survival benefits of a biobehavioral mechanism that signals gaps in social support and prompts affiliation for beneficial communal responses to stress. Tending to offspring in times of stress would be vital to ensuring the survival of the species. Oxytocin may be at the core of such tending responses in threatening circumstances. Evidence from a broad array of animal studies shows that central administration of oxytocin enhances maternal behavior (see Taylor et al., 2000, for a review; Taylor, 2002). Such tending also has a wide array of immediate benefits—for example, reducing HPA and SNS activity in both mother and offspring.[2]

Evidence concerning the biological bases and consequences of maternal–infant contact in humans is more limited. Oxytocin is believed to be implicated initially in bonding between mother and infant. Oxytocin is at high levels in the mother following giving birth and may promote bonding; however, mother–infant attachment may soon become independent of its hormonal bases, maintained instead by neuromechanisms in the brain that underlie attachment (Taylor, 2002).

BENEFITS OF BEFRIENDING UNDER STRESS

A large social-support literature documents that "befriending" leads to substantial mental and physical health benefits in times of stress. Social isolation is tied to a significantly enhanced risk of mortality, whereas social support is tied to a broad array of beneficial health outcomes, including reduced risk of mortality (see Taylor, 2007, for a current review). Whether oxytocin is implicated in these processes has been unknown. However, in one study (Detillion, Craft, Glasper, Prendergast, & DeVries, 2004), Siberian hamsters received a skin wound and were then exposed to immobilization stress. The stressor increased cortisol concentrations and impaired wound healing, but only in socially isolated animals and not in socially housed ones. Thus, social housing acted as a stress buffer. Removing cortisol via adrenalectomy (removal of the adrenal glands) eliminated the impact of the stressor on wound healing, thereby implicating the HPA axis in the healing process. Of particular relevance to the current arguments, treating the isolated hamsters with oxytocin eliminated the stress-induced increases in cortisol and facilitated wound healing; treating socially housed hamsters with an oxytocin antagonist delayed wound healing. These data strongly imply that social contacts can protect against the adverse effects of stress through a mechanism that implicates oxytocin-induced suppression of the HPA axis. Thus, there appear to be discernible clinical consequences of oxytocin suppression of the HPA axis.

GENDER DIFFERENCES IN THE RELATION OF OXYTOCIN TO TENDING AND BEFRIENDING

The effects of oxytocin on social behavior have been heavily studied in estrogen-treated female animals and in women. The evidence that oxytocin plays an important role in male social relationships is less plentiful. Heinrichs et al. (2003) found that oxytocin had anti-stress effects in men. However, their paradigm used exogenous administration of oxytocin and therefore showed that oxytocin can have such effects in men, but not necessarily that it typically does.

There are several reasons to believe that oxytocin may play a more important role in influencing women's social behavior than men's, especially under stress. At the time when human stress responses evolved, work was largely sex segregated, with women more responsible for childcare. Thus, selection pressures for responses to threat that benefit both self and offspring may have been greater for females than for males—favoring social responses to stress in women especially (Taylor, 2002). Women's consistently stronger affiliative responses to stress compared to those of men (Tamres, Janicki, & Helgeson, 2002; Taylor, 2002) is consistent with this point. Estrogen strongly enhances the effects of oxytocin, which is also consistent with a greater role for oxytocin in women's behavior than in men's. At present, there appears to be a stronger basis for making inferences about the relation of oxytocin to social behavior in females than in males.

CONCLUSIONS

A large animal literature and a small human literature have tied oxytocin to separation distress, maternal tending, befriending responses to stress, and reduced psychological and biological stress responses. Exactly how oxytocin is implicated in these processes and how this may differ for males and females is not yet clear. Moreover, significant paradoxes remain, most especially the relation of oxytocin to both relationship distress and to reduced stress responses. Despite these gaps in knowledge, the mechanisms underlying oxytocin's relation to the reduction of stress and the beneficial effects of social responses to stress on health appears to be in view.

Clarifying the role of oxytocin in relationship processes—those implicated in both stressful and nonstressful times—will be valuable for scientific yield regarding the biological underpinnings of social bonds. Such knowledge will also help to clarify oxytocin's potential role in social dysfunction and disease processes. For example, the centrality of social deficits to mental disorders such as depression and autism suggests that with greater understanding of the oxytocin system, these disorders might become better understood as well.

Basic research issues for the future include resolution of significant methodological issues regarding oxytocin-based underpinnings of social relationships, especially the differences between experimental findings manipulating oxytocin and findings relating plasma oxytocin and social processes. More broadly, whether affiliation is best characterized as an appetitive need with dynamics approximating those in Figure 1 remains to be seen. The model proposed here hopefully provides a heuristic for further examination of these processes.

Recommended Reading

Carter, C.S., Lederhendler, I.I., & Kirkpatrick, B., eds. (1999). (See References)
Taylor, S.E. (2002). (See References)

Acknowledgments—Preparation of this article was supported by National Science Foundation Grant SES-0525713.

Notes

1. Address correspondence to Shelley E. Taylor, UCLA Department of Psychology, 1282A Franz Hall, Los Angeles, CA 90095; taylors@ psych.ucla.edu.
2. All the animal data are based on responses of mothers, not those of fathers.

References

Baumeister, R.F., & Leary, M.R. (1995). The need to belong: Desire for interpersonal attachments as a fundamental human motivation. *Psychological Bulletin, 117*, 497–529.

Carter, C.S. (1998). Neuroendocrine perspectives on social attachment and love. *Psychoneuroendocrinology, 23*, 779–818.

Carter, C.S., Lederhendler, I.I., & Kirkpatrick, B. (Eds.). (1999). *The integrative neurobiology of affiliation*. Cambridge, MA: MIT Press.

Depue, R.A., & Morrone-Strupinsky, J.V. (2005). A neurobiobehavioral model of affiliative bonding: Implications for conceptualizing a human trait of affiliation. *Behavioral and Brain Sciences, 28*, 313–395.

Detillion, C.E., Craft, T.K., Glasper, E.R., Prendergast, B.J., & DeVries, C. (2004). Social facilitation of wound healing. *Psychoneuroendocrinology, 29*, 1004–1011.

Grewen, K.M., Girdler, S.S., Amico, J., & Light, K.C. (2005). Effects of partner support on resting oxytocin, cortisol, norepinephrine, and blood pressure before and after warm partner contact. *Psychosomatic Medicine, 67*, 531–538.

Heinrichs, M., Baumgartner, T., Kirshbaum, C., & Ehlert, U. (2003). Social support and oxytocin interact to suppress cortisol and subjective responses to psychological stress. *Biological Psychiatry, 54*, 1389–1398.

Insel, T.R. (1997). A neurobiological basis of social attachment. *American Journal of Psychiatry, 154*, 726–735.

Light, K., Grewen, K., & Amico, J. (2005). More frequent partnerhugs and higher oxytocin levels are linked to lower blood pressure and heart rate in premenopausal women. *Biological Psychiatry, 69*, 5–21.

Light, K.C., Smith, T.E., Johns, J.M., Brownley, K.A., Hofheimer, J.A., & Amico, J.A. (2000). Oxytocin responsivity in mothers of infants: A preliminary study of relationships with blood pressure during laboratory stress and normal ambulatory activity. *Health Psychology, 19*, 560–567.

Panksepp, J. (1998). *Affective neuroscience*. London: Oxford University Press.

Panksepp, J., Nelson, E., & Bekkedal, M. (1999). Brain systems for the mediation of social separation distress and social-reward: Evolutionary antecedents and neuropeptide intermediaries. In C.S. Carter, I.I. Lederhendler, & B. Kirkpatrick (Eds.), *The integrative neurobiology of affiliation* (pp. 221–244). Cambridge, MA: MIT Press.

Tamres, L., Janicki, D., & Helgeson, V.S. (2002). Sex differences in coping behavior: A meta-analytic review. *Personality and Social Psychology Review, 6*, 2–30.

Taylor, S.E. (2002). *The tending instinct: How nurturing is essential to who we are and how we live.* New York: Holt.

Taylor, S.E. (2007). Social support. In H.S. Friedman & R.C. Silver (Eds.), *Foundations of health psychology* (pp. 145–171). New York: Oxford University Press.

Taylor, S.E., Gonzaga, G., Klein, L.C., Hu, P., Greendale, G.A., & Seeman S. E. (2006). Relation of oxytocin to psychological and biological stress responses in older women. *Psychosomatic Medicine, 68*, 238–245.

Taylor, S.E., Klein, L.C., Lewis, B.P., Gruenewald, T.L., Gurung, R.A.R., & Updegraff, J.A. (2000). Biobehavioral responses to stress in females: Tend-and-befriend, not fight-or-flight. *Psychological Review, 107*, 411–429.

Turner, R.A., Altemus, M., Enos, T., Cooper, B., & McGuinness, T. (1999). Preliminary research on plasma oxytocin in normal cycling women: Investigating emotion and interpersonal distress. *Psychiatry, 62*, 97–113.

Critical Thinking Questions

1. Compare and contrast the *fight-or-flight* response and the *tend and befriend* response to stress.

2. Describe the role of oxytocin in the tending and befriending response.

3. In her conclusion, the author states that understanding the role of oxytocin in the tending and befriending response will increase scientific understanding of the "biological underpinnings of social bonds." Why might this understanding be important? What are some possible implications of such an understanding?

This article has been reprinted as it originally appeared in *Current Directions in Psychological Science*. Citation information for this article as originally published appears above.

Positive Affect and Health

Sheldon Cohen[1] and Sarah D. Pressman

Carnegie Mellon University

Abstract

Negative affective styles such as anxiety, depression, and hostility have long been accepted as predictors of increased risk for illness and mortality. In contrast, positive affective styles have been relatively ignored in the health literature. Here we highlight consistent patterns of research associating trait positive affect (PA) and physical health. The evidence we review suggests an association of trait PA and lower morbidity and decreased symptoms and pain. PA is also associated with increased longevity among community-dwelling elderly. The association of PA and survival among those with serious illness is less clear and suggests the possibility that PA may be harmful in some situations. We conclude by raising conceptual and methodological reservations about this literature and suggesting directions for future research.

Keywords

positive emotion; positive affect; morbidity; mortality; health; symptoms

The role of emotions in physical health has been a central topic in health psychology for some time. Emotions are thought to represent the principal pathway linking psychological stress to disease, and enduring affective styles such as anxiety and depression have been found to be associated with greater morbidity and mortality. However, when health psychologists have referred to the roles of emotions and affect in health, they have typically meant negative emotions such as anger, depression, and anxiety. Only recently has there been any serious discussion of the potential effect of positive affect (PA).

One challenge in making sense of the literature on PA and health is that there is little agreement on what is meant by PA. We define positive emotion or affect as feelings that reflect a level of pleasurable engagement with the environment, such as happiness, joy, excitement, enthusiasm, and contentment (Clark, Watson, & Leeka, 1989). These can be brief, longer lasting, or more stable trait-like feelings. Importantly, the lack of positive engagement does not necessarily imply negative affect such as anger, anxiety, and depression.

REVIEW

The strongest links between positive emotions and health are found in studies that examine trait affective style, which reflects a person's typical emotional experience, rather than state affect, which reflects momentary responses to events. Here we provide short descriptions of the associations between trait PA and mortality (longevity), morbidity (illness onset), survival from life-threatening disease, and reports of symptoms and pain. (For a comprehensive review of this literature see Pressman & Cohen, 2005). The studies we review use prospective designs that help to eliminate the explanation that being sick resulted in lower PA. This is done by measuring PA and health at study onset (base-line) and assessing whether PA predicts changes in health over the follow-up period. Because the measure of PA is given before the change in health, it cannot have been caused by that change. Many, but not all, of the studies also include controls for spurious (third) factors such as age, sex, socioeconomic status, and race/ethnicity. Overall, the literature reviewed here is provocative, although it suffers from a range of methodological and conceptual limitations. It does however allow us to highlight both consistencies in results as well as the issues that need to be addressed to ultimately determine if a positive affective style is an important predictor of good health.

Mortality

A study that has received considerable attention evaluated PA by coding autobiographical writing samples collected from a group of nuns when they were in their early twenties (Danner, Snowdon, & Friesen, 2001). The greater the number of positive emotion words and sentences, the greater was the probability (adjusting for age and education) of being alive 60 years later. In contrast, the number of negative emotions reported was not associated with mortality.

However, the overall evidence on PA and mortality is more complex. Most (seven) of these studies have been done in elderly persons (average age over 60) living either on their own or with their families. These studies are virtually unanimous in linking positive emotional dispositions to longer life. But positive emotions are not generally associated with increased longevity in studies of other populations. For example, two studies suggest that institutionalized elderly with high PA are at increased risk of mortality (Janoff-Bulman & Marshall, 1982; Stones, Dornan, & Kozma, 1989) and an analysis of a sample of gifted children found that PA during childhood was associated with greater risk for death 65 years later (Friedman et al., 1993).

Illness Onset

In a study from our own laboratory (Cohen, Doyle, Turner, Alper, & Skoner, 2003), 334 adult volunteers were phone interviewed seven times over a 3-week period. For each interview, participants rated how accurately each of nine positive and nine negative adjectives described how they felt over the last day. Examples of PA items included *lively, energetic, happy, cheerful, at ease,* and *calm.* Examples of negative-affect (NA) items included *sad, depressed, nervous,* and *hostile.* Daily mood scores were calculated and averaged across the 7 days to create summary measures of trait PA and NA. Subsequently, subjects were exposed to one of two viruses that cause a common cold and were monitored for 5 days for the development of clinical illness. Colds were defined by objective markers of illness, including infection, mucus production (assessed by weighing tissues), and congestion (assessed by the amount of time it took for a dye put into the nostrils to reach the back of the throat). Those with high levels of PA were less likely to develop a cold when exposed to a virus (see Fig. 1). This relationship remained

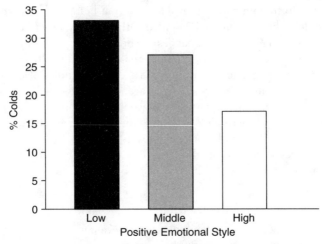

Fig. 1. The association between trait positive emotional style and the incidence of the common cold as diagnosed through objectively assessed markers of disease (infection, mucus weights, and congestion). Adapted from data reported in Cohen, Doyle, Turner, Alper, & Skoner (2003).

after controlling for age, sex, immunity (baseline antibody to the experimental virus), education, and NA.

In other morbidity studies, trait PA has been associated with lower rates of stroke among noninstitutionalized elderly (Ostir, Markides, Peek, & Goodwin, 2001), lower rates of rehospitalization for coronary problems (Middleton & Byrd, 1996), fewer injuries (e.g., Koivumaa-Honkanen et al., 2000) and improved pregnancy outcomes among women undergoing assisted fertilization (Klonoff-Cohen, Chu, Natarajan, & Sieber, 2001). These studies are often limited by a lack of control for factors such as NA, optimism, and personal control that may influence both PA and disease susceptibility, and many do not rule out the possibility that PA itself (e.g., endorsing of items such as *energetic, full-of-pep,* and *vigorous*) is merely a marker of subclinical disease processes.

Survival

A popular hypothesis is that trait PA increases longevity of persons suffering from life-threatening disease. However, comparatively few studies have examined whether PA predicts survival among people with chronic diseases, and available findings are at best mixed. A pattern of results does however suggest a hypothesis. Individuals with diseases that have decent prospects for long-term survival, such as early-stage breast cancer, coronary heart disease, and AIDS, may benefit from PA. However, high levels of trait PA may be detrimental to the health of individuals who have advanced diseases with poor and short-term prognoses—e.g., patients with melanoma, metastatic breast cancer, and end-stage renal disease—possibly as a consequence of underreporting of symptoms resulting in inadequate care, or of a lack of adherence to treatment (Pressman & Cohen, 2005).

Symptoms and Pain

There is considerable evidence linking PA to reports of fewer symptoms, less pain, and better health. These outcomes have practical importance, but there is reason to think that this association may be driven primarily by PA influences on how people perceive their bodies rather than by affect-elicited changes in physiological processes (e.g., Pennebaker, 1983).

For example, a study from our own lab suggests that trait PA is associated with less symptom reporting when objective disease is held constant (Cohen et al., 2003). As described earlier, PA and NA were assessed by averaging responses across seven nightly interviews. Volunteers were then exposed to a virus that causes the common cold and monitored for objective signs of illness. To test whether trait affect could influence symptom reporting, we predicted self-reported cold symptoms (collected for 5 days following viral exposure) from trait affect, controlling for the objective markers of disease mentioned earlier. When objective signs of illness were held constant, those higher in trait PA reported less severe symptoms, and those higher in trait NA reported more severe ones. Figure 2 presents the residual scores derived from the PA analysis. These scores represent the extent to which one reports more (+ scores) or fewer (− scores) symptoms than would be predicted from the objective markers of disease. Interestingly, when both PA and NA were entered in the same regression

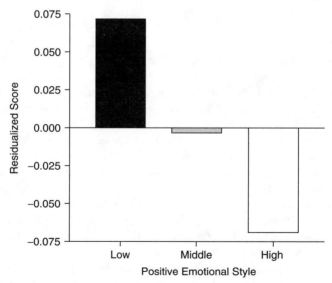

Fig. 2. The association between trait positive emotional style and self-reported symptoms, controlling for objective markers of disease (infection, mucus weights, and congestion). Residualized score represents the extent to which one reports more or fewer symptoms than is predicted by objective signs of illness. Scores above 0 indicate more symptoms than expected and those below 0 indicate fewer symptoms than expected. Adapted from data reported in Cohen, Doyle, Turner, Alper, & Skoner (2003).

equation, only PA continued to predict symptom reporting, suggesting that low PA (not high NA) may be the driving force in the reporting of unfound symptoms.

Other prospective evidence also reveals that trait PA predicts better self-reported health, fewer symptoms in the elderly, and less pain among rheumatoid arthritis and fibromyalgia patients. Interestingly, experimental evidence suggests that inducing state PA in both healthy and mildly ill individuals results in more favorable self-evaluations of health as compared to individuals induced to feel NA and a neutral control condition (e.g., Salovey & Birnbaum, 1989).

Although these data are provocative, many of these studies also found that NA was associated with greater symptom reporting and poorer self-reported health, begging the question of whether NA or PA is responsible for the effects found. However, there are several studies, like the one described at the beginning of this section, that provide evidence that PA effects on self-reported health are independent of, and often stronger than, those of NA.

LIMITATIONS OF THE EXISTING LITERATURE

Overall, there is provocative evidence that trait PA may influence health and well-being. Strong inferences are not yet possible, however. One problem in interpreting this literature is that in many cases it is difficult to distinguish between the effects of positive and negative emotions. For example, do community-residing elderly live longer because they are happy or because they are not sad? Interestingly, people's experiences of positive and negative emotions are partly independent in some circumstances (e.g., Diener & Emmons, 1985). For instance, in looking back over the last year of one's life (a typical trait PA measure), one can reasonably report having been both happy and sad. A definitive answer to whether positive or negative emotions are making independent contributions to a health outcome can only come from studies that measure both types of emotions separately. Surprisingly, studies that have focused on the effects of negative emotions on health have similarly failed to control for positive emotions. Consequently, it is difficult to conclude from the existing literature whether sadness results in a less healthy, shorter life or whether happiness leads to a healthier and longer one.

There is also concern that some measures of positive emotions may themselves be markers of associated cognitive and social dispositions such as extraversion, self-esteem, personal control, and optimism. In general, these factors have moderate associations with trait PA, but few existing studies control for the possibility that they, and not PA, are responsible for any associations with health that are found. A further issue with PA measurement is that some types of PA may themselves be direct indicators of physical health. For example, endorsing adjectives such as *energetic, full-of-pep,* and *vigorous* may reflect a positive mood, but may also reflect how healthy one feels. Self-rated health has been found to predict illness and longevity above and beyond objective health measures such as physician ratings. Consequently, it is important for future work to include standard measures of self-rated health to help exclude the possibility that we are merely predicting good objective health from good perceived health masquerading as positive emotions.

Another issue is the potential importance of differentiating activated (e.g., enthusiastic, joyful) and nonactivated (e.g., calm, content) affect. Health researchers consider physiological arousal to be a primary pathway through which emotions may influence health. It is thus likely that the arousing nature of an emotion, not only its valence, plays into its potential influences on health outcomes. This is especially relevant given that most measures of PA assess primarily activated emotions.

It is also unclear whether it is important to distinguish among the various subcomponents of PA, such as happiness, elation, and joy, or whether these affects cluster together in experience or in the manner by which they influence health. Few studies explicitly compare different positive emotions or compare individual emotions to a PA aggregate. Finally, there is evidence that the expression of PA varies across cultures, even Western cultures. Consequently, it is difficult to know to what extent this work would apply outside of the United States.

HOW COULD PA IMPROVE HEALTH?

Higher trait PA has been associated with better health practices such as improved sleep quality, more exercise, and more intake of dietary zinc, as well as with lower levels of the stress hormones epinephrine, norepinephrine, and cortisol (Pressman & Cohen, 2005). PA has also been hypothesized to be associated with other health-relevant hormones, including increases in oxytocin and growth hormone and secretion of endogenous opioids. Induced PA in the laboratory has been shown to alter various aspects of immune function, although the direction of changes are not entirely consistent and seem to be dependent on details of the manipulation and the degree of arousal produced via the induction (see Pressman & Cohen, 2005). PA may also influence health by altering social interactions. Persons who report more PA socialize more often and maintain more and higher-quality social ties. PA may result in more and closer social contacts because it facilitates approach behavior and because others are drawn to form attachments with pleasant individuals. More diverse and closer social ties have been associated with lower risk for both morbidity and premature mortality. Finally, health care providers may be more attentive to persons with more pleasant affect.

As an alternative to the arguments above, which assume that PA directly affects health, PA may influence health primarily through its ability to ameliorate the potentially pathogenic influences of stressful life events. For example, Fredrickson (1998) suggests that positive emotions encourage exploration and creativity and result in the building of social, intellectual, and physical resources. Similarly, Salovey, Rothman, Detweiler, and Steward (2000) suggest that positive emotions generate psychological resources by promoting resilience, endurance, and optimism.

WHERE DO WE GO FROM HERE?

Some key strategies to move this literature forward include (a) using more sophisticated measures of PA to differentiate between dimensions of affect (e.g., activated vs. unactivated; discrete positive emotions); (b) including both PA and

NA in studies in order to assess whether they have independent associations with health outcomes; (c) including social and cognitive factors that correlate with PA, such as extraversion, personal control, purpose, self-esteem, and optimism, in order to assess whether these factors are responsible for associations attributed to PA; (d) including measures of self-reported health to exclude it as an alternative explanation; and (e) assessing alternative pathways through which PA could influence health.

Overall, we consider the literature associating trait PA with health provocative but not definitive. Nonetheless, the current findings should encourage those interested in affect and health to include PA as a potential predictor and to test the potential pathways that may link PA to health.

Recommended Reading

Lyubomirsky, S., King, L., & Diener, E. (2005). The benefits of frequent positive affect: Does happiness lead to success? *Psychological Bulletin, 131*, 803–855.
Pressman, S.D., & Cohen, S. (2005). (See References)
Salovey, P., Rothman, A.J., Detweiler, J.B., & Steward, W.T. (2000). (See References)

Acknowledgments—Preparation of this article was facilitated by support from Pittsburgh NIH Mind-Body Center (Grants HL65111 & HL65112), the John D. and Catherine T. MacArthur Foundation Network on Socioeconomic Status and Health, and a Postgraduate Scholarship from the Natural Science & Engineering Research Council of Canada.

Note

1. Address correspondence to Sheldon Cohen, Department of Psychology, Carnegie Mellon University, Pittsburgh, PA 15213; e-mail: scohen@cmu.edu.

References

Clark, L.A., Watson, D., & Leeka, J. (1989). Diurnal variation in the positive affects. *Motivation and Emotion, 13*, 205–234.
Cohen, S., Doyle, W.J., Turner, R.B., Alper, C.M., & Skoner, D.P. (2003). Emotional style and susceptibility to the common cold. *Psychosomatic Medicine, 65*, 652–657.
Danner, D.D., Snowdon, D.A., & Friesen, W.V. (2001). Positive emotions in early life and longevity: Findings from the nun study. *Journal of Personality & Social Psychology, 80*, 804–813.
Diener, E., & Emmons, R.A. (1985). The independence of positive and negative affect. *Journal of Personality and Social Psychology, 47*, 1105–1117.
Fredrickson, B.L. (1998). What good are positive emotions? *Review of General Psychology, 2*, 300–319.
Friedman, H.S., Tucker, J.S., Tomlinson-Keasey, C., Schwartz, J.E., Wingard, D.L., & Criqui, M.H. (1993). Does childhood personality predict longevity? *Journal of Personality & Social Psychology, 65*, 176–185.
Janoff-Bulman, R., & Marshall, G. (1982). Mortality, well-being, and control: A study of a population of institutionalized aged. *Personality & Social Psychology Bulletin, 8*, 691–698.
Klonoff-Cohen, H., Chu, E., Natarajan, L., & Sieber, W. (2001). A prospective study of stress among women undergoing in vitro fertilization or gamete intrafallopian transfer. *Fertility & Sterility, 76*, 675–687.
Koivumaa-Honkanen, H., Honkanen, R., Viinamaki, H., Heikkila, K., Kaprio, J., & Koskenvuo, M. (2000). Self-reported life satisfaction and 20-year mortality in healthy Finnish adults. *American Journal of Epidemiology, 152*, 983–991.

Middleton, R.A., & Byrd, E.K. (1996). Psychosocial factors and hospital readmission status of older persons with cardiovascular disease. *Journal of Applied Rehabilitation Counseling, 27,* 3–10.

Ostir, G.V., Markides, K.S., Peek, M.K., & Goodwin, J.S. (2001). The association between emotional well-being and the incidence of stroke in older adults. *Psychosomatic Medicine, 63,* 210–215.

Pennebaker, J.W. (1983). *The psychology of physical symptoms.* New York: Springer-Verlag.

Pressman, S.D., & Cohen, S. (2005). Does positive affect influence health? *Psychological Bulletin, 131,* 925–971.

Salovey, P., & Birnbaum, D. (1989). Influence of mood on health-relevant cognitions. *Journal of Personality & Social Psychology, 57,* 539–551.

Salovey, P., Rothman, A.J., Detweiler, J.B., & Steward, W.T. (2000). Emotional states and physical health. *American Psychologist, 55,* 110–121.

Stones, M.J., Dornan, B., & Kozma, A. (1989). The prediction of mortality in elderly institution residents. *Journals of Gerontology, 44,* P72–P79.

Critical Thinking Questions

1. Describe some positive and some negative outcomes of positive affect using evidence from research on mortality, illness onset, survival, and pain.

2. Identify three problems in interpreting the existing literature on positive affect and well-being, and explain why each presents a problem. Speculate on ways to overcome each of these problems.

3. The authors conclude the article by presenting five key strategies to move this research area forward. Choose the three you find the most compelling and defend the importance of such a strategy. In doing so, be sure to explain the strategy and point out the implications of such research.

This article has been reprinted as it originally appeared in *Current Directions in Psychological Science.* Citation information for this article as originally published appears above.

Resilience in the Face of Potential Trauma

George A. Bonanno[1]

Teachers College, Columbia University

Abstract

Until recently, resilience among adults exposed to potentially traumatic events was thought to occur rarely and in either pathological or exceptionally healthy individuals. Recent research indicates, however, that the most common reaction among adults exposed to such events is a relatively stable pattern of healthy functioning coupled with the enduring capacity for positive emotion and generative experiences. A surprising finding is that there is no single resilient type. Rather, there appear to be multiple and sometimes unexpected ways to be resilient, and sometimes resilience is achieved by means that are not fully adaptive under normal circumstances. For example, people who characteristically use self-enhancing biases often incur social liabilities but show resilient outcomes when confronted with extreme adversity. Directions for further research are considered.

Keywords

loss; grief; trauma; resilience; coping

Life is filled with peril. During the normal course of their lives, most adults face one or more potentially traumatic events (e.g., violent or life-threatening occurrences or the death of close friends or relatives). Following such events, many people find it difficult to concentrate; they may feel anxious, confused, and depressed; and they may not eat or sleep properly. Some people have such strong and enduring reactions that they are unable to function normally for years afterward. It should come as no surprise that these dramatic reactions have dominated the literatures on loss and trauma. Until recently, the opposite reaction—the maintenance of a relative stable trajectory of healthy functioning following exposure to a potential trauma—has received scant attention. When theorists have considered such a pattern, they have typically viewed it either as an aberration resulting from extreme denial or as a sign of exceptional emotional strength (e.g., McFarlane & Yehuda, 1996).

RESILIENCE (NOT RECOVERY) IS THE MOST COMMON RESPONSE TO POTENTIAL TRAUMA

Over a decade ago, my colleagues and I began an ongoing investigation of this supposedly rare response, and the means by which people might achieve such presumably superficial (or exemplary) functioning in the aftermath of a potentially traumatic event. The results of our research have consistently challenged the prevailing view on the subject. We took as our starting point the burgeoning developmental literature on resilience. Developmental researchers and theorists had for several decades highlighted various protective factors (e.g., ego-resiliency, the presence of supportive relationships) that promote healthy trajectories among children exposed to unfavorable life circumstances such as poverty (e.g., Garmezy, 1991; Rutter, 1987). We sought to adapt this body of research to the study of resilient outcomes among adults in otherwise normal circumstances who are exposed to isolated and potentially highly disruptive events.

Our research led to three primary conclusions, each mirroring but also extending the insights gained from developmental research. First, resilience following potentially traumatic events represents a distinct outcome trajectory from that typically associated with recovery from trauma. Historically, there have been few attempts to distinguish subgroups within the broad category of individuals exposed to potential trauma who do not develop post-traumatic stress disorder (PTSD).When resilience had been considered, it was often in terms of factors that "favor a path to recovery" (McFarlane & Yehuda, 1996, p. 158). However, studies have now demonstrated that resilience and recovery are discrete and empirically separable outcome trajectories following a dramatic event such as the death of a spouse (e.g., Bonanno, Wortman, et al., 2002) or direct exposure to terrorist attack (e.g., Bonanno, Rennicke, & Dekel, in press). Figure 1 depicts the prototypical resilience and recovery trajectories, as well as trajectories representing chronic and delayed symptom elevations (discussed later).

In this framework, recovery is defined by moderate to severe initial elevations in psychological symptoms that significantly disrupt normal functioning and that decline only gradually over the course of many months before returning to pre-trauma levels. In contrast, resilience is characterized by relatively mild and short-lived disruptions and a stable trajectory of healthy functioning across time. A key point is that even though resilient individuals may experience an initial, brief spike in distress (Bonanno, Moskowitz, Papa, & Folkman, 2005) or may struggle for a short period to maintain psychological equilibrium (e.g., several weeks of sporadic difficulty concentrating, intermittent sleeplessness, or daily

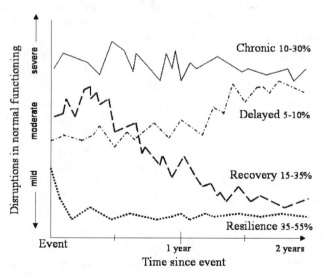

Fig. 1. Prototypical trajectories of disruption in normal functioning during the 2-year period following a loss or potential trauma.

variability in levels of well-being; Bisconti et al., in press), they nonetheless manage to keep functioning effectively at or near their normal levels. For example, resilience has been linked to the continued fulfillment of personal and social responsibilities and the capacity for positive emotions and generative experiences (e.g., engaging in new creative activities or new relationships), both immediately and in the months following exposure to a potentially traumatic event (Bonanno & Keltner, 1997; Bonanno, Wortman, et al., 2002; Bonanno, Rennicke, & Dekel, in press; Fredrickson et al., 2003).

A second conclusion that emerges from our research is that resilience is typically the most common outcome following exposure to a potentially traumatic event. It has been widely assumed in the literature that the most common response to such an occurrence is an initial but sizeable elevation in trauma symptoms followed by gradual resolution and recovery (McFarlane & Yehuda, 1996). However, although symptom levels tend to vary for different potentially traumatic events, resilience has consistently emerged as the most common outcome trajectory. In one study, for example, over half of the people in a sample of middle-aged individuals who had lost their spouses showed a stable, low level of symptoms; and stable low symptoms were observed in more than a third of a group of gay men who were bereaved after providing care for a partner dying of AIDS, a considerably more stressful context (Bonanno, Moskowitz, et al., 2005). Resilience was also readily observed in a random phone-dialing survey of Manhattan residents following the September 11 terrorist attack (Bonanno, Galea, Bucciarelli, & Vlahov, 2005). Following conventions established in the study of subthreshold depression, we defined a mild to moderate trauma reaction as two or more PTSD symptoms and resilience as one or no PTSD symptoms in the first 6 months following the attack. Over 65% in the New York metropolitan area were resilient. Among people with more concentrated exposure (e.g., those who had either witnessed the attack in person or who were in the World Trade Center during the attack), the proportion showing resilience was still over 50%. Finally, even among people who were physically injured in the attack, a group for whom the estimated proportion of PTSD was extremely high (26.1%), one third (32.8%) of the individuals were resilient.

In establishing the validity of the resilient trajectory it is imperative to distinguish stable, healthy functioning from denial or other forms of superficial adjustment. To this end, several studies have now documented links between resilience and generally high functioning prior to a potentially traumatic event (Bonanno, Wortman, et al., 2002; Bonanno, Moskowitz, et al., 2005). Several studies have also documented resilient outcomes using relatively objective measures that go beyond participant self-report, including structured clinical interviews and anonymous ratings of functioning from participants' friends or relatives (e.g., Bonanno, Rennicke, & Dekel, in press; Bonanno, Moskowitz, et al., 2005). For example, we (Bonanno, Rennicke, & Dekel, in press) recruited the friends and relatives of high-exposure survivors of the World Trade Center terrorist attack and asked them to assign the survivors to either the resilience trajectory or one of the other outcome trajectories depicted in Figure 1. The assignments of friends and relatives closely matched the survivors' actual symptom levels over time, and thus provided important validation for the resilience trajectory.

THE HETEROGENEITY OF RESILIENCE: FLEXIBLE AND PRAGMATIC COPING

A third conclusion to emerge from our research, again extending the conclusions of developmental researchers, is that there are multiple and sometimes unexpected factors that might promote a resilient outcome. At the most general level, many of the same characteristics that promote healthy development should also foster adult resilience. These would include both situational factors, such as supportive relationships, and individual factors, such as the capacity to adapt flexibly to challenges (Block & Block, 1980). The capacity for adaptive flexibility was mirrored in a recent study associating resilience among New York City college students in the aftermath of September 11 with flexibility in emotion regulation, defined as the ability to effectively enhance or suppress emotional expression when instructed to do so (Bonanno, Papa, LaLande, Westphal, & Coifman, 2004).

In addition to these general health-promoting factors, however, our research also underscores a crucial point of departure from the developmental literature. Childhood resilience is typically understood in response to corrosive environments, such as poverty or enduring abuse. By contrast, adult resilience is more often a matter of coping with an isolated and usually (but not always) brief potentially traumatic event. The key point is that whereas corrosive environments require longer-term adaptive solutions, isolated events often oblige a more pragmatic form of coping, a "whatever it takes" approach, which may involve behaviors and strategies that are less effective or even maladaptive in other contexts. For instance, considerable research attests to the health benefits of expressing negative emotions. Although most resilient bereaved individuals express at least some negative emotion while talking about their loss, they nonetheless express relatively less negative emotion and greater positive emotion than other bereaved individuals (e.g., Bonanno & Keltner, 1997), thereby minimizing the impact of the loss while "increasing continued contact with and support from important people in the social environment" (p. 134).

Another example of pragmatic coping is illustrated by trait self-enhancement, the tendency toward self-serving biases in perception and attribution (e.g., overestimating one's own positive qualities). People given to self-serving biases tend to be narcissistic and to evoke negative reactions in other people. However, they also have high self-esteem and cope well with isolated potential traumas. Our research team examined self-enhancement among people dealing with two powerful stressor events, the premature death of a spouse and exposure to urban combat during the recent civil war in Bosnia (Bonanno, Field, Kovacevic, & Kaltman, 2002). In both samples, trait self-enhancement was positively associated with ratings of functioning made by mental health experts. In the bereavement study, however, untrained observers rated self-enhancers relatively un-favorably (lower on positive traits, e.g., honest; and higher on negative traits, e.g., self-centered). Yet, these negative impressions did not appear to interfere with self-enhancers' ability to maintain a high level of functioning after the loss.

This same pattern of findings was observed among high-exposure survivors of the September 11 attack (Bonanno et al., in press). Trait self-enhancement was more prevalent among individuals exhibitingthe resilient trajectory, whether established by self-reported symptoms or ratings from friends or relatives. Self-enhancers also had greater positive affect and were rated by their friends and relatives as having consistently higher levels of mental and physical health, goal accomplishment, and coping ability. However, self-enhancers' friends and relatives also rated them as decreasing in social adjustment over the 18 months after September 11 and, among those with the highest levels of exposure, as less honest. This mixed pattern of findings suggests again that self-enhancers are able to maintain generally high levels of functioning in most areas except their social relations. Interestingly, however, self-enhancers themselves perceived their social relationships in relatively more positive terms than other participants, and this factor fully mediated their low levels of PTSD symptoms. In other words, self-enhancers appear to be blissfully unaware of the critical reactions they can evoke in others, and this type of self-serving bias evidently plays a crucial role in their ability to maintain stable levels of healthy functioning in other areas following a potentially traumatic event.

DIRECTIONS FOR FUTURE RESEARCH

The study of adult resilience is nascent and there are myriad questions for future research. An obvious imperative is to learn how the various costs and benefits of resilience vary across different types and durations of potentially traumatic events. Is there a point, for example, when the long-term costs of a particular type of coping might outweigh whatever crucial short-term advantages it provides? Might such trade-offs vary by gender or culture? Western, independence-oriented societies, for example, tend to focus more heavily than collectivist societies on the personal experience of trauma. However, little is known about the extent that loss and trauma reactions vary across cultures. A recent comparative study showed that bereaved people in China recovered more quickly from loss than did bereaved Americans (Bonanno, Papa, et al., 2005). However, as is typical of Chinese culture, Chinese bereaved also reported more physical symptoms than Americans. These data raise the intriguing questions of whether resilience has different meanings in different cultural contexts and, perhaps even more important, whether different cultures may learn from each other about effective and not-so-effective ways of coping with extreme adversity.

These questions in turn raise multiple practical and philosophical uncertainties about whether resilience can or should be learned. On the one hand, the observed link between resilient outcomes and personality variables suggests that resilient traits may be relatively fixed and not easily inculcated in others. And, given the social costs associated with some of the traits found in resilient people (e.g., self-enhancement), the advantage of simply imitating resilient individuals is questionable. On the other hand, a more promising avenue for training people to cope resiliently with trauma is suggested by the evidence linking resilience to flexible adaptation (Block & Block, 1980; Bonanno et al., 2004). Because adaptive flexibility can be manipulated experimentally (e.g., people's ability to engage in various cognitive or emotional processes can be measured under different stress or conditions; Bonanno et al., 2004), it should be possible to systematically examine the stability of such a trait over time and the conditions under which it might be learned or enhanced.

A related question pertains to how resilient individuals might view their own effectiveness at coping with potential trauma. Although at least some resilient individuals are surprised at how well they cope (Bonanno, Wortman, et al., 2002), it seems likely that others (e.g., self-enhancers) might overestimate their own resilience. This issue is particularly intriguing in relation to the distinction between stable resilience and delayed reactions. Although delayed reactions are not typically observed during bereavement (e.g., Bonanno, Wortman, et al., 2002), a small subset of individuals exposed to potentially traumatic events (5–10%) typically exhibit delayed PTSD. Preliminary evidence indicates that delayed-PTSD responders have higher initial symptom levels than do resilient individuals (e.g., Bonanno et al., in press). Further evidence of this distinction would hold potentially important diagnostic implications for early intervention.

Finally, another question pertains to how resilient individuals experience the crucial early weeks after an extreme stressor event. A recent study by Bisconti, Bergeman, and Boker (in press) shed some welcome light on this issue by examining daily well-being ratings in the early months after the death of a spouse. Although resilient bereaved typically show only mild and relatively short-lived overall decreases in well-being, examination of their daily ratings indicated marked variability across the first 3 weeks and then a more stable but still variable period that endured through the second month of bereavement. Perhaps similar research using larger samples and Internet methods might illuminate how resilient individuals manage to continue functioning and meeting the ongoing demands of their lives while nonetheless struggling, at least for a short period, to maintain self-regulatory equilibrium.

Recommended Readings

Bonanno, G.A. (2004). Loss, trauma, and human resilience: Have we underestimated the human capacity to thrive after extremely aversive events. *American Psychologist, 59*, 20–28.

Bonanno, G.A., & Kaltman, S. (2001). The varieties of grief experience. *Clinical Psychology Review, 21*, 705–734.

Gilbert, D.T., Pinel, E.C., Wilson, T.D., Blumberg, S.J., & Wheatley, T. (1998). Immune neglect: A source of durability bias in affective forecasting. *Journal of Personality and Social Psychology, 75*, 617–638.

Luthar, S.S. (in press). Resilient adaptation. In D. Cicchetti & D.J. Cohen (Eds.), *Developmental psychopathology: Risk, disorder, and adaptation*. New York: Wiley.

Acknowledgments—This research was supported by grants from the National Institutes of Health (R29-MH57274) and the National Science Foundation (BCS-0202772 and BCS-0337643).

Note

1. Address correspondence to George A. Bonanno, Clinical Psychology Program, 525 West 120th St., Box 218, Teachers College, Columbia University, New York, NY 10027; e-mail: gab38@columbia.edu.

References

Bisconti, T.L., Bergeman, C.S., & Boker, S.M. (in press). Social support as a predictor of variability: An examination of recent widows' adjustment trajectories. *Psychology and Aging.*

Block, J.H., & Block, J. (1980). The role of ego-control and ego-resiliency in the organization of behavior. In W.A. Collins (Ed.), *The Minnesota Symposia on Child Psychology* (Vol. 13, pp. 39–101). Hillsdale, NJ: Erlbaum.

Bonanno, G.A., Field, N.P., Kovacevic, A., & Kaltman, S. (2002). Self-enhancement as a buffer against extreme adversity: Civil war in Bosnia and traumatic loss in the United States. *Personality and Social Psychology Bulletin, 28,* 184–196.

Bonanno, G.A., Galea, S., Bucciarelli, A., & Vlahov, D. (2005). Psychological resilience after disaster: New York City in the aftermath of the September 11th terrorist attack. Manuscript submitted for publication.

Bonanno, G.A., & Keltner, D. (1997). Facial expressions of emotion and the course of conjugal bereavement. *Journal of Abnormal Psychology, 106,* 126–137.

Bonanno, G.A., Moskowitz, J.T., Papa, A., & Folkman, S. (2005). Resilience to loss in bereaved spouses, bereaved parents, and bereaved gay men. *Journal of Personality and Social Psychology, 88,* 827–843.

Bonanno, G.A., Papa, A., Lalande, K., Nanping, Z., & Noll, J.G. (2005). Grief processing and deliberate grief avoidance: A prospective comparison of bereaved spouses and parents in the United States and China. *Journal of Consulting and Clinical Psychology, 73,* 86–98.

Bonanno, G.A., Papa, A., LaLande, K., Westphal, M., & Coifman, K. (2004). The importance of being flexible: The ability to both enhance and suppress emotional expression predicts long-term adjustment. *Psychological Science, 15,* 482–487.

Bonanno, G.A., Rennicke, C., & Dekel, S. (in press). Self-enhancement among high-exposure survivors of the September 11th terrorist attack: Resilience or social maladjustment? *Journal of Personality and Social Psychology.*

Bonanno, G.A., Wortman, C.B., Lehman, D.R., Tweed, R.G., Haring, M., Sonnega, J., Carr, D., & Neese, R.M. (2002). Resilience to loss and chronic grief: A prospective study from pre-loss to 18 months post-loss. *Journal of Personality and Social Psychology, 83,* 1150–1164.

Fredrickson, B.L., Tugade, M.M., Waugh, C.E., & Larkin, G.R. (2003). What good are positive emotions in crisis? A prospective study of resilience and emotion following the terrorist attacks on the United States on September 11th, 2001. *Journal of Personality and Social Psychology, 84,* 365–376.

Garmezy, N. (1991). Resilience and vulnerability to adverse developmental outcomes associated with poverty. *American Behavioral Scientist, 34,* 416–430.

McFarlane, A.C., & Yehuda, R. (1996). Resilience, vulnerability, and the course of posttraumatic reactions. In B.A. van der Kolk, A.C. McFarlane, & L. Weisaeth (Eds.), *Traumatic stress* (pp. 155–181). New York: Guilford.

Rutter, M. (1987). Psychosocial resilience and protective mechanisms. *American Journal of Orthopsychiatry, 57,* 316–331.

Critical Thinking Questions

1. The author uses developmental research and theories to support his three main conclusions about resilience. Explain each of these conclusions and describe the research used to support each.

2. Explain how self-enhancement can be used as a coping strategy. What are some of the pros and cons of this strategy?

3. Identify four directions for future research in the study of adult resilience. Evaluate each direction in terms of its potential importance and practical value.

This article has been reprinted as it originally appeared in *Current Directions in Psychological Science*. Citation information for this article as originally published appears above.

Topic Index